PARK CHUNG-HEE

From Poverty to Power

Chong-Sik Lee

The KHU Press
Palos Verdes, CA

Kyung Hee University Korean Studies
No. 1

ISBN: 0615560288
EAN-13: 9780615560281

Available at Amazon.com,
www.CreateSpace.com/3712656, and Other Retailers

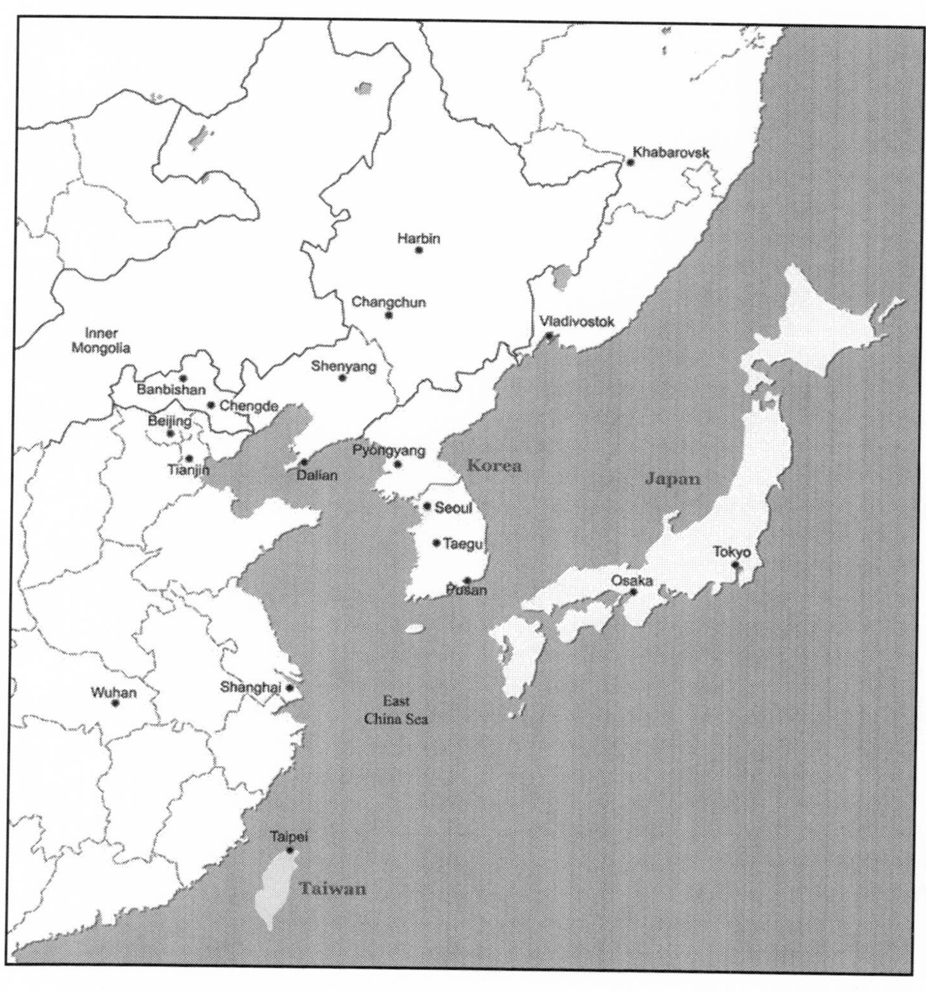
Khabarovsk
Harbin
Changchun
Vladivostok
Inner
Mongolia
Shenyang
Banbishan
Chengde
Beijing
Tianjin
Dalian
Pyŏngyang
Korea
Japan
Seoul
Taegu
Pusan
Tokyo
Osaka
Wuhan
Shanghai
East
China Sea
Taipei
Taiwan

To

Roger

CONTENT

✡ ✡ ✡

Preface

My interest in Park Chung-Hee goes back to 1961, when he first made news by leading a military coup against the incipient democratic regime. The short and stern-faced man in a dark-green army jacket with dark glasses and his hands behind his back was impressive but puzzling. What kind of a man must he have been to lead the first military coup in Korea since 1392? Was he a power-mad maniac? These questions were in my mind as I reported on American reactions to the coup in *Sasanggye* (The World of Thought) magazine in Seoul, which strongly supported the coup.

I avidly followed the news about the junta. The arrests and trials of business tycoons and others for corruption were remarkable. General Park appeared to be a ruthless man as he put many of his junta colleagues on trial on counterrevolutionary charges. No one knew what Park's next move would be, and a chill swept through society. He rushed a series of reform programs through, but later in 1963, we all watched Park's tearful farewell ceremony in which he swore to retire from politics. He said he did not wish to see another miserable soldier like himself endure so much hardship. A total reversal followed soon after. He was not going to retire after all.

His government sent troops to Vietnam to assist President Johnson's war against the Vietcong, and strange things began to happen. The soldiers started to send U.S. dollars home. The small, relatively unknown Hanjin Company jumped onto the scene as a military contractor, and thousands of young men flocked there, sending more dollars home. South Korea's economic boom was on. Park presided over weekly meetings of business leaders to review and plan the export of goods not only to Vietnam, but all over the world. Park even coerced Hanjin to take over a bankrupt two-plane "airline" called Air Korea. Cho Choong-Hoon, the head of Hanjin, had started his career in the field of transportation, and under his leadership, the fledgling company grew into one of the largest airlines in the world, Korean Air. Though Cho had started as a lowly trucker hauling trash, the conglomerate he formed handled billions of dollars of business a year by the time he passed away. The Hyundai Construction Company was involved in Vietnam, too.

Then the earth shook as the United States lost the war in Vietnam. The world churned around in a dizzying swirl. The Nixon Doctrine, the Sino-American détente, Nixon's unilateral withdrawal of one of the two U.S. divisions in South Korea, and the July 4 joint communiqué of North and South Korea in 1972 followed one after another. Meanwhile, President Park declared a state of emergency in 1971, followed by a constitutional revision. The new constitution gave him the power to appoint one-third of the members of the National Assembly and even outlawed criticism of the constitution and of the president. There was no doubt that Park Chung-Hee was turning himself into a generalissimo. I became a vocal critic, in public and private, writing op-ed pieces for newspapers. I even criticized him at U.S. Congressional hearings, even though I acknowledged that he had been placed in a vise between Nixon's détente policy and North Korea's hard line. I also chose to stay away from Korea for the duration of the *Yushin* constitutional system, which meant an absence of nine years, until 1981. President Park was assassinated in October 1979, and General Chun Doo Hwan had installed himself as president by the time I revisited Seoul.

I recount these events because readers ought to know where I stand politically vis-à-vis Park Chung-Hee, the subject of this book. I did admire his achievements but abhorred his dictatorship. Some called me a Park supporter, and others charged me for being an ambivalent critic. Perhaps readers of this book will reach similar conclusions. But my objective has been to look at the person Park Chung-Hee with an open mind, trying to understand him from as many angles as possible.

Many books and articles have been published on Park Chung-Hee, but I was particularly impressed by two works in Korean, one by Cho Kap-je, who published several books on Park's life, and the other by Chŏng Yŏng-jin, who wrote a three-volume historical novel on Park's early years. These two authors collected enormous amounts of information, both documentary and oral, which has been very helpful to me. I would not even have started this project had their works not been available. But I found their works wanting in some respects as I began to ask different questions. I wanted to know how certain events affected Park or what his thoughts were as he witnessed them, but all I could do in many cases was to provide educated guesses. Access to Park's diaries or later writings would have helped, but they were not available. How I envy those biographers who had access to diaries, letters, and recollections of friends and neighbors! The reader will notice that I have used many conditional phrases, such as *could have*, *would have*, and *might have*. I hope more material will become available in the future to answer some of my remaining questions.

I was surprised after starting my research on Park Chung-Hee that he and I shared certain affinities. No, I did not grow up in dire poverty as he did, although I did suffer enough in my childhood. Nor was I the last son of a poor peasant farmer. I was in fact the first son of a teacher-turned-businessman. I was lucky enough to be taller than most of my classmates, while Park was the shortest of his peers. But I believe I can understand him better than most of the younger generation today, because both of us grew up as loyal subjects of Emperor Hirohito and went through the same Japanese educational system. Even though he was fourteen years older than I, militarism was firmly established in the educational system in Korea when he attended and taught at schools. Since Japanese was the only language permitted at school at that time, both of us became fluent in it. Both of us read the war-oriented *manga* (comics), magazines, and history books. We sang Japanese military songs and recited the Imperial Rescript on Education. As I said, the schools taught and trained us to be perfect subjects of Emperor Hirohito. Parents and family members did not dare to interfere in this process even if they disagreed. One would never know when a child might blurt out an "un-Japanese" or anti-Japanese remark that could land the whole family in hell. I never experienced such an event, but I was denied admission to the middle school in Pyongyang because I was caught speaking Korean on the day of the entrance examination. I did not intend to become a hero. It just happened that way, but it was enough to change the course of my life. I did not know it then, but it was a significant turning point in my life.

Another affinity that helped me to understand Park was his Manchurian experience. He spent three years of his youth in that part of China, where the Japanese military had established Manchukuo, the Manchu Empire, under Emperor Pu Yi, better known as the "Last Emperor."

It seems bizarre now seventy years later, but it was too real to us then. Japan had firm control of that big piece of land surrounded by Siberia, the maritime provinces of the Soviet Union, the Korean Peninsula, Mainland China, and Mongolia. Had the Japanese been content with that conquest and not tried to expand into China's mainland in 1937, they might still be holding onto that land with Hirohito's empire intact.

In any case, Park's experience in Manchuria played a large role in his life, and it was the same for me. In fact, our lives in Manchuria overlapped for a year or so. He was stationed there between 1944 and 1945 as a lieutenant of the Manchukuo army in the northwestern corner of what was then a part of Manchukuo; I attended a middle school in Liaoyang, just southwest of Shenyang. I spent a good part of my childhood in Liaoyang and Tiehling, which is further north, closer to Sinjing (now Changchun) where Park attended the Manchukuo Military Academy. My experience in Manchuria led me to write a book about the anti-Japanese movement there, *Revolutionary Struggle in Manchuria*. The knowledge I gained in writing that book did help me to better understand the events in which Park was involved. This was also the case for the seven months he was stranded in Beijing after Japan capitulated in August 1945. My family was stuck in Liaoyang for a much longer period. Both of us spent our days under the Chinese Nationalist government headed by Generalissimo Chiang Kai-shek.

All this is not meant to say that I understand Park perfectly. The truth is far from it. I encountered many questions about the various phases of his life to which I found no answers. I hope someday someone will answer these questions, which are scattered throughout this book. This is important because I believe understanding Park Chung-Hee is vital to understanding what has happened in Korea since 1961.

Acknowledgments

I wish to acknowledge my debt to Professors Ch'oe Yŏng-Ho and Helena Meyer-Knapp for reading a number of my drafts and giving me valuable advice. I am afraid I tried their patience by sending them so many drafts through the three or four years it took to write this book. This was truly a learning experience. Professor Meyer-Knapp and Professor Kwon Gibung also served as my sounding boards and sources of ideas through our daily promenades and dialogues at Kyung Hee University's Graduate Institute of Peace Studies (GIP). I am also indebted to others, including Professors Fred Dickinson, Lee Jung-Bok, Oh Myeng-Ho, Ch'oe Hyentai, and Kim Dong Han, who read portions of the manuscript at different stages and gave me valuable advice. Professor Dickinson's expertise on Japanese history, in particular, saved me from committing a number of grievous errors. I benefited much from conversations with Professor Lee Chae-Jin and Dr. Kim Young Hoon.

I also wish to thank Mr. Kim Jae-ch'un, Park's close associate, for sharing his thoughts with me. The same goes for Ambassador Ch'oe P'illip, who had been Park's assistant. Professor Jeon Hyun-soo was kind enough to escort me to Kumi where Park Chung-Hee grew up. Mr. Yu Byŏng-chŏl took me to Munkyŏng to breathe the fresh air of the mining town where Park Chung-Hee taught and endured the drought of 1939. Professor Kim Yong-Ho urged me to take a trip to Banbishan in northwestern China where Park Chung-Hee spent thirteen months of his youth and arranged the details of my travel. It was an adventure I will never forget. Readers interested in how we discovered Banbishan may read appendix 3, which covers our trip together.

I troubled Mr. Kim Dong-Wook, head of the library at the GIP, for many esoteric materials in Japanese and Korean; he spared no effort in locating them for me, and I am grateful to him. Ms. Han Ji-soo, Mr. Kim's assistant, was very efficient in helping me. Mr. Ishimatsu Hisayuki, the Japanese librarian at Berkeley, was a godsend. He undertook the search for Japanese material in Japan and the United States. In Tokyo, Ms. Jung Ji-yun, "my Tokyo representative," searched the horizon for many valuable Japanese materials. I also wish to thank Ghim Taedeog for gathering Park Chung-Hee's photographs for me. My gratitude also goes to Messrs. Watanabe Takashi and Kanno Naoki at the National Institute for Defense Studies for rendering assistance beyond the call of duty.

By a fortuitous turn of events, Captain Kim Chang-Kon of the Republic of Korea Army served as my research assistant for two years at the Graduate School of Peace Studies, and he was a true blessing. He found not only many unexpected materials for me but also gave me valuable advice as the manuscript progressed.

I read an earlier version of this work at a conference held in honor of the ninetieth birthday of Professor Robert A. Scalapino at the Institute of East Asian Studies, Berkeley, in September 2009. Dr. Scalapino is responsible in part for this work, because he is the one who launched me into the study of Korea in 1957, and he has continued to teach me since then. It would be unfair, however, to blame him or anyone else for my shortcomings.

I am indebted also to Mark Shoffner, who plowed through the thicket of Chinese, Japanese, and Korean names and words to make my writing more readable. Sharon Yongnan Lee did the second round of editing, and I give my warm thanks to her as well.

Last but not least, I wish to offer my special thanks to President Choue Inwon of Kyung Hee University for his generous support of this work. I also wish to thank the Yeon Kang Foundation in Seoul whose grant many years ago enabled me to continue my study of Korea. I must emphasize that I am solely responsible for the content of this book. None of the individuals and institutions mentioned here should be held responsible for my opinions or my defects.

Introduction

Park Chung-Hee remains a controversial figure among Koreans. On one hand, many believe he ranks among the greatest leaders Korea has ever had. Without him, they say, Korea would not have been able to join the ranks of advanced nations. His leadership transformed a backward economy, which was far behind that of the Philippines and Nigeria, into a member of the G20. His leadership nurtured Hyundai, Samsung, and LG into world-renowned companies. He is credited with the creation of the "Miracle of the Han River."

On the other hand, some argue that Park's role in South Korea's development has been exaggerated. Korea was on the threshold of a rapid takeoff in 1961 when Park Chung-Hee overturned the democratic government led by Premier Chang Myŏn. Korea had the human resources; it could have obtained the capital from abroad, as Park subsequently did. The international environment was also quite favorable for South Korea's development. The country might have developed even faster had the junta not disrupted the democratic process, they argue.

His detractors further denounce Park Chung-Hee for the convolutions in his political affiliations. They accuse him of having been a national traitor, who faithfully served the Japanese colonial masters. They say that although he became a member of the Communist Party after Korea's liberation from Japan in 1945, he then betrayed the party by exposing their secrets to the authorities. The turncoat then led a coup d'état against the democratic regime and ruled the country as a ruthless dictator. Park may have led South Korea's economic advances, but he did so at the expense of the workers he suppressed. Kim Chae-gyu, Park's intelligence director, did the right thing when he shot him to death in 1979, they contend.

Such polarized views continue to make the study of Park Chung-Hee interesting and important. Whatever one may think of him as a person, there is no doubt about his role in putting South Korea on the map. He was the locomotive that propelled the modernization train. As the junta leader and subsequently as president of the Republic of Korea, he pushed his program through like a commander attacking an enemy's fort. As some of the efforts began to bear fruit, he had even more soaring ambitions for his country.[1]

The heated controversy reflects in part the ideological atmosphere of South Korea in the late twentieth and early twenty-first centuries but also highlights the character of the period Park's generation had to go through. They lived through one of the most, if not the most, turbulent periods in Korean history. Even a cursory sketch would persuade the uninitiated.

He was a Korean, to be sure, but was born a subject of the Japanese emperor because he was born in 1917, twelve years after Korea lost its sovereignty and became a part of the Japanese empire. Japan had to let go of Korea in 1945 after it was defeated by the allied powers, including the United States and the Soviet Union, in the Second World War, but that did not mean Korean independence. Instead, the two allied powers

---

1 Please see the epilogue for my rendering of how economic development occurred.

divided the Korean Peninsula into two parts, each of the great powers occupying one. The Koreans regained independence three years later, in 1948, but two separate regimes emerged rather than one, and the two republics bitterly opposed each other. The result was a war between 1950 and 1953 that killed multitudes of people and deepened the enmity between the two sides. The truce was signed in July 1953, but two large armies confront each other on the Korean Peninsula even today with no sign of the tension abating.

If such kaleidoscopic changes were not complicated enough, there was more. The Japanese empire that ruled the Koreans went through precipitous changes too. The Japan he knew during his elementary school years was very different from the one he faced in later years as the country changed around him at breakneck speed. Japanese leaders were not content with having Korea and Taiwan as their colonies; they invaded Manchuria and China also. Domestically, the Japanese empire appeared headed for parliamentary democracy when Park Chung-Hee was a child, but by the time he was in his teens, Japan had fallen captive to the militarists. Eventually, the military hotheads threw Japan against the United States, which had been critical of Japanese expansionism, and that war led to the dropping of the atomic bombs in Hiroshima and Nagasaki followed by Soviet attacks in Manchuria and Korea in August 1945. So Park spent his formative years, between ages thirteen to twenty-eight, under Japanese militarism.

The Japanese surrender and Korean liberation opened a new phase in Park Chung-Hee's life, but the trauma of liberation turned out to be more nightmarish than anyone could have imagined. No one had thought that the victors in the war against Japan would divide Korea into two parts and turn it into the front line of an ideological conflict they could not reconcile. The Americans prided themselves on their capitalism and individual freedom, while the Russian Communists dedicated themselves to Communist revolution, which in reality meant the building of a collective society headed by an autocrat. The two powers worked together when they faced common enemies, but the defeat of the Axis Powers, including Nazi Germany and Militarist Japan, restored the cold war atmosphere that had already prevailed before the Second World War. Thus, Korea became the microcosm of an international confrontation, and Park was obliged to find his way through the middle of it.

The ideological confrontation between the Soviet Union and the United State inflicted a greater burden on Park Chung-Hee than on most of the Korean people in that it killed his older brother outright and put Park Chung-Hee through a torture mill. It is truly a wonder that Park Chung-Hee survived these ordeals and emerged as Korea's modernizing leader.

My aim in this book is to trace the development of Park Chung-Hee's mind-set, which led to the coup d'état of 1961 and his efforts for modernization. Some may dismiss such an effort as useless; he was motivated by nothing more than a hunger for power, they would argue. But I obviously do not subscribe to that view. I was struck by a series of statements Park made soon after he overthrew the incipient democratic regime in 1961 and decided to investigate. The statement published on June 15, 1961, a month after the coup, was extraordinary. Major General Park Chung-Hee denounced "all the leaders of the past" for letting the people suffer in misery and putting the country in jeopardy.[2] The result had been devastating to the people, he argued. While the powerful abused their authority, engaged in corruption, and accumulated wealth, the people came to accept intrigues, slander, and false accusations as a means of advancing in the world. Moreover, they became irresponsible and lazy, wishing to reap fruits without planting, exercise freedom without responsibility, and hope for miracles and magic to liberate them from poverty. Illegal transactions became the norm, a way of life. Korea had become a den of thieves where no one put in an honest day's work.[3] The surprise was not that Korea remained poor and decadent but that it survived at all.

One could easily dismiss such lambast as an excuse invented by a man who overthrew a legally constituted democratic regime, but he went further two years later. "Our five thousand years of history was a continuation of degeneration, crudity, and stagnation,"[4] Park said. "We should set ablaze all our history that was more like a storehouse of evil."[5] One would expect a new political leader to glorify the country's traditions and history, but Park was definitely not following the norm. Instead, he elaborated on his denunciatory theme.

It is doubtful that many people at that time paid much attention to what Park wrote. Those who did could not help but be skeptical about

---

2 Park Chung-Hee, *Chidojado* [The Leader's Way] (Seoul: Supreme Council of National Reconstruction, 1961), 9. It is dated June 15, 1961, a month after the coup. My thanks go to Kim Chang-kon and Lee Jo-a for locating this essay for me. Of the thousands of copies that were published in 1961, only the Chosŏn University library preserved one.

3 Ibid., 29.

4 Park Chung-Hui, *Kukka wa hyŏngmyŏng kwa na* [The Nation, Revolution, and I] (Seoul: Kwangmyŏng, 1963), 245.

5 Ibid., 249.

his statements. But there was something strange about Park's remarks. It would have been sufficient for him to denounce the regime he had just overthrown; he did not have to attack all of Korean history. Chang Myŏn's Democratic Party was simply not ready to fill the political vacuum created by the Student Revolution of April 1960. This revolution had forced out the octogenarian Syngman Rhee, who had been president of the republic since 1948. Chang's party was nothing more than a makeshift coalition of two divergent political groups, and there was not a dynamic enough leadership to unite the two. Hence, the politicians waged their internal strife in public, Premier Chang announcing the replacement of cabinet ministers every few days as if the cabinet were a merry-go-round. In the meantime, the people clamored for everything they did not have previously, and chaos prevailed.[6] Many in 1961 assumed that Park's coup was the military's response to the immediate situation.

Why, then, the denunciation of all the leaders of the past and the wish to set ablaze "five thousand years of history"? How did Park come to form such a perspective? What kind of a man was he? How was his character formed? How did his perspective affect his actions in subsequent years? These, I believe, are important questions because Park set out to reform not only Korea's economy and its landscape, but also its "national character," the behavior and thinking patterns of the people. While "national character" was not something Park could change overnight, he did leave a deep imprint in setting the nation's course in that direction. My hope now is to answer some of the questions posed above.

---

6 Cf. Sungjoo Hahn, *The Failure of Democracy in South Korea* (Berkeley: University of California Press, 1974).

I. THE LEGACY OF THE FATHER

Park Chung-Hee once said that poverty was both his teacher and his benefactor. Park's struggles to overcome poverty became the motivating force behind his crusade against it. Lasswell was right when he said that the power seeker "pursues power as a means of compensation against deprivation."[1] But one would be amiss to concentrate solely on Park's childhood poverty and not probe the reasons behind it. Park's father, Park Sŏng-bin, had not been a son of an ordinary poor peasant. In fact, his father was the son of a *yangban*, the ruling class. The family's poverty was the result of an intrepid political action Sŏng-bin had taken in his youth. Park's statement, therefore, must be amended to read, "The poverty that my father imposed on me was my teacher and benefactor." I attach much importance to the phrase "imposed on me" because the poverty Park had to endure epitomized the suffering of the family, which deeply affected the young man's perspective on Korean history.

The Father

The immediate cause of Park's poverty was his father's involvement in the Tonghak movement, which swept the country in the late nineteenth century. His grandfather[2] had inherited enough land to feed the family.[3] Having the heritage of *yangban*, he naturally wanted his first son, Sŏng-bin (1871–1938), to climb the ladder of success, which meant preparing for and taking the civil service examinations.[4] He probably

1 Harold D. Lasswell, *Power and Personality* (New York: Viking Press, 1962), 39 (original edition by W.W. Norton, 1948).

2 Park Yŏng-gyu (1840–1914).

3 Cho Kap-je, *Na ui mudŏm e ch'im ul paett'ŏra* [Spit on My Grave] (Seoul: Chosŏn Ilbosa, 1998), 331. One of his cousins said his grandfather used to receive piles of rice sacks from his tenants each autumn. The author based his information on interviews with Park's cousin Park Chae-sŏk, the son of Park Mu-hui and the second elder brother of Park's father.

4 See Choe Yŏng-Ho, *The Civil Examinations and the Social Structure in Early Yi*

hoped that his son would follow the example of his ancestor Park Mun-su (1691–1756), who had shaken the region in the early 1700s as a royal inspector, traveling with his men incognito and smashing the corrupt officials who had turned their offices into dens of thieves. Park Mun-su did this not only once but twice, saving the hungry public in the neighboring Ch'ungch'ŏng Province in 1730.[5] But Sŏng-bin, Park Chung-Hee's father, had a severe handicap in his efforts to emulate his distinguished ancestor; he was born at the wrong time in the wrong branch of the Koryŏng Park clan.[6] Sŏng-bin's branch of the Koryŏng Park clan, known as the "Chik-kang-gong-p'a," had not produced many passers of the civil service examination since their fifteenth-generation ancestor Mang-dal moved to Sŏngju, a village some twenty miles west of Taegu. The sixteenth- to eighteenth-generation ancestors passed the examinations and obtained minor government positions,[7] but for ten generations after that, no one had passed them.[8] The odds were stacked against Sŏng-bin, because while the civil service examination was open to all *yangbans* in theory, it had been skewed to allow the dominance of a small number of clans.[9] Unfortunately for Sŏngbin, the Koryŏng Park

---

Dynasty Korea, 1392–1600 (Seoul: Korean Research Center, 1987).

5 Pak Mun-su was later appointed the Minister of Rites. His achievements as a Royal Inspector was dramatized in a movie, *Amhaeng ŏsa Pak Munsu*, in 1962. It was probably not a coincidence that Pak Mun-su was one of Park Chung-Hee's ancestors and that the latter had just carried out the coup d'état in 1961, stating the elimination of corruption as one of his slogans.

6 "Koryŏng" in "the "Koryŏng Park" clan indicates the name of the place where one of Chŏng-Hee's ancestors established himself and started a new branch of the Park clan. It is located about ten kilometers south of Sŏngju.

7 Ch'ambong, Changsarang, Hogun, and Pu-hogun.

8 I have examined the record of each of Park's ancestors in the clan's lineage books.

9 JaHyun Kim Haboush, *A Heritage of Kings* (New York: Columbia University Press, 1988), 16; Edward Wagner, "The Ladder of Success in Yi Dynasty Korea," *Occasional Papers on Korea*, 1 (April 1974): 1–18 (at p. 4).

was not one of them. Sŏng-bin, therefore, could not count on the extra help needed to pass the highly competitive qualifying examinations.

Park Chung-Hee's mention of his father passing the *mukwa* or the military branch examination[10] says much about the situation. The military examination was not a part of the civil service examination system and carried much less prestige than *munkwa* (moon-kwa), the civil examinations. It was open not only to the yangban but to commoners as well. Sometimes, in cases of war and famine, the military examination was used as a means of mobilizing people or raising revenues for the state, allowing thousands who sought to elevate their status to do so. All this indicates that Sŏng-bin's clan had been reduced to a marginal yangban position—in all probability, they were desperately struggling to hold onto their yangban status.[11]

Park Chung Hee's account of his father joining the Tonghak rebels is quite credible in this context. A young man in his position, whether he had passed the *mukwa* examination or not, would have wanted a change, a revolutionary change, hoping for something better. It was a society where politics dominated everything, but the government had fallen into such a state of decadence that honesty and hard work simply did not pay.

---

10 Park Chung-Hee, "Na ui sonyŏn shijŏl" [My Childhood Days], dated April 26, 1970. Reprinted in *Wŏlgan Chosŏn* [Chosŏn Monthly] (May 1984): 84–95; Chŏng Chae-gyŏng, *Wiin Park Chung-Hee* [Park Chung-Hee, the Great Man] (Seoul: Chipmundang, 1992): 12–24. Page numbers for this work are from Chŏng Chae-gyong's volume. Hereafter noted as Park, "My Childhood Days." Park mentioned his father's title as "*hyoryŏk puwi,*" a 9th(b) rank.

11 I am grateful to Professor Ch'oe Yŏng-Ho of the University of Hawaii for enlightening me on these matters. For a more detailed examination of the military examination, see the excellent work by Eugene Park, *Between Dream and Reality: The Military Examination in Late Chosŏn Korea, 1600–1894* (Cambridge, MA: Harvard University Press, 2007).

The Old Regime in Decay

This was not a situation General Yi Sŏng-gye (1335–1408), the founder of the Chosŏn Dynasty, would have wanted. He had overthrown the decadent Koryŏ Dynasty (918–1392) in 1392 and instituted cataclysmic changes, eradicating the abuse and corruption the Buddhist-dominated regime had allowed. His regime adopted Confucianism as the state ideology and built the new dynasty accordingly. But, in time, the Chosŏn Dynasty suffered from the same malaise that had afflicted the previous dynasty. Lethargy and corruption set in, and the reigning ideology became rote and form, rather than a dynamic guide for the improvement of society. Even worse, it became a tool for political struggle, a weapon to attack opponents. Once opponents were defined as heretics, there was no room for compromise. Extremism became the norm, and a multitude of able men were persecuted or exterminated in the name of upholding orthodoxy. The conservative and classically oriented ideology left little hope for rejuvenation.

Some Koreans today sing the praises of this dynasty, which lasted five hundred years, but it would have been unlikely that any bloodline could produce able leaders for so many generations. The dynasty was fortunate to produce two right-minded kings in the eighteenth century, Yŏngjo (1724–1776) and Chŏngjo (1776–1800), but upon the latter's death in 1800, the Chosŏn Dynasty fell into the hands of ravenous and rapacious families, who paid no attention to the fate of the nation. A victorious patriarch in the political struggle would install a child-king as a puppet, have him marry his own daughter or granddaughter, and then proclaim himself the father or grandfather-in-law of the king. Thus Sunjo (r. 1800–1834) was enthroned at eleven, Hŏnjong (r. 1834–1849) at seven, and Ch'ŏljong (r. 1849–1863) at eighteen. The latter had a legitimate bloodline but was not remotely prepared to be a king. He was an impoverished peasant in Kanghwa Island, barely earning a living. He could neither read nor write when he was installed as king, and even though he was provided a queen and a host of palace ladies, he did not produce a male heir. In the meantime, the in-law families plundered the people and treated them with "as much arrogance and greed as if they had been conquered in a war."[12]

The dynasty needed someone else with the founder's bloodline, and it fell on Yi Myŏng-bok (1852–1907) to inherit the throne in 1863 at the age of eleven. His father, Yi Ha-ŭng (1820–1898), better known by his title Taewŏn'gun, had seen enough abuse of power, and set out to restore royal authority and order. He made much progress in reforming the government, but he had to yield power to his son, King Kojong, after ten years. Boisterous opposition against Taewŏn'gun's reform programs was to be expected, but some of his efforts to bolster royal authority were too much of a burden for the masses to bear. Taewŏn'gun's xenophobic stand against the West also created serious problems. But his most serious error was in the selection of his daughter-in-law. His intent was to avoid the abuse of in-laws who had virtually ruined the nation for so many decades. He chose, therefore, a daughter of an impoverished Min clan, which had very few male offspring. But he could not have chosen a craftier, stronger-willed, or more power-hungry woman. Taewŏn'gun may have shared the same qualities, but he could not win the contest against her. His good-natured son had a character that was exactly the opposite of his wife's.

---

12 I borrowed the expression Plutarch (ca. AD 45–120) used to describe the plundering of the people at the time of Brutus (85–42 BC) to show that the ancient Romans and the nineteenth-century Koreans had much in common! *Makers of Rome*, trans. Ian Scott-Kilvert (London: Penguin Books, 1965), 228.

Kojong was timid and lacked the vision and will to make tough decisions. Instead, he was easily swayed by those around him, particularly his queen, commonly referred to as Queen Min (1864–1895), who was steeped in superstition and relied heavily on sorceresses for major decisions. All efforts to enlighten the queen and the Min clan were in vain. The legacy of grinding poverty had ingrained resistance to change.[13]

The following observation, recorded by a Western-educated young man named Yun Ch'i-ho (1864–1945) in the 1890s, provides the background for the rise of the Tonghak Rebellion of 1894–95. These paragraphs are also relevant in understanding Park Chung-Hee's scathing criticism of Korea's history. Yun's father, Yun Ung-ryŏl (1840–1911), was a successful politician under Kojong and tried to steer his son down the same path.

> *Success at Any Cost*[14]
>
> Knowing, as my father does, the poisonous and disastrous effects of Haingsei [wielding power and influence] upon the character of the individual and of the nation,

---

13 The United States government had just concluded a treaty of amity with Korea in 1882 and given Min Yŏng-ik, the queen's favorite nephew, an around-the-world tour in 1883. Even after seeing New York, London, Paris, Rome, and the Suez Canal, he preferred the old Chinese classics and Korea's subservient relations with the Qing Dynasty. For my study of Min Yŏng-ik and the Min clan, see Yi Chŏng-sik, *KuHanmal ui kaehyŏk tongnip t'usa Sŏ Chae-p'il* [Sŏ Chae-p'il: The Fighter for Reform and Independence at the End of the Old Korea] (Seoul: Seoul National University Press, 2003), 34–43. I attribute the backwardness of the Min clan to the dire poverty its members suffered before Queen Min rose to power. Min Yŏng-ik, for example, endured destitution until he reached the age of fourteen or fifteen but was thrust into the limelight and a decision-making position at twenty-three. Destitution at this time also meant he received no education of any kind.

14 I have added the subheadings for convenience. The question mark in the quotation here was in the original text.

knowing, as he does, that one in order to Haingsei, must part with honesty, righteousness, noble aims and high purposes, knowing all this better than any other person in Corea, my father still insists on my going into it. I must throw away every principle of honor and of morality if I want to "Haingsei." Father himself says that honesty and a sense of honor do not go well with Haingsei. The only thing that Haingsei hunts after is glory (?) and gain. No means is too mean or too wicked for the attainment of the end—office.[15]

The King Selling Magistracies

Since last January Kim Hong Niuk, the Russian interpreter has sold over 20 magistrates at the average price of $2,000, giving him $40,000. He gained, according to Mr. Tang, $60,000 in the ginseng trade. Within four months he has gained $100,000. [16]

My father had to pay 60,000.00 Yang ($12,000.00) for the governorship of Kwang Chu. He gave 10,000.00 Yang ($2,000.00) to the Palace on the birthday of the Prince. Various articles of furniture etc. to the worth of 20,000.00 Yang ($4,000.00) were ordered by the Palace at the expense of my father. Thus scarcely four months have passed since he was appointed the governor, whose monthly salary is $200.00 only: yet he has already spent $18,000.00 or twenty two and half times as much as his salary for 4 months! A very poor investment, I should say.[17]

---

15 February 23, 1895; Kuksa P'yŏnch'an Wiwonhoe [The Committee for the Compilation of National History], *Yun Ch'i-ho ilgi* [The Yun Ch'i-ho Diary], vol. 4 (Seoul: T'amkudang, 1975), 33. The question mark in parentheses was in the original text.

16 April 22, 1898; ibid., vol. 5, 153.

17 May 6, 1901; ibid., vol. 5, 292–293.

Kojong's Character

> Poor King! He is surrounded by hundreds of people who are hurrying him and his country to ruin. Yet what can be done with a gentleman for whom experience has no lessons: patriotism no meaning, and honesty no attractions? Woe unto the land whose destiny has been placed in the hand of such a master. Every time I see His Majesty I feel like crying: for I love as well as pity him: but I can't get near him because I wouldn't lie and cheat him.[18]

It is not surprising that the author of these comments joined with Sŏ Chae-p'il in 1896 to organize and lead the Independence Club to advocate Korea's reform. Sŏ Chae-p'il had just returned from his ten-year exile in the United States and shared Yun Ch'i-ho's opinion about the king and the officialdom. The student debate group Sŏ organized expanded into large public gatherings on the Seoul streets under the auspices of the same club. It was only natural for everyone to assume, therefore, that those playing an active part in these meetings were the reformers who would lead Korea to a brighter future. Yun Ch'i-ho evidently held such hopes, but he was utterly disappointed. Here is his diary entry of February 1, 1899:

The Character of the "Progressive Activists"

> But what has made me sick and hopeless is the discovery of the thorough rottenness of many, or nine-tenths, of the members of the Independence Club or the People's Meeting. Not one of them seems to have been able to withstand the temptation of stealing as much as possible of the money contributed by others. Such men as Mun

18 November 14, 1897; ibid., vol. 5, 115–116.

> T'aewon, Kim Kwangt'ae, Pang Handok, Rim Chinsu etc., in whom I had reposed unbounded trust as to their honesty and integrity, have turned out to be regular thieves. The young men who had come from Japan after a few years' stay there are worse. They have become so rotten that they deem it weakness nay even crime not to be able to cheat money out of some unsuspecting fools. Those who were loudest in denouncing the corruption etc. of officials have turned out, to my disgust and amazement, to be as unscrupulous and unreliable as the worst of the worst officials![19]
>
> Was it for these rascals that some of us sacrificed the welfare of body and mind during the year[s] past? With such a people and for such a people, to start any popular demonstrations would be madness. The blood of the race has to be changed by a new education, a new government and a new religion.[20]

One can begin to see why Park Chung-Hee later brought up the question of "national character." Discussion of that weighty subject, however, must be postponed for the time being.

It was not surprising that the subjugated masses occasionally exploded into revolts under such conditions. The Hong Kyŏng-rae Rebellion of 1811–1812 displayed the intensity of hostility against the regime in the northwestern region. The rebellion lasted five months, requiring concentrated efforts of the central government. Half a century later, those in the three southern provinces revolted in 1862, continuing well into the following year. Rebellion in Chinju spread to the nearby towns, and soon, a chain reaction spread throughout the southern provinces

---

19 February 1, 1899; ibid., vol. 5, 207–208.
20 Ibid.

of Kyŏngsang, Chŏlla, and Ch'ungchŏng, the disgruntled masses sacking government offices and murdering the hated officials. The government sent its troops to contain the rebellion and tried to take corrective measures, but a just and efficient government could not be expected when magistracies were bought and sold like merchandise. While the Tonghak Rebellion of 1895 was of sectarian origin, it was fueled by the peasants' anger and frustration against the corrupt sociopolitical system that had brought on economic destitution.[21]

The Tonghak Movement

Why did Park Sŏng-bin join the Tonghaks? Why did the government condemn the rebels to the extent of meting a death sentence upon Park Sŏng-bin? Sŏng-bin himself did not leave us any record, but one of his contemporaries did. Kim Ku (1876–1949), six years younger than Park Sŏng-bin, wrote the following, beginning with how he became interested in the Tonghak movement[22]:

> It was rumored at that time that O Ong-sŏn, who lived in Kaetgol, about twenty ri south of my village,[23] and Ch'oe Hyŏn, who lived in the next village, had been learning Tonghak principles...It was said that in going in and out of houses they did not use doors; they appeared or disappeared instantaneously; they could walk in the sky and go to visit Ch'oe To-myŏng, the leader in Ch'ungch'ŏng Province, within a night. I began to develop a curiosity about Tonghak and decided to visit them.

---

21 See Yi Ki-baek, *New History of Korea,* trans. Edward Wagner with Edward Shulz (Seoul: Ilchokak, 1996), 283–285.

22 Quotations are from *Paekbŏm ilji: Kim Ku Chasŏjŏn* [Memoirs of Paekbŏm: Autobiography of Kim Ku] (Seoul: Koryŏ Sŏnbongsa, 1947). 26–33.

23 About eight kilometers or five miles.

Kim Ku then related what impressed him the most during his first visit.

> As I approached Mr. O's house, I could hear people reading something aloud. It was different from the tone of chanting Buddhist sutras or other poems and sounded rather like singing songs in harmony. When I called at the house, a young and handsome man of the yangban class appeared, wearing a gentleman's hat. As I politely bowed, he politely bowed back. I was very much impressed and, after telling him my name and address, said, "Even if I were a mature man with a proper hat, a gentleman of yangban birth would not bow to me. Now, seeing that I am only a boy of the commoners' class, you are treating me over courteously."
>
> He smiled and said that he was a follower of Tonghak and that in the teachings of the founder there was no discrimination according to wealth or birth, and hence all were to be treated equally. When I told him the purpose of my visit, he politely explained to me the history and major principles of the religion…The principles were that the wicked people of the last era of the world should renew themselves and lead new lives in order to become a new people. By doing so they would be able to serve the true king in the future in constructing a new nation in Keryong Mountain. I was overjoyed to hear his teachings…

What follows is his summation:

> Since I had previously determined to become a man of good heart…it was very important for me to have God within me and act according to the way of Heaven. Also, for a man who was of the commoners' class and filled with indignation,

> the egalitarianism preached by Tonghak was extremely precious. Also the prediction [that] the Yi dynasty was coming to an end was well received by me, because I had been disappointed by the corruption in the government. I was filled with a desire to join Tonghak and asked the procedure for entering. I was told that I should bring one mal [30 lb.] of rice, three dozen sheets of window paper, and one pair of candles. I looked through Tonggyŏng Taejŏn, P'alpy'on Kasa, and Kungwolga and returned home. After joining Tonghak I studied diligently and strove to propagate the teachings…
>
> At this time there were few yangbans joining, and most of those entering were of the lower classes. Within a few months I obtained several hundred followers. My name was widely known in the district. Many came to ask me about the teachings, and rumors were circulated about me…Some said that they saw Kim Ch'ang-am[24] walking in the air more than two meters above the ground. With these rumors becoming widespread, I gained several thousand followers.

We do not know where the rumor of leaders' supernatural powers originated, but it appears that this played an important role in attracting followers. An unidentified Western missionary backed up Kim Ku's account. The Tonghaks not only had magical power, but they promised everything short of paradise:

> No sickness would enter the house; crops would never fail; debts would not be paid nor taxes; in the battle the bullets of the enemy would be changed to water. Indeed the magical power of the leaders was limitless. It gave an opportunity also to pay off an old score with an enemy.[25]

---

24 Kim Ku's childhood name.

25 "Seven Months among the Tong Haks," *Korean Repository*, vol. 2 (June 1895),

So assured, the mob occasionally burst into violence:

> Magistrates were seized, books burned, guns, ammunition, spears, and banners plundered. To the ordinary Korean such power so quickly acquired seemed to substantiate their reports of magical power. Little persuasion or threatening was now needed to swell the ranks. Thousands joined in a day, several who attended our Christian meeting in the morning were on the warpath in the evening. Great were the promises and bright the prospects of the initiated. They struck a very effective chord in the Korean's heart.[26]

The strongest attraction, however, was political, that is, the advocacy of egalitarianism and the replacement of the corrupt political regime. It is quite obviously what the lower classes wanted to hear. Park Sŏng-bin may have been a yangban, but he was marginalized, frustrated, and indignant at the corruption and injustice that surrounded him. We do not know how large the Tonghak group in Kumi was or how violent the rebellion there became, but Park Sŏng-bin would have emerged as a leader because of his yangban status and his ability to read and write. He was also a large, robust man with strong character.

Spontaneous rebellions rarely succeed against the established government, however, and the Tonghaks were no exception. The regime squashed them, and Park Sŏng-bin became a prisoner. It was sheer luck, as his wife told his son later, that he escaped the hands of the executioners.

Park Sŏng-bin's wife and children may have been glad that he survived, but his father was not and did not forgive his errant son. This is

---

201–208. The quotation is from p. 203. The author is not identified.

26 Ibid., 202–203.

where the young Park Chung-Hee's troubles began. Regardless of Park Sŏng-bin's justification for joining the revolt, his father had good reason to be outraged. To join the rebels against the authorities constituted a monstrous crime for a yangban. Sŏng-bin's actions were particularly painful for his father, as they could have jeopardized the yangban status of his whole family. No official codes have been written on how a yangban would lose his privileged status, but becoming a traitor certainly would have been a sufficient reason. Maintaining the yangban status was not just a matter of prestige. It immunized the family from taxes, the military draft, corvée, and other burdens the government imposed upon the commoners. Park Sŏng-bin risked too much when he joined the Tonghaks. One can understand why Sŏngbin's father ousted him from the clan, depriving him of his birthright as the first son to inherit the family farm. Instead, he chose his third son as the beneficiary. These harsh actions were not only proper for a self-respecting yangban; they were necessary. Not punishing his errant son would also be seen by the officialdom as the father's condoning of his actions. The father had to worry about the other members of the Park clan also, particularly in view of the second-class status of his branch.

The seriousness of the punishment inflicted on Park Sŏng-bin can be seen from the fact that he had to move to Sangmo-dong, his wife's village a few miles north in Sŏnsan County. His brother-in-law, who taught Chinese classics to children, let him (or his sister) till a small plot, just over an acre, adjacent to the family cemetery.[27] The income from the plot was to be used for the semi-annual memorial services for ancestors. Such land was known as *wit'o* and was large enough for a couple with

27 Park Chung-Hee said it was 1,600 p'yong, approximately 1.2 acres; "My Childhood Days," 15.

a child or two, but not when they had more children. Thus, the son of a yangban was relegated to the status of a grave keeper, known in Korean as *myojik* or *myojigi*, a position that does not accrue much respect in any society.[28] Most likely, it is for this reason that Park Sŏng-bin never helped his wife with the farmwork. To do so would have meant the acceptance of, or resignation to, myojik status, which would have tarnished his yangban rank. This was not a trivial matter in the highly stratified society. Hence, Park Sŏng-bin became a lifelong loafer or wastrel, not willing to engage in any productive activity from his early twenties on. Instead, he whiled away his time with wine and travels. Perhaps it was also his way of protesting the harsh punishment his father and the clan had imposed upon him. Whatever the reason, it fell on his wife to manage the family. We do not know how old she was when all this happened, but she would have been very young. The yangban custom was to marry their children in their early teens, from thirteen to sixteen. The wife had no choice but to support her family, even after the disgrace.

I must ask the reader's indulgence at this point to explain the evidence concerning Park Sŏng-bin's involvement in the Tonghak movement, because this act essentially shaped his son's life and because the claim is not based on the solid documentary evidence that historians require. But I believe Park Chung-Hee's story about his father to be credible for two reasons. First, Park specifically mentioned hearing it from his mother, and such a source cannot be doubted. No mother would invent such a story; what she told her son was equivalent to a twenty-first-century mother in South Korea telling her son that his father had joined a Communist rebellion and escaped the hands of the executioner.

28 See Yi Man-gap, *Han'guk nongch'on ui sahoe kujo* [Social Structure in Korean Farming Villages] (Seoul: Han'guk Yŏn'gu Tosŏgwan, 1960), 122–124.

The mother would whisper such a story to her son only if it were true, because it was not something to be proud of. His mother told him the story not once, but repeatedly. She evidently enjoyed teasing her youngest son about the possibility of his not having been born had his father been executed.

The disinheritance of Park Sŏng-bin also serves as strong evidence of his joining the Tonghaks. Primogeniture is not a simple matter of transferring property to the first son. In Korean tradition, first sons have always been responsible for carrying the family name from generation to generation, a responsibility not treated lightly. The first son's family was called the *chong-ga* (pronounced "jong-ka") and was responsible for holding ceremonies for each of the ancestors of many generations on their birthdays and their days of death. This was in addition to the two national memorial days in the spring and autumn. Since all of the clan members participated in the ceremony and had to be fed a number of meals, the chong-ga household required a great many working hands. The chong-ga also had to lodge and feed the relatives. In other words, the first son had to work for the privilege of inheriting the family estate. If Sŏng-bin's treason against the state had not soiled the family's honor, his father would never have disinherited his first son. There is little doubt that Sŏng-bin's father's wrath stemmed from his involvement in the Tonghak movement.

Some have argued that Sŏng-bin's father gave his inheritance to his third son because Sŏng-bin had spent too much money to prepare and take the examinations. Others have argued that it was because of Sŏng-bin's drinking habits. But these are not adequate reasons for disinheritance. The yangban was expected to spend as much of his fortune as he could to educate his sons, because the family's future depended on the sons' success. It was an investment rather than an indulgence. The notion of Sŏng-bin losing his birthright because of his drinking is questionable, because it is not known when he started to indulge in liquor, or to what extent. It is possible that he acquired the habit of drinking after he lost his birthright, rather than before. Such trauma would drive many men to hit the bottle.

The Mother

Whatever he did among the Tonghaks, Park Sŏng-bin survived the ordeal and sired another son upon returning home. His wife was horrified when she found herself pregnant again at the age of forty-three. Feeding another mouth was not a small problem in 1917, because southern Korea, where the Park family lived, had been hit by a severe case of wind and flood damage that year.[29] On top of the added economic burden of feeding another child, it was very embarrassing for a woman of her age to become pregnant. Indeed, her first daughter was expecting a baby at this time too. She drank bowls of soy sauce, threw herself off piles of firewood, and otherwise tried every known means to abort the fetus, but to no avail.[30] He was a tenacious baby. Eventually, she gave birth to Chung-Hee all alone on November 14, 1917. His sister, Chae-Hee, had run to seek adult help when his mother started to moan in pain, but the baby arrived without any assistance.[31] Perhaps the circumstances of his birth presaged his lonely life.

---

29 Chōsen Sōtokufu (Korean Government General), *Shisei 30nen shi* [A 30 Year History of Administration] (Seoul, 1940, 897). The same region suffered severe flooding the previous year; ibid., chronology section, 18.

30 Cho Kap-je quoted from Park Chung-Hee's sister Pak Chae-hui in his *Spit on My Grave*, vol. 1, 318.

31 Ibid., 320.

Park's mother, Paek Nam-ui, had grown up in a relatively well-to-do family and had experienced no hardships before her marriage. She was even able to read and write the Korean script, a skill very few village women possessed. While she had tried her best to abort him, she poured her affection on her youngest son. Park's short autobiography devoted many paragraphs to her dedication: how she woke him early each morning with breakfast and a wash bowl of warm water ready; how she stood at the edge of the pine forest to watch her son leaving for the two-hour walk to school before sunrise and waited for his return after dark; how she washed his muddy cotton-padded socks every night and laid them on the heated floor to dry for the next day; and how she wrapped eggs in socks for him to carry to the Japanese-owned store by the school to exchange for pencils or notebooks. The family had no clock or watches with which to tell time. Only her inner clock told her when to get up and ready her child for school. In fact, no one in the village had such a modern contraption as a "time machine." Electricity and running water would come to the village many decades later. In any event, Park's mother's love undoubtedly gave the young child the confidence he needed at school.

Poverty

Depending on a small plot of land on the high ground meant poverty, of course, but the growing family made the situation even worse. The Park family's third daughter-in-law, the wife of the third son, Park Sang-Hee, best described the situation:

> How would I have known my husband's family was so poor?! Hanging on the entrance to the kitchen was a straw mat rather than a door! Their ceiling was made out of apple box pieces. I found it strange that my mother-in-law would not let me enter the kitchen, insisting that the new-style daughter-in-law should not get into the old-style kitchen. I found out later that they had no rice, nor the soy sauce [to whip up a meal].[32]

She was shocked because she was a daughter of a prosperous businessman in the town of Kimch'ŏn. The mother could not let the middle-school-educated "modern girl" into the hole in the ground that served as the kitchen. The daughter-in-law outclassed the Park family not only in terms of wealth but also in education. Park Sang-Hee had made history in the village by entering and graduating from the elementary school in Kumi, located five miles away from Sangmo-dong, but that was all the education he had received. Nor did his education improve the family's economic situation. His mother would have been horrified by her daughter-in-law's visit. It was definitely thoughtless of Sang-Hee to allow his wife to visit the hovel that served as their home.

---

32 Ibid., 410.

Park Sŏng-bin's family would have resented the poverty and the wastrel who had caused it all, but Chung-Hee came to appreciate his father more and more as he matured. Eventually, he came to share his father's views about the old Korean kingdom. His assessment of the Tonghak movement in 1963 was very positive. He called it "the surprising spontaneous resistance movement of the people rare in our history."[33] His account in 1969 was even more glowing:

> The Tonghak Rebellion was the first democratic revolution the people of our country started in history. It was among the farmers that the leading forces to construct a new society germinated. They further developed the thoughts of the masses with self-identity (chuch'e), which became the foundation for reconstruction and revolution. It became the spiritual source to realize revolutionary thoughts and new democracy. [The Tong-

33 Park Chung-Hee, *Minjok ui chŏryŏk* [Underlying Strength of the Nation] (Seoul: Kwangmyŏng, 1971), 40. He devoted pages 40 through 44 to the Tonghak movement. In this version, he restricted the denunciatory statement of Korean history from the late nineteenth century to the middle of the twentieth.

> hak Rebellion] became the spiritual foundation of such later democratic revolutions as the March First movement (of 1919), the April 19th movement (of 1960) and the May 16th movement (of 1961).[34]

Park's characterization of the Tonghak rebellion, however, contains many questionable points. It would be a distortion to call the Tonghak movement a "democratic revolution," some would argue. It was rather a peasant rebellion with a strong conservative orientation.[35] But it was certainly the largest peasant rebellion the Chosŏn Dynasty had witnessed, with a strong sense of egalitarianism that challenged and shook the old order. Many would also disagree with Park Chung-Hee on the causal links between that movement and the other events he cited, particularly the military coup of May 16, 1961. Such discrepancies, however, highlight the extent to which Park Chung-Hee came to share his father's thoughts. Some may say the son shared his father's rebellious streak. Others may say he shared his father's inability to contain his rage against injustice.

---

34 Park, vol. 1, 1969, 122.

35 See Young-Ick Lew, "The Conservative Character of the 1894 Tonghak Peasant Uprising," *The Journal of Korean Studies*, vol. 7 (1990), 149–180; Yu Yŏng-ik, *Tonghak nongmin pong-gi wa Kap-o kaengjang* [The Tonghak Farmers' Uprising and the Kap-o Reform] (Seoul: Ilchokak, 1998).

II. KUMI ELEMENTARY SCHOOL

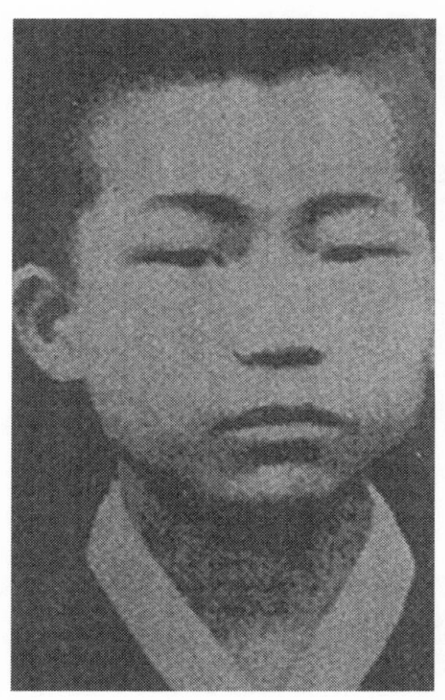

By the time Park Chung-Hee was born in 1917, the Tonghak Rebellion was nothing but a memory. The old Korean saying "even the rivers and mountains change in a decade" proved to be true, and much had happened between the Tonghak movement of 1894–95 and Chung-Hee's birth. Those years changed not only Korea's topography but also turned the entire region upside down. The time-honored China-centered civilization of East Asia crumbled with the Japanese defeat of China in 1895. The "island dwarfs," as the Chinese and Koreans had scornfully called the Japanese, then gained world-power status a decade later by defeating tsarist Russia in a war that involved not only the armies but also the navies, with their gigantic and ominous warships, which symbolized modernity.

King Kojong of the Chosŏn kingdom watched the movements of endless columns of Japanese soldiers marching through the capital city with equanimity. He had declared neutrality after the Russo-Japanese War erupted in 1904 but had placed his bets on the winning side; his government and the people actively supported the Japanese in the course of the war. He also thought he could depend on American support if he faced unexpected problems. The United States and the Korean kingdom had signed the Treaty of Peace, Amity, Commerce, and Navigation in 1882; surely the Americans would keep their word.[1] But the Japanese

---

1 In 1904, Yi Yong-ik, Kojong's confidant and the minister in charge of royal properties, told the British war correspondent F. A. McKenzie three days before Japan attacked Russia that "Korea was safe, for her independence was guaranteed by America and Europe." The following is their conversation:

> McKenzie: Don't you understand that treaties not backed by power are useless? If you wish the treaties to be respected, you must live up to them. You must reform or perish.
> Yi: It does not matter what the other nations are doing; we have this day sent out a statement that we are neutral and asking for our neutrality to be respected.

had their own designs. They wanted to take over Korea, and not much more effort was necessary to accomplish this aim. They already had a large army in Korea. All they had to do was to convert this army into the "Korea Garrison Army" (*Chōsen Chūtōgun*) to occupy Korea permanently. Since the Korean kingdom had only a few battalions of military forces trained by Chinese advisors, King Kojong did not even have a chance to protest the imposition. The Americans the king relied on at this time were more sympathetic to the Japanese, who had fought against Russia and thus prevented it from taking over Manchuria, and they had no intention of intervening against them. The treaty of 1882, in any event, did not bind the United States to protect the defenseless Korean kingdom.[2]

In spite of Kojong's inaction, however, some of the Korean soldiers rose in revolt against the Japanese in 1907, and thousands of others joined them. They could not, however, match the Japanese army, which had been strong enough to defeat the Russian forces. Thousands of Koreans fell on the battlefields, and the revolt had ended by 1911. Some of the resistors fled to Manchuria, contiguously located directly north of the Korean Peninsula, and tried to continue their fight, but they

---

(The Korean government declared neutrality in the Russo-Japanese war on January 21, 1904.)
McKenzie: Why should they protect you, if you do not protect yourself?
Yi: We have the promise of America. She will be our friend whatever happens.
F. A. McKenzie, *Korea's Fight for Freedom* (New York and London: Fleming H. Revell), 77–78.

2 King Kojong believed the United States would intervene for Korea because he believed in the 1882 treaty that had provided for "mutual assistance" if a third country caused problems for either of the two countries. That clause was in the Chinese language text that Li Hung-jang of China negotiated for Korea. The English text of the treaty, however, said one of the contracting parties would provide "good offices" to resolve the problems when requested. I have noted the discrepancy in my *KuHanmal ui kaehyŏk tongnip t'usa Sŏ Chae-p'il*, 280–281.

dissipated over the years. Japan, in the meantime, turned Korea into a protectorate in 1905 and made it an integral part of the Japanese empire in 1910.[3] In legal terms, therefore, Park Chung-Hee was born a subject of Emperor Yoshihito of Japan, better known as Emperor Taishō.

These momentous changes, however, did not affect the Park family's economic situation, as the new rulers paid no attention to the peasants struggling to eke out a living in the mountain villages. The peasants were unlike the landowners who had lost much of their property during the first decade of Japanese colonial rule. Imitating the Taikō survey carried out by Hideyoshi in the sixteenth and seventeenth centuries, the colonial government required the Koreans to register their landownership within a certain period for administrative purposes. But many local landowners ended up losing what they owned either because they were not aware of the new registration requirement or because they did not register properly. The Park family had none to lose, and life in the mountain village continued as before.

Even Sangmo-dong, however, could not be immune from the current of change sweeping through the country. The old custom of according deferential treatment to the yangban families faded very slowly in the countryside, but it was definitely on the way out. The abolition of the civil service examination system in 1894 accelerated the change because that system, known as *kwagŏ*, had been a special privilege reserved for the *yangban*. The old system of teaching Chinese classics was becoming obsolete, and Park Chung-Hee's uncle, the *sŏdang* (schoolhouse) teacher, became a relic of the past. What the world demanded now was modern education, and it had to begin with elementary school.

---

3 Cf. Chong-Sik Lee, *The Politics of Korean Nationalism* (Berkeley: University of California Press, 1963), chapters 5 and 6.

But the colonial government was slow in building such schools, and the first one to open in the vicinity of Sangmo-dong was in the town of Kumi, some eight kilometers (five miles) away. This was the school that Park Sang-Hee, Chung-Hee's third older brother, attended. The first two older brothers did not, either because the school opened too late for them or because the family could not afford to send them there. The tuition was only sixty sen or pennies a semester, equivalent to sixty eggs,[4] but cash, whatever the amount, was a scarce commodity for a farmer. The pencils and notebooks also cost money. Besides, eight kilometers was not a short distance for a child to travel early mornings and late afternoons, particularly because he had to traverse the treacherous mountain paths.

The paths to school were particularly harsh in the winter for a small child walking alone. Two older children from Park's village of some ninety families had enrolled in the same school, but they soon dropped out after their parents saw the school's exercise program. The chin-ups and other exercises on the iron bar, in particular, looked too dangerous. Chung-Hee, therefore, had to walk ten miles a day all alone, just as his brother had a few years earlier.[5] He later wrote that he often could not find the path to school during blizzards or after a snowstorm. The rice fields and the narrow paths became indistinguishable as snow blanketed everything. He missed some classes because wolves were at play in

4 The stationary store in front of the school accepted an egg in lieu of one penny, which means the tuition was sixty eggs a semester. Park Chung-Hee, "Na ui sonyŏn shijŏl" [My Childhood Days], dated April 26, 1970, 19; Chŏng Chae-gyŏng, *Wiin Park Chung-Hee* [Park Chung-Hee, the Great Man] (Seoul: Chipmundang, 1992), 12–24. Page numbers for this work are from this volume, hereafter noted as Park, "My Childhood Days."

5 Park Sang-hee was then the only one from the village attending the Kumi Elementary School; Park, "My Childhood Days," 5, of the handwritten version.

the forest on the way.[6] In the summer, the rain would soak him and his books, even though he wore a straw hat and had the books strapped to his back.[7] He often suffered indigestion in the winter because the cooked barley in his lunch box froze and would not thaw in time for lunch. The classrooms evidently had no stoves, and he could not get hot water to thaw his lunch. He had to seek help from the neighborhood acupuncturist for relief from indigestion, as other digestive medicine was not available in the village.[8] His favorite lunch was *kaettŏk*, the steamed cake made of ground wheat wrapped in pumpkin leaves. His mother would get some unhusked wheat, grind it with grinding stones, shape the dough into round cakes, and steam them. The wheat shells remained in the cake because husked wheat was more expensive.[9] But such treats were rare. Many years later, Park Chung-Hee attributed his short stature to not having had enough to eat.

> When I returned home after school, walking the 20 ri (8 kilometers or 5 miles) distance, I would get very hungry. I would go to the kitchen and lift the lid of the cooking pot but it was all empty. I wanted to chew some seasoned turnip but there was none. So I would dip a little soy source on my finger and suck it. I wish we had a chestnut tree or two in the back of our house. I would have loved to eat boiled chestnuts. Do you know why I have a small body? It is because I did not have enough to eat when I was a child.[10]

6 Ibid., 17.
7 Ibid., 16.
8 Ibid., 18–19.
9 Park Chung-Hee told this to Kim Chae-ch'un (Jae-ch'un), his longtime associate. Chong-Sik Lee interview with Kim Chae-ch'un, May 4, 2009 (Seoul).
10 Kim Chŏng-ryŏm, *Ah, Park Chung-Hee* (Seoul: Chungang M & B, 1997), 318; Kim served as Park's' chief of staff in the President's Office for nine years between 1969 and 1978.

Kim Chŏng-ryŏm, who recorded this remark, said President Park encouraged the planting of chestnuts and other fruit-bearing trees. The memory of poverty was deeply ingrained in his mind.[11]

One of his classmates, Pak Sŭng-yong, recollected the content of Park Chung-Hee's lunch boxes later, because they had the distinct mark of the poor family. Most of the other children's lunch boxes contained barley mixed with some rice, but Park Chung-Hee's had barley with millet, the yellow grain that was much cheaper than rice. The classmates, therefore, could tell even from a distance the economic status of his family. The yellow color stood out because the cooked barley in the background was light beige in color. But there were many days Park Chung-Hee could not or would not bring lunch and would instead go to the home of his best friend Yi Chun-sang, which was only a five-minute walk from the school. Chun-sang's father was an herb doctor with a thriving business and was known for his wealth. His father and grandfathers had been herb doctors, too, and evidently managed their wealth well. The two boys had established a friendship early on and became inseparable in the eyes of others.

The injury Chun-sang suffered at the school's athletic meet in the spring of 1928 cemented their ties further. His knee injury was bad enough, but his father's status as the town's "medical person" made it much worse. He was good at curing Chung-Hee's indigestion, but he was no surgeon. He poured heated mercury on the knee not once but three times, having others hold the screaming boy's body. The treatment killed off whatever germs the knee had attracted but also burned off the knee cartilage, making it impossible for his son to bend his right knee thereafter. The poor boy needed mental and physical support more than

11 Ibid.

ever, and Park Chung-Hee was at his side constantly. His reputation as a tough class leader was already well-established by then, and no one even dared to insult or slight Chun-sang for his handicap.[12]

Chun-sang's situation graphically illustrated the need for better medical facilities in town, and Park Sang-Hee, Chung-Hee's third brother and an aspiring young journalist, assumed the role of spokesman. Health care was, in fact, the topic of his debut article in the first-ever publication of the national newspaper, *Chosŏn Ilbo* (Korea Daily) on January 14, 1933.[13] Park Sang-Hee was listed as a reporter for the Sŏnsan branch office of the same paper, although he had previously been appointed as a reporter by the rival *Dong-a Ilbo* (the East Asia Daily) on June 8, 1928.[14] His article deserves our attention here not only because it tells us much about the condition of the times but also because he reveals much about himself. This piece may have served as the catalyst for Mr. Cho, the businessman in Kimch'ŏn, to permit his daughter to marry the young man from the mountain village the following year. Here is what it said:

---

12 http://kr.blog.yahoo.com/ppis4988/23746; the friendship lasted until Yi Chun-sang died in 1973. While Park Chung-Hee was pursuing his military career, Chun-sang was barely surviving with his handicap. His father's wealth perished during the war, and his father died too; he had learned no useful skills and had no means to support himself. In October 1963, however, his old friend made him the town's top VIP and removed all his worries. Park's special train arrived at the Kumi railway station soon after he was elected president of the republic on the fifteenth. He probably wanted to pay homage to his ancestors with the auspicious news. The Koryŏng Park family indeed had something to be proud of. The first thing he did after shaking a few hands was to search for his old friend Chun-sang among the crowd. Park then had his jeep driven to his old home with the thin old man in a ragged outfit sitting behind him. It thus became a moral—and political—duty of all those following the jeep in the motorcade to take care of Yi Chun-sang.

13 Cho Kap-je, vol. 1, 410–411.

14 Ibid., 407.

> There are a few herb doctors in Sŏnsan, but there is only one new (or Western) style Korean public doctor [Kong-ui][15] in the town of Sŏnsan. While there are two other "restricted to locality doctors" in Changch'ŏn and Kumi, medical facilities are so limited that the residents suffer real inconvenience. The number of doctors being only three in a county of 80,000 people means there is only one doctor for each 27,000 people, and that includes the "restricted to locality doctors."
>
> Kumi is a small cultural town which the Seoul-Pusan Railroad traverses. There are more than 600 households living in it, but only one Japanese "restricted to locality doctor," who is over fifty years of age, resides there. If a person becomes seriously ill, (s)he not only could not obtain the medicine needed but his or her life could not be saved unless (s)he is carried to Kimch'ŏn or Taegu. This is indeed a shame for the entire county in an age when we have advanced culture. Not only is it a shame but a grave humanitarian problem. An immediate increase in medical facility is required.[16]

Whether the article made any impact on ordinary readers is unclear. However, the piece was impressive in that it was written by a man with barely four years of elementary education.[17] More important for Mr. Cho, however, was that the article was published in a national newspaper. Sang-Hee's bride would have been awestruck too by the man who put Kumi and Sŏnsan on the national map. Hwang T'ae-sŏng of Kimch'ŏn would not have had a difficult time in persuading

---

15 Kong-ui, translated as "public doctor" here, is most likely a doctor licensed to practice medicine without restrictions. The "restricted to locality doctor," on the other hand, is one with very limited medical training, most often limited to correspondence courses, and licensed to practice medicine in remote localities where no alternatives were available.

16 The entire article is reprinted in Cho Kap-je, vol. 1, 411.

17 The elementary school at his time was for four years. It was expanded to six years when Park Chung-Hee attended it.

Mr. Cho and his daughter that Sang-Hee was a promising young man. Hwang, a close friend of Sang-Hee, served as the intermediary for the two families and affected the lives of the Park family for many years thereafter. No one knew then that three decades later, it would fall to Sang-Hee's younger brother, Park Chung-Hee, to order Hwang's execution.

Like his brother Sang-Hee, Park Chung-Hee was intelligent. He was also tenacious and able to endure hardship. He certainly needed these qualities to survive the travails he was to face. One wonders where those qualities came from, given their father's reputation for being a "good-for-nothing" loafer. It may be that the biographers who painted Park's father in such unflattering colors were in error. His father had other qualities, as Park Chung-Hee related in his autobiographical notes: "My father was a cheerful and intrepid man who liked drinks. When he was young he happened to meet a tiger on the Sŏngju mountain road at night. He was all alone. He sat down, filled his pipe and stroked the flint stones. The tiger moved away as the stones sparkled and lit the pipe. I thought he was brave."[18] One can be certain that these were the qualities the son admired. Being scared in the face of danger is human; it is quite another to dispose of such fear without panic. Park Chung-Hee inherited his father's intelligence and taste for liquor. Perhaps he inherited fearlessness too.

Chung-Hee endured and eventually became the second child in the Park family to graduate from Kumi elementary school, but the cost he paid troubled him the rest of his life. The long commutes, hunger, and

18 Park Chung-Hee, "My Childhood Days," 22.

indigestion stunted his growth.[19] He was 119.8 centimeters (47 inches) during the second grade; he reached only 135.8 centimeters (4 feet 5.5 inches) in the sixth grade He was one of the shortest students at every school he attended. His classmates quickly discovered his sensitivity to his short stature and learned to avoid mentioning it. His weight was only 22.0 kilograms (48 pounds) by the second grade and 30 kilograms (66 pounds) in sixth grade.

One might suppose that a child with so many handicaps would have done poorly in classes, but quite the opposite was the case. Table 1 shows that Park earned 8 out of 10 points in three non-academic classes (*shūshin* or social ethics, drawing, and physical education) during the third year, when he reported sixteen absences due to illness, but he earned 9 or 10 points for all subjects during the other five years. During the sixth year, he earned 10 points in all academic subjects. One of the two 9s was in physical education.

Park's school record did not indicate class ranking, and we cannot be certain whether he ranked number one every year, as some biographers have claimed. We also do not know how many students received the excellence award or summa cum laude (*Yūtō-shō*) each year. But school records show that Park received the award every year except the fourth and fifth; he received additional awards for diligence (*seikinshō*) during the third and sixth years.

---

19 Ibid., 19. Here, he mentioned the commute and indigestion only.

Table 1

Pak Chung-Hee's Transcript at Kumi Elementary School[20]

Subject/Year	First	Second	Third	Fourth	Fifth	Sixth
Years	1926–27	1927–28	1928–29	1929–30	1930–31	1931–32
Shūshin	9	9	8	10	10	10
Japanese	10	10	9	9	10	10
Korean	10	9	9	10	10	10
Arithmetic	10	9	9	9	10	10
Japanese History					10	10
Geography					10	10
Science				9	10	10
Occupations				10	9	10
Drawing	9	10	8	9	10	10
Music	9	9	9	9	9	10
Physical Ed.	9	9	8	9	9	9
Home Economics and Sewing						9
Moral demeanor	A	A	A	A	A	A
Days attended	233	231	234	242	251	249
Sick days	18	20	16	0	1	3
Abs. / Accidents				9		

20 Source: Chŏng Yŏng-jin, *Ch'ŏngnyŏn Pak Chung-Hui*, 34; Chŏng Wun-hyŏng, *Sillok Kunin Pak Chung-Hui* [Veritable Record of the Soldier Pak Chung-Hui] (Seoul: Kaema Kowŏn, 2004), 23. The latter is more legible.

Park's teachers rewarded his excellence by appointing him the class leader for at least some of the years he attended. An episode Park Chung-Hee recorded in this connection is extremely interesting, bearing in mind his later accomplishments. The story has to do with a strong and stubborn classmate who would not listen to his commands. Chung-Hee saw that the fellow was weak in math, always getting reprimanded by the teacher. Therefore, during the recess periods, the class leader taught the boy how to solve math problems and even helped him do the homework. The strategy, of course, was foolproof. Thereafter, the fellow "obeyed me unconditionally, whatever I said."[21] Chung-Hee was not only tough but wily. It is important to note that he jotted down this note in 1970 when he was fifty-three years old and had been in control of South Korea for seven years. But he cherished the triumph of his childhood days. Such a memory does not go away easily.

That episode, of course, tells us that Park Chung-Hee was good at arithmetic, and school records confirm this. It also tells us that he carefully calculated his strategy. He might have mobilized the bullies in the class to force the fellow to obey him, but instead, he used his craftiness to tackle the problem. He was confident about his ability to teach and lead others. However, some of his classmates reported later that the diminutive class leader was not always subtle with his classmates. He reportedly used his authority quite liberally; almost everyone in his class suffered his slapping at one time or another, and they feared him.[22] Was this an act to let off his frustrations? One should take note of the word *obeyed* in his own account. Some may wonder how the tiny class leader could get away with slapping his classmates, but this was a

21 Park Chung-Hee, "My Childhood Days," 23.
22 Cho Kap-je, vol. 1, 353–354.

society where authority figures at any level could exercise the "authority of position." He was following the practices of the Japanese army, which were also adopted at schools. A corporal was entitled to kick and beat a private whenever he found an excuse. The latter could do the same the following year when he had a new enlisted man under him.

Chung-Hee's experience of wielding authority deserves special attention. He undoubtedly enjoyed exercising the authority given him. By the same token, he would have accepted the structure of authority that he lived in. It is in this context that his longing to become a military leader must be seen. His fascination with the military started very early in his life. The Eightieth Army Regiment in Taegu often held maneuvers in Kumi near his home.[23] Evidently, the terrain there suited the army. Multitudes of soldiers moved in unison at the command of an officer and the blaring of trumpets. Some may attribute Park's attraction to the military to his father having passed the *mukwa*, or the military branch examination, which is a possibility. His fascination with military maneuvers, though, is very clear. As a child living in a remote village, he had not experienced such dramatic scenes before. Whatever happened beyond the village, his home community was still basically a primitive village where electricity was not available and "moving pictures" could not be seen. Park would have started to read about wars and battles in books and magazines after he started school, but no written material could provide as vivid a picture as the real soldiers marching in front of him. The military maneuvers, therefore, are likely to have left a much deeper impression on young Park than on a child then living in a city with access to movie houses.

The power of commanding officers would have attracted Park's attention in particular. The saber-rattling police officers represented the

---

23 Park Chung-Hee, "My Childhood Days," 23.

zenith of power to the village child, but these fearsome agents of the state humbled themselves before the military officers. Obviously, the army officers outranked the policemen, and Park longed to join the powerful. We do not know when he saw his first military maneuver, but it determined the course of his life. The village policemen had been a matchless terror for the villagers, paralyzing passersby with their shouts of "Kora!" (Hey, rascal!). Most of the villagers did not understand the language the policemen spoke because, like Chung-Hee's uneducated brothers, they had not gone to school to learn Japanese. Hence they feared policemen even approaching them. The policemen, whose ability for verbal communication with the villagers was very limited, would have used only gestures, shouts, and violence to express their frustration and displeasure. What's more, the villagers knew the policemen had ample reasons to beat and kick them with their heavy boots because they knowingly violated the laws. They often played prohibited card games in the off-season and drank moonshine.[24] We do not know whether any members of the Park family bet money on cards, but Chung-Hee recollected the times when someone hastily wrapped up the urns containing the moonshine and headed for the hills. It would have given the villagers great pleasure to see someone humbling the devils who harassed them.

Chung-Hee's longing for power intensified in the fifth grade, when he read Yi Kwang-su's historical novel about Admiral Yi Sun-shin. In 1597, the admiral led a small Korean fleet of thirteen ships, which against all odds managed to forestall and create havoc for an invading Japanese fleet of 133 ships. He used his knowledge of local waters and the terrain to destroy so many enemy transport ships ferrying troops and supplies that the Japanese had to abandon the invasion. It was

---

24 Ibid., 23.

impossible for any Korean child reading the account of the admiral's actions not to be moved. The following year, Park read three books on Napoleon Bonaparte.[25] He was particularly impressed that Napoleon's short stature did not prevent him from greatness. He adored Napoleon so much that he later, when he was a teacher himself, set a large framed picture of the diminutive, potbellied French general on his desk at his boardinghouse. One of his students at Munkyŏng Elementary School saw it when she visited her teacher and asked him who it was. Park replied that it was "Hero Napoleon" and gave the young student and the rest of her classmates a long recitation about the man.[26]

Napoleon Bonaparte

Park Chung-Hee's adoration of Napoleon presents an interesting case for us to ponder. As is well known, Napoleon's father, Carlo Bonaparte, had struggled as a Corsican fighter under Pasquale Paoli in opposition to the French until the movement was crushed. He then accepted the position of assessor for Ajaccio working for the French and sent his sons to France to be educated. It was easy for Napoleon, therefore, to adapt to French rule and enter the Military College of Brienne and the French Military Academy in Paris.[27] Nevertheless, Napoleon continued to see French rule of Corsica as "French tyranny" and Paoli as his hero.[28] His military and political acumen eventually made him the French emperor; nevertheless, it was said, "France has not been able to make Napoleon a Frenchman."[29]

25 Ibid., 23.

26 Kwon Yŏng-ki, 357.

27 Jacques Godechot, "Napoleon Bonaparte," Encyclopedia Britannica, online.

28 Henri Calvet, *Napoléon* (Paris: Presses Universitaires de France, 1943), 8–9.

29 Henri Calvet, *Napoléon*, Japanese trans. Inoue Kōji (Tokyo: Hakusui-sha, 1952), 14. Inoue may have found this sentence in an edition other than the one published in 1943. I could not find the last sentence in the 1943 edition I consulted.

In other words, the son of a rebel not only ruled the country his father fought against but turned it into an empire. Did young Chung-Hee fantasize about following Napoleon's footsteps to be the absolute ruler?

We are aware, of course, that the Japanese severely discriminated against the Koreans, and everyone would declare that there was no possibility for Park Chung-Hee ever to become a Japanese army general. But the young Corsican faced no less discrimination from the French. His sheer brilliance as a strategist and tactician were the keys to his success. We know that likewise, Park Chung-Hee's road to South Korea's presidency was not an easy one.

Admiral Yi Sun-shin

Yi Sun-shin's effect on Park Chung-Hee is more complicated. The writer Yi Kwang-su heaped adulation on Admiral Yi, and Park became a lifelong devotee of the admiral. Yi Sun-shin was not only a dedicated patriot but also an unparalleled strategist and commander. Even the Japanese navy admired him. But Yi's novel detailed much more. It recounted the hardships the admiral had to endure due to the malicious slander of jealous politicians. One of the false accusations in particular was so vicious that government rascals had the admiral arrested, tortured, and tried for treason even while his forces were smashing the Japanese navy. Fortunately, Yi Sun-shin was spared his life, but he was demoted to a low-ranking sailor until sometime later when he was once again restored to his former position to resume his attacks on the Japanese fleets. Yi Kwang-su, the equivalent of Korea's Pushkin, did not shield the readers from the shameful details of deceit, cowardice, ineptitude, and spinelessness that surrounded the king and his ministers. While the novel put the admiral on a high pedestal, readers could not help but condemn the Chosŏn Dynasty. It may be because of this very criticism that the Japanese censors and "Thought Police" [Tokkō] allowed *Dong-a Ilbo* (the East Asia Daily) to publish the novel in serialized form in 1931.

What the novelist said of the admiral helps us to assess the effect of the novel on young Park Chung-Hee. The following is the first statement of Yi Kwang-su about the admiral:

> I do not revere Yi Sun-shin for having invented the iron-clad turtle ship. Nor do I admire him for his accomplishments during the Imjin War. Of course his achievements were great, but the real reason for my admiration and veneration is his self-sacrificing and boundless loyalty (patriotism) that transcended rewards and punishments. He gave his all to his duty and his belief regardless of how those small men around him slandered him. He did not falter in his loyalty until even up to the last moment of his life. I admire that loyalty and that personality…I do not wish to create him through my imagination. I simply wish to amplify his person depicted in historical records with the best of my ability.[30]

Yi Kwang-su's second statement is also useful in understanding Park Chung-Hee's eventual assessment of Korean history.

> There is a story about my work "Yi Sun-shin." Dr. Horace Underwood of Yŏnhui College published a book in English entitled "A Study of Ships."[31] He said in his preface that he learned much from Yi Kwang-su's work on Yi Sun-shin and that there is no other work available now that is more complete on the history of the Imjin War. So he wanted to translate the work into English but gave it up because the book too graphically depicted the shortcomings of the Korean people. He was

30 *Dong-A Ilbo*, May 30, 1931.

31 It appears that Yi Kwang-su was referring to Underwood's article, "Korean Boats and Ships," *Transactions of the Korean Branch of the Royal Asiatic Society*, 33 (1934).

afraid that the translation might give Western readers a bad impression of the Korean people.

> Dr. Underwood was the only one who really understood me. Yi Sun-shin was the one who transcended self-interest and glory. He pushed through what he believed in regardless of the cost. This was Yi Sun-shin. But the typical Korean was like those cunning court officials who were filled with ambition and jealousy.[32]

The "cunning officials" Yi Kwang-su mentioned were the ones who had persecuted the admiral. Their intrigues would have reinforced Chung-Hee's negative views about the dynasty he had acquired from his father and helped explain the reasons for the misery he inherited. One might compare Park's indignation to what the British people might feel if Admiral Nelson had been arrested while he was devastating the Spanish fleet at Trafalgar, or what Americans would think had Admiral Chester Nimitz been bound and dragged to Washington DC after his fleet sank four Japanese aircraft carriers at Midway. Park Chung-Hee's historical perspective may have been determined by his father's involvement in the Tonghak movement, but Yi Kwang-su definitely played a large role in reinforcing Park's historical perspective. The Chosŏn Dynasty should have been replaced by another more vibrant one long before Hideyoshi's invasion started in 1592,[33] two hundred years after the Chosŏn had begun. Park Chung-Hee revered Admiral Yi so much that when he became South Korea's president, he had a grandiose monument built to commemorate him in Asan and his statute built in the center of Seoul.

---

32 Quoted from *Samch'ŏlli* [Three Thousand Ri] (1931) by Kim P'al-bong, postscript, *Ch'unwon munhak* [Ch'unwon Literature], vol. 6, Yi Sun-shin (Seoul: Sŏnghan, 1978).

33 For a brief but cogent analysis of Korea's military condition before and during Hideyoshi's invasion, see Nam-lin Hur, "Politicking or Being Politicked: Wartime Governance in Chosŏn Korea, 1592–98," paper presented at the Association for Asian Studies, March 2006.

Park Chung-Hee and the Sunday School

Park Chung-Hee had no direct contact with Dr. Underwood, but he did come under his influence while he was attending the elementary school. As a young boy, Park attended the Sangmo Church about five hundred meters south of his home at Sangmo-dong, which was led by "a disciple of Underwood," according to Cho Kap-je.[34] Horace Grant Underwood (1859–1916) was a London-born American Presbyterian missionary and one of the first two Protestant missionaries to arrive in Chemulpo (now Inchŏn) in 1885. He founded the John D. Wells Training School for Christian Workers, which grew into Kyŏngshin Middle and High School and Yŏnhui College, which then evolved into Yonsei University. We do not know the identity of the founder and hence cannot establish a direct link between the Sangmo Church and Underwood, but Park Chung-Hee attended the Sunday school there while he was in the elementary school, according to his contemporaries.[35] He was one of about twenty children regularly attending the Sunday school, carrying Bibles and hymn books while wearing traditional Korean clothing. On Christmas mornings, one of his classmates recalled, the children accompanied the choir groups touring the church members' homes to sing Christmas carols and hymns. The church at that time was not much different from the Korean-style tile roof homes, except it had four large rooms. The yangban families in the Sangmo-dong neighborhood rejected Christianity, because it opposed the traditional custom of paying homage to ancestors, but they did not overtly interfere with church activities or the ringing of church bells. None of the Park family members joined Chung-Hee in going to the church,

---

34 http://kr.blog.yahoo.com/ppis4988/23746.

35 The unidentified author of the Web site interviewed a number of old church elders who knew the young Park Chung-Hee, http://kr.blog.yahoo.com/ppis4988/23746.

and evidently, Park Chung-Hee did not become a devout Christian. His church attendance ended when he graduated from the elementary school. He later acknowledged his church attendance and even donated some money for the reconstruction of the Sangmo church after the Korean War, but that was the extent of his ties with Christianity.[36] One can only speculate about the influence of Christianity on Park Chung-Hee.

36 By 2010, the Sangmo Presbyterian Church had grown into a thirty-thousand-member congregation—a mammoth institution. Its Web site says it was founded by "the ancestors who received the gospel message from the missionary Underwood" (www.sangmo.or.kr. accessed on November 23, 2010).

III. THE TAEGU NORMAL SCHOOL: THE YEARS OF DESPAIR

Park Chung-Hee's intelligence, in any event, got him accepted by the Taegu Normal School, the secondary school to train elementary-school teachers. This was the third such school the colonial government had established in Korea after the ones in Seoul and Pyongyang, and the competition was fierce. Not only did the school not charge tuition, but it also promised a teaching position after graduation. Teaching has been a respected profession throughout Korea's history; hence, it offered a chance for social advancement too. Since normal schools were known to select only the very best of the brightest, the cap with the normal school logo served as a mark of distinction. Each student had to promise to teach for two years after graduation if he did not receive living expenses from the school and four years if he did. The latter benefit was provided only to those with a class rank of forty or above. The school eventually admitted ten Japanese students and ninety Koreans out of 1,070 applicants, or about one in ten for Koreans.[1] The ratio was kept relatively low because elementary school principals allowed only the very best to apply.

Applicants for Taegu Normal School came not only from the southern part of Korea but from the southern part of Japan as well. The school accepted more Korean students than Japanese because it was a class B school with the mission to train teachers for Korean schools, called common schools (*futsū gakkō* in Japanese and *pot'ong hakkyo* in Korean). The ratio at Seoul Normal School, a class A normal school, was eight Japanese to two Koreans. It was intended mainly for teach-

1 Kwon Yŏng-ki, "Kongkae kŭmji. Taegu Sabŏm sŏngjŏkp'yo ui pimil" [Not for the public: The Secret of the Taegu Normal School Transcript], *Wŏlgan Chosŏn* [Chosŏn Monthly], May 1991, 351–361 (at p. 351).

ers of Japanese children in Korea, who studied at what was known as normal elementary schools (*Jinjō shōgakkō*).[2]

Park Chung-Hee's ranking at the time of admission in 1932 was 51 out of 100 or 51 among the 1,070 applicants. He was the first Taegu Normal School student that Kumi Elementary School had ever produced, and big celebrations followed. Park's mother had earnestly prayed that her youngest child would fail, but she would have rejoiced, too. It was the family's economic situation that worried her. The tuition was free, but someone had to provide for the train fares, meals, shoes, and so on. The students also had to pay for dormitory meals (6.50 yen[3]) and a 4.5 yen monthly deposit for school trips.[4] All that meant cash, and a peasant farmer simply had no means to produce money. Chung-Hee could not carry eggs to Taegu to exchange for notebooks as he had before.

Why were all the farmers so strapped? The answer requires a brief survey of the Parks' environment.

Socioeconomic Conditions of the 1930s

Chung-Hee's "educated brother" won over their mother's misgivings about sending Park to Taegu Normal School, but even he would have had occasion to share his mother's concerns later on. The period between 1932 and 1937, when Chung-Hee attended the normal school, happened to be the most difficult years for his family. The Great Depression that affected most of the globe also slowed down

---

2 Kim Ch'ang-guk, *Kankokujin ga chi'nichika ni narutoki* [When a Korean Becomes a Japanophile], (Tokyo: Heibonsha, 2000), 42.

3 The exchange rate at this time was two yen to a U.S. dollar. Hence, his dormitory meals would have cost $3.25 a semester.

4 Kim Pyŏng-hee in his autobiography on the Internet, see http://home.megapass.co.kr/~gimbyngh/hoigorog00.html (The Taegu Normal School, I).

the Japanese and Korean economies,[5] but even more serious was the Japanese colonial policy of using Korea as Japan's "bread basket." This policy made Korean farmers extremely vulnerable to the vicissitudes of the Japanese economy, having exported 42 percent of their total rice production to Japan between 1927 and 1931.[6] Korea exported over a third of its other agricultural products, such as fruits, chestnuts, cattle, and silk worms, to Japan in 1929.[7] The problems began the year that Japan had a bumper rice harvest and did not need Korean rice. And since Korea too had bumper crops in 1930, 1931, and 1933, the glut pushed prices down 38 percent, from 27.82 yen per *koku* in 1929 to 17.17 yen in 1931.[8] The situation did not improve until 1935, and the effect was disastrous for Korean farmers. They produced more but earned less. They could not pay back the money owed for fertilizers at harvest time, and their debt burdens mounted higher and higher. The colonial government, which had encouraged the farmers to borrow money for fertilizers to increase production, offered no relief when the farmers faced the glut. The Japanese banks and corporations that had provided the loans took over the mortgaged lands, forcing the

5 Cf. Charles P. Kindleberger, *The World in Depression, 1929–1939*, revised and enlarged edition (Berkeley: University of California Press, 1986).
6 Kim Mun-sik, "Iljeha ui nongŏp konghwang kwa nongch'on bunhae" [Agricultural Depression and the Disintegration of Farming Villages under Japanese Imperialism]," *Nongŏp kyŏngje yŏn'gu*, 12(1), September 2005, 1–23 (at pp. 3–4).
7 Ibid., 3.
8 Ibid., 4; Chōsen Ginkōshi Kenkyūkai (ed.), *Chōsen Ginkōshi* [History of the Bank of Chōsen], (Tokyo: Tōyō Keizai Shinpōsha, 1987), 390. A *koku* (sŏm or sŏk in Korean) of rice is equivalent to about 5 bushels (4.9629 bushels).

small landowners to leave.[9] It was unthinkable for the Park family to produce the cash needed for Chung-Hee's education.[10]

Table 2[11] shows the average income of the average Korean farmer. The Park family's farm, however, was on high ground and below average in size and soil quality, and its annual income would not have reached the national average.[12] The family would have felt the effect of the depression much longer than the statistics indicate, because most farmers survived the worst years by piling more debts onto what they already owed. Interest rates on farmers' debts were often exorbitant. It was impossible for tenant farmers to escape the cycle of debts and payments.[13] We do not know the exact condition of the Park family, but it is worth noting that the junta Park headed in 1961 set up the elimination of farmers' usurious debt obligations as its first task.

---

9 See Edwin H. Gragert, *Landownership under Colonial Rule: Korea's Japanese Experience, 1900–1935* (Honolulu: University of Hawaii Press, 1994), 140–161.
10 The stationary store in front of the school accepted an egg in lieu of one penny; Park Chung-Hee, "My Childhood Days," 19.
11 Please see table 2.
12 According to Cho Kap-je, Park Sŏng-bin's second son, Mu-hui or Mu-Hee, tilled a rice farm belonging to Chang Sŭng-won. His son Chang Taek-sang later became famous as the head of the Metropolitan (Seoul) Police under the U.S. Military Government; Cho Kap-je, vol. 1, 392–393.
13 A study conducted by the Agriculture and Forestry Bureau of the Korean Government-General in 1938 indicated that 80 percent of tenant farmers in North Kyŏngsang Province owed an average of 92 yen per household; Nōrin-kyoku, *Nōka keizai gaikyō chōsa: Kosaku nōka, 1933–1938* [A Study of the General Condition of Farmers' Economic Condition: Tenant Farmers] (Seoul: 1940), 75.

Table 2[14]

Agricultural Production and Per-Far

	Rice (cleaned) in 1,000 koku	Barley in 1,000 koku	Production in 1,000 yen (A)	Farm household (B)	Income per household in Yen (A/B)	Index
1926	15,300	9,591	1,139,594	2,835,042	401.97	100.0%
1927	17,298	9,070	1,122,853	2,812,766	399.20	99.3%
1928	13,511	8,746	1,022,604	2,793,540	366.06	91.1%
1929	13,701	9,387	964,280	2,800,565	344.32	85.7%
1930	19,180	9,964	724,227	2,892,267	250.40	62.3%
1931	15,872	10,207	702,855	2,858,744	245.86	61.2%
1932	16,345	10,619	831,816	2,875,277	289.30	72.0%
1933	18,192	10,370	920,841	2,905,039	316.98	78.9%
1934	16,717	11,116	1,020,147	2,906,314	351.01	87.3%
1935	17,884	12,311	1,147,045	2,983,112	384.51	95.7%
1936	19,410	10,405	1,208,911	3,056,503	395.52	98.4%
1937	26,796	14,680	1,560,487	3,058,755	510.17	126.9%
1938	24,138	11,760	1,574,787	3,052,392	515.92	128.3%
1939	14,355	13,138	1,644,404	3,023,133	543.94	135.3%

14 Source: Korean Government-General, *Shisei 25nen shi* (1935); appendix table 15 and Chosŏn Kyŏngje T'ongshinsa, *Chosŏn kyŏngje t'ongge yoran* (1949), 26, reproduced from Kim Mun-sik, "Iljeha ui nongŏp konghwang kwa nongch'on bunhae" [Agricultural Depression and the Disintegration of Farming Villages under Japanese Imperialism], *Nongŏp kyŏngje yŏn'gu*, 12, no. 1 (September 2005), 8.

*Rice production is a rice-year basis, November to May

Park Sang-Hee: The Older Brother

The news of Sang-Hee's loss of job in 1935 was nothing less than a calamity for Park Chung-Hee under this condition. Sang-Hee had established himself in Kumi, the town where he went to school, and had become one of the local leader-activists there. As noted earlier, he served as a reporter or correspondent for the nationwide newspapers *Dong-a Ilbo* (the East Asia Daily) and *Chosŏn Ilbo* (Korea Daily), both published in Seoul. He also became known among the town's residents because he was an officer of the Young Men's Association and the Shin-kan-hoe, the nationwide Korean political organization that the colonial government had allowed between 1927 and 1931. Above all, he had charisma. His wife's niece told the author Cho Kap-je that she often saw Sang-Hee serving as the town's arbiter. He would listen to arguments from both sides and quickly render a judgment that was accepted without protest.

The colonial police paid close attention to Sang-Hee not only because of his local influence but also because his range extended beyond the little town of Kumi. He was chosen to be the general secretary of the Research and Investigation Department of Shin-kan-hoe's Sŏnsan County. *Chosŏn Ilbo* reported in November 1927 that the provincial police had arrested Sang-Hee and his cohorts, creating a fearful atmosphere in town.[15] Evidently, the speakers he had invited for a public meeting had said something that touched the nerves of the local police.[16]

---

15 Chŏng Yŏng-jin's book carries a facsimile of the *Chosŏn Ilbo* article of November 14, 1927, about his arrest on I, 24.

16 Kim Chin-hwa reports in his *Ilje ha Taegu ui ŏnron yŏn'gu* [A Study of Taegu Journalism under Japanese Imperialism] (Taegu: Hwada Ch'ulp'an, 1978) that he was arrested for allegedly subversive speeches delivered by two individuals he had invited from nearby Ch'ilgok for a public meeting (p. 164).

Most of Sang-Hee's activities did not produce much income, but his work for *Chosŏn Chungang Ilbo* (Korea Central Daily News) was different. A man of substance opened its Taegu office and paid Sang-Hee a small but regular salary. But the position did not last long, as the office did not produce enough income to sustain it. Nor did the *Chosŏn Chungang Ilbo* Company headed by Yŏ Un-hyŏng have a solid financial base. Sang-Hee's heyday lasted only eleven months, between September 1934 and July 1935.[17] The depression impinged on every place and everyone.[18]

School Curriculum

Training schoolteachers is a serious business for any country, and much thought was given to the problem by the founders of the Meiji regime (1868–1912), which began Japan's process of modernization. The students at Taegu Normal School may not have known, but their school was carrying on the tradition established by Mori Arinori (1847–1889), the first Minister of Education in modern Japan, who emphasized the need for mental as well as physical training.[19] The mental training was to be based on Nishimura Shigeki's writings on "ethics," or *shūshin*, but the physical training was entrusted to army drill-masters. "It resulted in…regulations that were designed to give teachers and

---

17 Chŏng Yŏng-jin, vol. 1, 134, 217.

18 Kim Chin-hwa suggested another possibility for Park Sang-hui's loss of the *Chosŏn Chungang Ilbo* job. He allegedly collected 3,000 yen from a Mr. Kim living in Taegu for Yun Myŏng-hyŏk from Beijing to be used for the Korean independence movement. Mr. Kim was of Sŏnsan origin but was doing business in Taegu. If Park Sang-hui had been arrested for this activity, he would not only have been fired from his job but would have served at least three years in prison. So far, I have not discovered any independent source for this episode.

19 Marius B. Jansen, *The Making of Modern Japan* (Cambridge, MA: Harvard University Press, 2000), 409.

school heads sweeping authority," according to the scholar of Japan's history Marius Jansen. "Ultimately, the ethos of the parade ground was deliberately extended to the dormitory, refectory, and study hall of the normal school, whence it eventually spread to infect the classrooms of an entire nation."[20]

Kisi Yonesaku, who later taught Park Chung-Hee at Taegu Normal School, recounted how Mori's policy was implemented at his alma mater, the Shizuoka Normal School, in 1919. The students went through a twenty-four-hour education system, from the dormitory to the classrooms. Every student lived in the dormitory under strict, army-like rules, including rising in the morning, eating at the dining hall, and attending classes. One had to fold all clothing into a one-foot-square bundle and pile it up neatly. A trumpet signaled lights-out. Underclassmen had to salute the upperclassmen and treat them with respect in speech and manner. While military officers (*haizoku shōkō*) were only assigned to other middle schools in Japan starting in January 1925, normal schools had them much earlier. In the autumn, the entire school participated in *enshū*, or military maneuvers.[21]

It is easy to see in this system the roots of militarism that rose up within Japan starting in the late 1920s, but the Meiji leaders had their own logic. They saw the way Great Britain had humiliated and carved up China for refusing to allow the sale of opium, specifically the Indian opium that Englishmen wanted to force China to buy. Imperial China paid dearly after the Opium War (1839–1842), including the ceding of the territory of Hong Kong. The only way for Japan not to fall victim

---

20 Ibid.

21 Kishi Yonesuke, *Ryūten kyōiku rokujū nen* [Sixty Years of Meandering Education], (Kawasaki, 1982, private publication), 13.

to Western imperialism was to develop its industries and to maintain a strong military force—hence the slogan "*fukoku kyōhei*," meaning "rich nation and strong army." The system of universal education that the leaders wanted required elementary-school teachers to train the young both in body and mind. The normal schools, secondary schools to train elementary-school teachers, were to serve as the key bridge between the army and the elementary schools, but even this was not enough. In 1925, in response to the popular demand to reduce the compulsory service period of young men from two years to sixteen months, the army instituted a program to train all middle-school students directly.[22] The mental part of the program was defined in the new directive for elementary-school teachers issued in 1881: "Loyalty to the Imperial House, love of country, filial piety toward parents, respect for superiors, faith in friends, charity toward inferiors, and respect for oneself constitute the Great Path of human morality." The Imperial Rescript for Education, promulgated in 1890, amplified these points. The government had the school children memorize the entire text of the rescript and recite them in unison each morning before classes began.

Taegu Normal School followed the example of its counterparts in Japan, and Park Chung-Hee found no problem adjusting to the new environment. He not only liked military drills but excelled at them, to the extent that he caught the eye of Lieutenant Colonel Arikawa Kazuichi (1891–1945), the officer in charge of military education at the school, with whom he developed a close relationship. The colonel found Chung-Hee's reaction to commands unusually crisp. The boy performed rifle and bayonet drills so well that he decided to use him as a training

22 Endō Yoshinobu, *Kindai nihon guntai kyōikushi kenkyū* [Study of the History of Modern Japanese Military Education], (Tokyo: Aoki shoten, 1994), 615.

model.[23] Park also enjoyed *kendō* (Japanese swordsmanship) and playing the trumpet; he became one of the school trumpeters. Park reveled in being a trumpeter at military maneuvers the normal school jointly conducted with the Eightieth Army Regiment during the two summers before graduation.[24] He was also a good sprinter and enjoyed soccer, becoming the school team's goalkeeper.[25] Arikawa's fondness for Park Chung-Hee was extraordinary. He was usually contemptuous not only of all Koreans, but also of the Japanese people living in Korea.[26] A graduate of the Japanese Military Academy and Army College, Arikawa was to play an important role in Park Chung-Hee's life. The school's military training in most cases involved nothing more than lectures and weekly drills, but selected students engaged in target practice using rifles provided by the army. Park's classmate Kim Pyŏng-hui mentioned that he was the only Korean student chosen to participate in this "special privilege,"[27] his ten teammates all being Japanese; according to Chŏng Yŏng-jin, Park was the head of the team during his last year at the school.[28]

It is not surprising that Park Chung-Hee kept alive his hope for a military career at the normal school. A conversation his classmate recorded is very revealing. Park Chung-Hee, according to Kim Pyŏng-hui, wanted to be a *rikugun taishō*, the highest-ranking army general. Kim's account is credible because the story revolves around

23 Kwon Yŏng-ki, "Kongkae kŭmji. Taegu Sabŏm sŏngjŏkp'yo ui pimil" [Not for the Public: The Secret of the Taegu Normal School], *Wŏlgan Chosŏn* [Chosŏn Monthly] (May 1991): 351–361 (at p. 352).

24 Cho Kap-je (2009), 39.

25 Kwon Yŏng-ki, 354.

26 Ibid., 356.

27 Kim Pyŏng-hui, Internet autobiography. For the web address, please see p. 47, FN 4.

28 Chŏng Yŏng-jin, *Ch'ŏngnyŏn Park Chŏnghui* [Young Man Park Chung-Hee] (Seoul: Riburo (Libro) Books, 1997), vol. 1, 179.

a "Japanese speech" by a non-Japanese-speaking provincial governor named Kim Yun-jŏng, who left a deep imprint on everyone who got to know him.[29] By necessity, Governor Kim read the supposedly Japanese text written phonetically in Korean (*hangŭl*), and the students enjoyed his annual speeches as a comedy performance. But his mispronunciation of "*zento tabō*" ("full of promise in the future") became a catch phrase among the students. He mispronounced it as "*zento taba*," which did not mean anything in either Japanese or Korean. So, one day when Park was with two classmates lying on the grass, he started a conversation.[30]

Park:	Do you think we have "zento taba"?
Yi Sŏng-jo:	We will end up teaching all our lives. If we're lucky, they say, we might become county chiefs.
Kim Pyŏng-hŭi:	What's so great about county chief? You will be a Japanese slave. No matter how sharp you are, they say the provincial governor is the limit for Koreans.
Park:	I want to give up teaching and become a soldier.
Kim:	You are good at trumpet. Maybe you will become the head of a military band.

29 Why the colonial government appointed the non-Japanese-speaking Kim Yun-jŏng as governor is an interesting story in itself. He rendered a valuable service to the Japanese empire in 1905, and the governorship was apparently what he desired as a reward. I have related his story in my *Yi Sungman ui kuhanmal kaehyŏk undong* [Syngman Rhee: From a Revolutionary to a Christian Nation-Builder], (Taejeon: Paichai University Press, 2005).

30 The story here is from Kim Pyŏng-hui's Internet autobiography, section 2, "The Taegu Normal School."

Park:	No, I will be a *rikugun taishō* (Army General).
Yi:	Everything as you wish? What about the obligatory teaching? I will become an inventor after I finish the obligation. What about you, Pyŏng-hui?
Kim:	I want to go to higher institutions. Then I will become a scientist. But we have our obligatory years. Don't we?

Kim Pyŏng-hui wrote that neither he nor Park Chung-Hee forgot the "zento taba" conversation. They joked about it twenty-five or so years later in 1959 at a small alumni gathering and again in 1961, after Park led the coup d'état that installed him as the de facto ruler of South Korea.

Park's adoration of Napoleon continued at the normal school. His classmate Yi Yŏ-wŏn remembered a conversation he had with Park on that specific topic. Park, according to Yi, had a strong interest in Western history: his reading list included Plutarch's *Julius Caesar* and Hitler's *Mein Kampf*. But Park's interest in Napoleon was more than ordinary. He told Yi that he was reading his third book on Napoleon. He was attracted to Napoleon because they shared very similar backgrounds. Napoleon was from a poor family; his mother poured her love on him; and he had dreams much like Park's when he was young. He had guts and intelligence; he jumped at opportunities. Both of them, Park added, were also short in stature.[31]

But which qualities in Napoleon did Park Chung-Hee admire most and wish to emulate? If I may use the advantage of knowing about Park Chung-Hee's later life, I would say it was Napoleon's

31 Chŏng Yŏng-jin, vol. 1, 181–183.

fortitude and dynamism that were most attractive to the young Korean. Napoleon did not let hardship overcome him, nor was he willing to allow events to overtake him. He was a proactive leader who took measures that others had not anticipated or even considered. He had the daring or "can-do" spirit to accomplish what others thought impossible. Napoleon was epitomized by the phrase "Impossible is not in my vocabulary."

Park Chung-Hee, however, could not follow in Napoleon's footsteps. Unlike the French Military Academy for Napoleon, the Japanese Military Academy was far out of his reach. It accepted very few Koreans each year, and his record at the normal school was so dismal that he could not even dream of becoming a military officer. His average grade fell from 72 points in the first year down to 71, 64, 62, and finally 61 in his final year. His class ranking was 47 out of 83 students in the second year but declined steadily afterward: 67th among 74 in the third year to 73rd out of 73 in the class in 1935.[32] The situation did not improve much in the fifth and last year, 1936–1937; Park ranked 69th out of the 70 graduating. He missed classes too often. He was absent ten days during the second year, but this increased to 41 days in the third year, and 48 days during the fourth year and 41 days in the final year.[33] It is a wonder that he was not expelled from the school with so many absences, but even a bright child could not catch up with others academically in these circumstances. Park's school records reveal a fuller picture.

32 Ibid., 217; Park Sang-Hee lost his reporter's job in July 1935.
33 From the school record reproduced in Kwon Yŏng-ki, 353, 355.

Table 3[34]

Academic Record of Park Chung-Hee at Taegu Normal School, 1932–1937

Subject/year	1st	2nd	3rd	4th	5th
Year	**1932–33**	**1933–34**	**1934–35**	**1935–36**	**1936–37**
Shūshin	60	72	72	62	68
Educational principles				64	
History of education					63
Teaching methods					65
Psychology			72		
Logic				67	
Management					71
Citizenship				67	62
Seminar in education					
J. language, readings	71	64	62	53	70
_________, expressions	76	72	66	62	57
_________, penmanship	70	68	60	62	
Korean, conversations				61	67
______, expressions					
Korean-Chinese, readings	76	75	63	66	76
_____________, expressions	66	82	63	72	68

34 Source: Chŏng Yŏng-jin, *Ch'ongnyon Pak Chung-Hee*, vol. 1 (Seoul: Libro, 1992), 269–271; Kwon Yŏng-gi, "Kongkae kŭmji. Taegu Sabŏm sŏngjŏkp'yo ŭi pimil" [Not for the public: The Secret of the Taegu Normal School], *Wŏlgan Chosŏn* [Chosŏn Monthly], (May 1991), 351–361 (at pp. 353, 355). Chŏng's book provided the facsimile of the record while Kwon printed it in reconstructed form. What appears in Chŏng's copy about history appears to be Kokushi or national history, but Kwŏn translated it as Yŏksa, history. I used numbers in Kwon's article because much of Chŏng's reprint is illegible.

Subject/year	1st	2nd	3rd	4th	5th
Year	**1932–33**	**1933–34**	**1934–35**	**1935–36**	**1936–37**
Engl. Language, readings	78	79	69	53	43
______________, expressions					
Geography	80	84	74	61	55
Japanese history	82	78	72	56	69
Mathematics, arithmetic	62				
______________, algebra	70	58	62	57	65
______________, geometry			53	70	67
______________, triangles					60
Botany	75	58	65	59	
Physics				55	44
Chemistry			59	49	43
Agriculture, theory	64	65	56	69	75
__________, practice	67	73	50	65	63
Commerce			63		
Industry					48
Drawing	74	74	68	60	60
Handicraft	64	67	60	59	58
Music	80	67	71	56	47
Phys. Education, Mil. training	79	66	66	61	60
______________, martial art					70

Subject/year	1st	2nd	3rd	4th	5th
Year	**1932–33**	**1933–34**	**1934–35**	**1935–36**	**1936–37**
____________, phys. exercise	76	69	63	67	60
____________, sporting game	67	72	61	61	51
Total points	1437	1357	1469	1609	1705
Average	72	71	64	62	61
Class ranking	60/97	47/83	67/74	73/73	69/70
Demeanor (sōkō)	B	B	B	C	B
Total class days	247	252	254	260	267
Class attendance	247	242	213	212	226
Absences		10	41	48	41
Early withdrawal from class		1	2	3	

His teachers may have wondered why a child who had enrolled as fifty-first among the 1,070 applicants was doing so poorly. The highest grades he received during the first year were 80, in geography and music. During the second year, the highest points he received were 84 in geography and 82 in Korean-Chinese expressions. The latter probably involved writing in Korean using both Chinese characters (*han-mun*) and Korean phonetic words. During the third year, the highest grade he received was 74 in geography. His best performance was in geography during the first three years, but his grades declined even in this subject to 61 and 55. Japanese history was his second best class, in which he earned 82, 78, and 72, before declining to 56 and 69 points. Park's mark of 84 in geography deserves special attention, as it was the highest grade he received throughout his five years at the normal school. His teachers' comments on his record sheets were not encouraging either. Their comments are as follows[35]:

Year	Comments on Park's character
First	Normal
Second	Gloomy, appears to be suffering from poverty
Third	Poverty; not active; a little *fumajime* [frivolous]
Fourth	Inactive; grouchy; *fumajime*

Poverty and Gloom

The teachers analyzed Park Chung-Hee's core problems and his resulting character formation. Park's problems were caused by dire poverty. A young man suffering from despair could not help but be gloomy and inactive. Unhappy circumstances naturally would make a person laconic and stern. Comments about Park got progressively worse each year. In the third year, it was "a little *fumajime*," meaning frivolous, insincere, or not serious, but it became an unqualified "fumajime" in the fourth year. In other words, he did not care about his studies. His demeanor (*sōkō*) had been a B previously, but this mark fell to a C in the 1935–1936 academic year.

Park's long absences from classes and his miserable ranking at Taegu Normal School require special attention, because they contrast so sharply with his performance at the elementary school. Unlike Kumi Elementary School, where he commuted by foot, the normal school was located an hour and a half by train away from home, which required money. The absences were most likely delays in enrolling at the beginning of each semester because his family had not yet scraped together enough money, rather than absences during the semester. His brother

35 Chŏng Yŏng-jin, vol. 1, 268.

Sang-Hee must have desperately tried every possibility for loans or gifts, but he could not collect the money in time for his younger brother. Being unemployed, he not only had to raise the money for tuition but for his family's livelihood as well. The year 1935 was particularly cruel to Park Sang-Hee. He not only lost his job but also his son and daughter to smallpox and measles.[36] It is a wonder that Park Chung-Hee went back to school at all that year. Sang-Hee and Chung-Hee could easily have given up everything that year, and no one would have blamed them. The two Parks endured, although Chung-Hee earned the comment "fuma-jime" from his teachers. The normal school tuition and boarding were free, but other costs nonetheless inflicted an unbearable burden on the son of a cash-strapped farmer. As noted earlier, students had to pay for dormitory meals. They also had to deposit 4.5 yen a month for annual school trips. These costs would not have burdened other students, but the Park family simply did not have any means of obtaining cash.

His classmate Kim Pyŏng-hui recollected one particular evening when Park was in tears. He was leaving for home that evening because the homeroom teacher had told him to go home and get the money due for the meals and school trips. Kim Pyŏng-hui shared Park's tears as they walked together to the railroad station.[37] They had to weep because they knew there was no money to be found at home, but Park Chung-Hee had no choice. Another classmate Kang Ŭng-gu remembered Park taking a walk in the yard each time his dormitory roommates pooled ten *sen* (pennies) each to buy snacks in the evenings. It was easier for him to absent himself. His pride would not allow him to share what the class-mates bought. We can only imagine what went through the young man's

---

36 Ibid., 218; Sang-Hee lost his two-year-old first son and his two-week-old daughter that year.

37 http://blog.chosun.com/blog.log.view.screen?blogId=11434&logId=4086192.

mind on those occasions. He could not share the joviality of classmates enjoying these forbidden fruits. Sneaking off campus to buy snacks was strictly forbidden, and the roommates took turns sharing the risk. Chung-Hee missed out not only on the food but also the resulting camaraderie with his classmates. He could not help but be gloomy, grouchy, and laconic. One can discern signs of pent-up anger in the eyes of the young man in photographs of the period. Chŏng Yŏng-jin, who wrote Park's biography, said Park was sometimes compared to a rattlesnake. His stern look could curdle anyone's spirit. Chŏng also characterized Park as a cold, self-centered realist.[38] There is no doubt that he became a careful calculator of his options. His survival required it.

Chung-Hee avoided anything that would jeopardize his chance of graduating from the normal school, but even he could not evade the sweetness of a love affair. By sheer chance, he met a girl who was attending the girls' middle school in Taegu. It turned out that Yi Chŏng-ok had graduated from the same elementary school, where her teacher had often bragged about a certain genius Park Chung-Hee, who had made it to Taegu Normal School. She was not a beauty, but Park liked and admired her other qualities. She was well-read, smart, quiet, and very supportive of him. Even though one of Park's classmates had been recently dismissed from the school for having a love letter hidden in his suitcase, Park dated Yi Chŏng-ok for a full year, even daring to take walks with her in parks and other public places and exposing himself to the danger of teachers finding him with a girl.[39] This was between 1934 and 1935, when Park Chung-Hee was in his third and fourth year of the school. He should have known better, but love did blind him. Each cared for the other deeply, and

38 Chŏng Yŏng-jin, vol. 1, 321.
39 Ibid.

it seemed nothing could separate them. Marriage, however, was out of the question, as Yi was from a well-to-do family in Kumi that was rich enough to send their daughter to the middle school in Taegu.

Park's First Marriage

Park Chung-Hee and Yi Chŏng-ok were not the only victims of poverty and a rigid class system. It also affected the life of another woman in a nearby village, whom Park's father forced him to marry. His father's health was declining, and he wanted his youngest son married. He knew nothing about his son's romance and chose a woman for him when Chung-Hee had finished his fourth year at the normal school. The son's protests had no effect. A modest wedding was held one evening at home, where the couple saw each other in the dim light for the first time. The marriage was consummated, but in the morning, both of them found the other far from ideal. Park Chung-Hee was still in love with Yi Chŏng-ok. The ghastly poverty in her husband's home also appalled Park's bride. They did produce a daughter, and the wife continued to live with the Park family, but the two avoided each other as much as possible. Chung-Hee, in any event, had another year to go at the normal school. Life was cruel to both of them.

The tears shed and the humiliation he suffered while attending the Taegu Normal School could easily have led Park to become a revolutionary seeking to overturn the political and economic system. However, later developments suggest that he not only rejected that road but chose to surmount the obstacles before him and ascend within the very society that had imposed so many handicaps on him. Perhaps he was too busy coping with the immediate tasks at hand to think otherwise. Alternatively, perhaps he had learned from his father's experience the futility of resisting environmental forces. In any event, there is no doubt that Park's normal school years deepened his resentment against poverty. Park Chung-Hee said in his 1963 book, *Kukka wa hyŏngmyŏng kwa na* (The Nation, Revolution, and I) that "poverty was my teacher and benefactor. My twenty-four hours cannot be separated from the work related to this teacher and benefactor."[40] Indeed, history would not have paid any attention to Park had his father not imposed poverty upon him.

Park's Japanese Teachers

We have noted earlier the teachers' comments on Park's environment and his resulting behavior. But what kind of teachers did he have? The following is based on Chŏng Yŏng-jin's exploration.

Taegu Normal School, of course, had many teachers other than Arikawa, the drill instructor, and many programs beyond military drills. The school had nineteen Japanese teachers and six Korean; each of them affected the young man differently. It is fortunate that his earlier biographers sought out Park's classmates and compiled profiles of his teachers.

Principal Hirayama Tadashi was a product of what is known as Taishō Democracy (between 1912 and 1926), the most liberal era in Japanese history, and proved to be an impeccable gentleman in every sense. In addition, his Korean was good enough to address the students' parents in Korean. Park Sang-Hee, who accompanied him to school on the first day, told his brother that he was lucky to have such a man as his principal.[41] He was in charge when the case of Teacher Hyŏn Chun-hyŏk broke out at the normal school in November 1931, and he not only declined to condemn Hyŏn and his disciples but implicitly supported

40 Park Chung-Hee, *Kukka wa hyŏngmyŏng kwa na* [The Nation, Revolution, and I], (Seoul: Hyangmunsa, 1963), 292.
41 Chŏng Yŏng-jin, vol. 1, 214–215.

them by visiting Hyŏn in prison. Hyŏn had led a reading group of students to study the forbidden ideology of Marxism. He also instilled Korean identity in them by teaching Korean history, contradicting official government policy. The court found Hyŏn and his students guilty of violating the Security Maintenance Law and incarcerated them in prison for many years.[42] The provincial authorities found Principal Hirayama's attitude unacceptable and transferred him to a lesser institution, where he was incapable of doing much "harm," as soon as they could.

Kishi Yonesaku, who taught psychology, pedagogy, and teaching methods, was another favorite of the Korean students. The Korean students also liked their painting and music teachers, who were not only liberal in outlook but sympathetic to the Korean students who suffered under some of the vicious Japanese teachers.[43] They were genuine educators who transcended nationality. In the case of Mr. Kishi, authorities objected to his liberal attitudes and sent him to Japan for a six-month training course in "Japanese Spirit" in 1937, subsequently dispatching him to other institutions.[44] Park Chung-Hee had taken the teaching methods course in his fifth year and presumably Kishi was his instructor. We do not know whether Park knew where Kishi received his spiritual training, but it was called the National Spiritual Cultural Research Center (Kokumin Seishin Bunka Kenkyūjo). Interestingly, Park, as South Korea's ruler in 1978, established the Korean Spiritual Cultural Research Center to infuse Korean spirit into his bureaucrats.

---

42 Hyŏn Chun-hyŏk emerged as a leader of the Communist Party in Pyongyang after Korea's liberation in 1945 but was killed by an assassin in September that year. See Robert A. Scalapino and Chong-Sik Lee, *Communism in Korea* (Berkeley: University of California Press, 1973), chapter 4.

43 Chŏng Yŏng-jin, vol. 1, 270.

44 Kishi, *Ryūten kyōiku*, 56–57.

Principal Hirayama's replacement and many other Japanese teachers fanned the anti-Japanese feelings among the Korean students. The principal and teachers may have wished to prevent a recurrence of the Hyŏn Chun-hyŏk "incident." Or perhaps they were sticklers, wanting to enforce school rules. The teachers would ransack students' possessions while they were away, searching for unauthorized publications or love letters, either a cause for dismissal or severe reprimand. The new principal prohibited not only Korean newspapers and magazines but even the reading of such Japanese magazines as *Chūo Kōron* (Central Review) or *Kaizō* (Reform).[45] These teachers enraged the students so much that some of them decided to punish the rascals. An incident occurred after Park Chung-Hee's graduation. Students beat up two teachers while on a field trip to Waegwan in 1939. They turned off the lights when the teachers were partying, put sacks over their heads, and beat them with bats and sticks. Only the intervention of respected Korean teachers prevented serious injuries. The authorities eventually identified the seven perpetrators and dismissed them from the school, but the damage was done. Those teachers had poisoned the atmosphere so much that it was impossible for the Korean students to forget their national identity.[46]

---

45 Chŏng Yŏng-jin, vol. 1, 94–95; Kishi, the teacher, referred to the searching of student possessions in their absence. He said it was just like what the secret police, or Tokkō Keisatsu, engaged in, but none ended up with dismissals. Notes written in the Korean language were prohibited; Kishi, *Ryūten kyōiku*, 53–54.

46 Cho Tŏk-song, then an editorial writer at *Chosŏn Ilbo*, wrote that upperclassmen beat up five (not two) teachers when they were all in Woegwan for voluntary labor (*kinrō hōshi*). He says scores of students were either dismissed or suspended from the school. Cho's account gives the impression that he depended on hearsay. He referred, however, to a preliminary court trial document about a students' literary club activity of thirty-five students from 1940 that resulted in the arrest of Teacher Kim Yŏng-gi and some three hundred others. Five of the thirty-five died in prison, and twelve of them died from illnesses acquired in prison. He did not identify the name of the court document; Cho Tŏk-song, "The Anti-Japanese Student Movement toward the End of Japanese Rule," *Sasangge* (November 1964): 82–90.

Hinomaru Bentō

Park's classmate Kim Pyŏng-hŭi wrote about a malicious teacher named Okamoto. The Korean students knew he would be difficult; he arrived at their school with a reputation for having aggressively prosecuted Korean students involved in the student strike in Kwangju in 1929. At Taegu, he lived up to his reputation by having a number of Park Chung-Hee's classmates expelled in 1934, when they were in their third year and had just returned from their school trip to Kyŏngju, the capital of the old Silla kingdom. At the center of the issue were the lunch boxes, or *bentō*, that the Japanese inn there had prepared for the students. The bentō happened to be *hinomaru bentō*, a box filled with white rice and a pickled plum in the center. Since the sour plum is pickled, red, and placed in the center, the Japanese called it hinomaru bentō, the word *hinomaru* here meaning "the round sun," a term used exclusively for the Japanese national flag emblem.[47]

The incident may sound bizarre to others, but not to Okamoto, who served as the prosecutor and judge in a hearing Kim Pyŏng-hŭi described as follows:

> Okamoto: So, you are Kim Pyŏng-hŭi. They say you don't like the Japanese.
>
> Kim: All of you here are Japanese and you are my teachers. I have no reason not to like my teachers. I have always respected you. I do not like those who violate laws whether they are Japanese or Korean.

---

47 Kim Pyŏng-hui's Internet autobiography; see http://home.megapass.co.kr/~gimbyngh/hoigorog00.html.

Okamoto: Why did you throw away the *hinomaru bentō* that symbolizes the national flag?
Kim: My father is an herb doctor. He always told me my body does not agree with plums. The *bentō* had a plum in it. So I left it in the inn's porch. I have never thought of throwing away *hinomaru*, our national symbol.
Okamoto: Why did you tell other students not to take the *bentō*?
Kim: I have never said anything to other students about the *bentō*.

Neither Kim nor Park Chung-Hee suffered punishment on this occasion, but others did. Some may have said they did not like sour tastes in general or that they could not eat the bentō with only a pickled plum, but a few others were not as quick-witted. Kim Pyŏng-hŭi said, however, no great harm was done in the long run. Those expelled excelled at other schools and grew up to be successful professionals. They were luckier than Park; their parents had the money to send them to other schools. Park had no margin for error.

The Korean Teachers

The six Korean teachers at Taegu Normal School are extremely interesting because collectively they represent a microcosmic panorama of Korean reaction to Japanese rule. Two of the teachers were absolutely indifferent to nationality or political questions. They simply did not show their sentiments or political leanings. (One of these two became the butt of jokes among the students, because he told a student visitor to fill up his tummy while producing only a few pieces of biscuit on the table.) Another one was a sheer opportunist. He did his best to create an impression among the students that he was a Korean nationalist, but he donned *haori* and *hakama*, uniquely Japanese habits, at home. Very few Koreans anywhere at this time even thought of acquiring such habits. Teacher Yŏm Chung-kwŏn, on the other hand, left no doubt that he was a Korean. He exuded the pride of being a Korean, along with his sharp intellect. But the most outspoken Korean nationalist was Teacher Kim Yŏng-ki, who told his students during their first session that "the Korean language is the Korean spirit. You can survive even in a tiger's den if you set your mind right,"[48] meaning that the students should not give up on their country. But Kim had no respect for the old kingdom that the Japanese had wiped out. He would burst into tears of anger and throw down the book he held in his hand as if to smash it in frustration at the way previous generations had ruined the country.[49]

It is not difficult to see that Kim Yŏng-ki was a favorite of the students, and it is quite likely that Park Chung-Hee shared Kim's nationalism, as well as his strong indignation against the old kingdom.[50] After all, as discussed earlier, Chung-Hee already had a negative opinion of that period of Korean history; Kim Yŏng-ki may have cemented these feelings.

We can sum up Park Chung-Hee's experience up to this point as follows: the young man endured a bone-chilling poverty that he could never forget. A bright boy who had been held back from achievement at school for the lack of meager sums of money could not forget the pain he suffered. Nor could he forget the humiliation he had endured.

---

48 Chŏng Yŏng-jin, vol. 1, 83.

49 Ibid., 88–93.

50 Kim's students celebrated his sixtieth birthday in Seoul sometime in 1961, after Park led the coup. See Kim Pyŏng-hui's autobiography; http://home.megapass.co.kr/~gimbyngh/hoigorog00.html; Park Chung-Hee appointed Kim the president of Kyŏngbuk National University in Taegu.

The class leader, who had never willingly yielded his top-ranking class position in elementary school, had been relegated to the last position at Taegu Normal School. The tears he shed in Taegu and the lonely walks he took while his classmates were enjoying snacks may have pushed him later to galvanize Korea's economy.

Park's father's indignation over the Chosŏn Dynasty needs to be stressed, because it played a large role in shaping Park's perspective on Korea's history and its relations with Japan. Park and his father shared Teacher Kim Yŏng-ki's condemnation of the old dynasty. Chung-Hee had already ruminated over the Korean people's fatal defects as he read Yi Kwang-su's account of Admiral Yi Sun-shin's life. Park's military training at the normal school also deserves to be noted. He had begun to adore Napoleon a year or two before he entered the normal school, but it was there that his military training started. Park's grades in academic subjects plummeted from his third year, but he continued to enjoy playing trumpet and *kendō*. Park also continued his military drills and target practice, as they were required courses. Park Chung-Hee was preparing himself for a military career even before he enrolled in the Manchukuo Military Academy a few years later.

Park's interaction with the many compassionate and humane Japanese teachers at Taegu Normal School, and perhaps at elementary school as well, would have affected his attitude toward Japanese rule. Such teachers as Principal Hirayama and Kishi Yonesaku of the normal school were rarities—even among Koreans, there were few teachers of this standard. They treated the Korean students with affection and compassion. The fact that they were the products of Taishō democracy, Japan's liberal era, should be emphasized. Had all Japanese teachers been like those two and had the colonial government been as compassionate, Japan would have found it easy to assimilate the Koreans.

IV. TEACHER PARK CHUNG-HEE: 1937–1940

Park Chung-Hee's class ranking at Taegu Normal School being sixty-nine out of seventy, it was unlikely that the authorities would assign him to a top elementary school. He was lucky that he got a teaching post at all and was assigned to Munkyŏng, a mining town not very far from his hometown of Kumi. The town of Munkyŏng has become a famous tourist attraction in the twenty-first century for its mountain scenery, but it was vastly different in the 1930s. Located literally at the end of the road, its only opening to the wider world was to the south, to Kimch'ŏn and Taegu. The situation had not changed since the days of the Silla Dynasty a thousand years earlier, when mountains divided tribes and nations. Right behind the Munkyŏng Elementary School was the imposingly high Chu-ŭl (Ju-eul) Mountain, which cast its shadow on the school each morning. To the left and the right were more impassable mountains. Coal mines were all Munkyŏng had. The situation changed more than a half century later, when tunnels and highways linked Munkyŏng with major urban areas to the north, including Seoul. The creation of these structures required digging five long tunnels immediately north of Munkyŏng. The closest tunnel to the town under Choryŏng Mountain is 2,645 meters, or 1.66 miles long.

The school drew its students from the town's families plus those living in more remote mountain villages some distance away. The miners' wages were low, and having little land to till, the people in the area could not help but be poor. Half of the students Park taught were not able to bring lunch to school each day, and many of them had very little to eat in the morning or evening.[1] Teacher Park Chung-Hee was accustomed to poverty, but his heart sank when he visited the homes of his students.

1 Chŏng Yŏng-jin, *Ch'ŏngnyŏn Park Chŏng-hui* [Young Man Park Chung-Hee], vol. 1 (Seoul: Riburo (Libro) Books, 1997), 283.

Many families chose not to send their children to school because they could not afford the tuition money. Park Chung-Hee helped some of them. He did have a steady monthly income at this time, which was much higher than that of older town officials; he could live comfortably even after sending some money home. The town offered absolutely nothing that he could spend his money on, though.

Some of his students later told interviewers that Park Chung-Hee was a kind and energetic teacher who liked to teach songs, swimming, and exercises. They had fond memories of school outings. On one occasion, he even saved a child from drowning when the entire school went to a nearby lake. Other teachers watched helplessly, but Teacher Park jumped into the water as soon as he saw what was happening.

It is not likely that Teacher Park had much of a social life in town. There were three Japanese teachers at Munkyŏng, including the principal; there were also three other Korean teachers, but no one recollected having much to do. Park Chung-Hee lived in a boardinghouse about two blocks away from the school with another man, and the only thing his roommate later recalled was their drinking sessions. Teacher Park preferred the local home brew over distilled liquor, and they drank a bucketful of it each time, the lady of the house joining in occasionally.[2] She was the one who brewed the *makkŏlle* or the local brew, and she taught Park how to brew it. He continued to play trumpet, either because he enjoyed it, to overcome his loneliness, or both. The townspeople became accustomed to the sound of an early morning trumpet from the nearby mountain. They were astonished to learn much later that Park had a wife and a daughter. Many had hoped to have him as

2 Ibid., 289–291.

their son-in-law. He evidently never had his wife and daughter visit him at Munkyŏng.

The Japanese Invasion of China, July 1937

If the mountains and the sleepy town of Munkyŏng did not stimulate Park, the Japanese empire did. The Japanese army started its invasion of the Chinese mainland in July 1937, soon after Park had assumed his teaching position at Munkyŏng, and the invasion deeply affected him. The Japanese army had impressed him since childhood, but now it loomed larger than ever before. The invasion proceeded smoothly, and the Japanese army appeared invincible. It quickly took over the main artery of transportation in Mainland China, the key cities along the major railways, and the great rivers. All that was left was to secure the adjacent towns and villages. The Chinese central government under Generalissimo Chiang Kai-shek abandoned the capital at Nanjing and moved up the Yangtze River to Hankow and then to Chungking. The young Japanese officers appeared to be ready to fulfill the dream of Toyotomi Hideyoshi who, in the sixteenth century, had dreamed of becoming China's emperor.

Japan's imminent conquest of China brought about a momentous change in Korean attitudes toward Japan. Even though Japan had fully controlled Korea since 1905 and even though most Koreans had accepted Japanese rule as a fait accompli, the Japanese may not have cowed them enough to squelch every aspiration for independence. But the news from the Chinese front made the Koreans take another look at Japanese might, resulting in reactions with grave implications. The Japanese colonial government in Korea noted the attitudinal change among the Koreans:

> Some of the nationalists who had held recalcitrant thoughts [against Japan] in the past have changed their views. Some of the religious and pseudo-religious groups that had been seen as anti-state in their orientation have begun to participate in patriotic events. The Korean vernacular press has begun to support national policies. Korean donations for national defense and for the soldiers have increased significantly to large amounts very comparable to the passion shown in Japan. The Koreans have begun to donate funds voluntarily for [purchasing] patriotic military airplanes and for anti-aircraft guns. The number of Koreans worshipping at Shinto Shrines has greatly increased. The Koreans held successive ceremonies to pray for the Japanese army's successes.[3]

One could, of course, discount the self-congratulatory tone of the above report as self-serving propaganda of the colonial government. But the government's internal and secret documents virtually echoed what it published for the public. The following is an excerpt from the report of the Police Department of the Kyŏnggi Province, classified as "secret":

> Especially the quick victory of the imperial army in China in July 1937 and ensuing conquests of Nanking, Canton and Wuhan, and the empire's alliance with the axis powers impressed on the masses the strength of the empire, and their trust in the government became stronger. Even some of the nationalist and Communist leaders who had been hostile to the government at the time of the Manchurian incident [1931] are voluntarily cooperating with the government giving lectures [to the public] or donating large sums of money for national defense.[4]

---

3 Chōsen Sōtokufu (Korean Government General), *Shisei 30nenshi* [History of Thirty Years of Administration] (Seoul, 1940), 801–802.

4 Keikidō Keisatsubu (The Police Department, Kyŏnggi Province), *Ch'ian jōkyō* [Security Conditions], 1939 (the section of special police), 9.

One still wishes there were some nongovernmental and non-Japanese accounts of the effect of the Japanese invasion of China on the Koreans, but I am inclined to believe that even the hardened nationalists began to wonder, if not doubt, the prospect of independence. Even before the Japanese began their attack on Chinese territory, the Chinese government under Chiang Kai-shek had made one concession after another to them. In the spring of 1933, by signing the Tangku Agreement, China ceded to Japan control over a part of the Hebei Province. More territory was ceded in 1935 in that region through two other agreements.[5] Unknown to most young people in Korea, there were a small number of Korean nationalists abroad still engaged in the struggle to win Korean independence, but until Sino-Japanese relations erupted into war, their leader, Kim Ku, had to spend his days and nights on a tiny fishing boat with a Chinese woman to evade the Japanese dragnet.[6] The Chinese government had promised to arrest and turn Kim over to the Japanese if they were able to find him.[7]

The young teacher in Munkyŏng cannot be blamed for thinking that Japan was invincible. In fact, the colonial government could not have found a more loyal teacher than Park Chung-Hee. One of his students recollected, for example, that his teacher took the sixth-grade boys to the mountains one weekend, where they played at soldiering. More active boys formed the Japanese army unit; lethargic ones became the Chinese soldiers. The two units engaged in mock battles, with predictable results. This was reenacted at the school's sports-day meet in the autumn, where parents and others gathered to watch. Undoubtedly, all

---

5 Nihon Koksai Seiji Gakkai, *Taiheiyō sensō eno michi* [The Road to the Pacific War], vol. 3 (Tokyo: Asahi Shinbunsha, 1962), 85–87.
6 Kim Ku, *Paekbom Ilji* [Autobiography of Kim Ku] (Seoul: Kinyŏm Saŏop Hyŏphoe, 1968), 318–319.
7 Nihon Koksai Seiji Gakkai, *Taiheiyō sensō eno michi*, vol. 3, 110–111, 223–224.

applauded with much enthusiasm when the "Japanese army" defeated the Chinese. Teacher Park also wrote a play entitled *The Korean Volunteer Soldiers Going to War*, which was enacted by the children.[8]

The Korean Volunteer Soldiers Going to War

The play Park wrote requires special attention because it shows how attuned he was to the political climate of the time. The colonial government had just instituted the Special Volunteer Enlistment System in February 1938 when the army inducted a small number (406) of young Korean men. A very large number of Korean youth responded to the call for volunteers (2,946 in 1938; 12,548 in 1939)[9]; some of them (45 in 1939 and 168 in 1940) even submitted the "oath in blood," pledging to do their best,[10] but, as noted, only a small portion were accepted.[11] Park Chung-Hee undoubtedly had his volunteer or volunteers submit such an oath for dramatic effect. The oath in blood refers to a sheet of white cloth with letters written in blood. One slices a finger to let the blood

---

8 Cho Kap-je (2009), 58.

9 Though 2,946 volunteered, only 1,381 passed the test in 1938. The number increased to 12,548 volunteers, and 7,007 passing the test in 1939; see Chōsen Sōtokufu, Korean Government-General, *Shisei 30nenshi* [Thirty Years of Administration] (Seoul, 1940), 806–897; Kōtō Hōin, Kenji-kyoku, High Court, Prosecutor's Office, *Shisō ihō* [Thought Report Series], vol. 22 (March 1940): 191–192.

10 Ibid.; the "oath in blood" received wide attention. See a photocopy of the news of such an oath reproduced in *Shisei 30nenshi* in the photo section at the end of the volume (unnumbered page).

11 Only 400 were enlisted in 1938, 600 in 1939, and 3,000 in 1940; see *Shisei 30nenshi*, 801–807. The number of recruits gradually increased to 6,300 in 1943 when the government instituted the universal draft system. Naimushō (Ministry of Home Affairs), *Chōsen oyobi Taiwan no genkyō* [The Present Condition in Korea and Taiwan] (July 1942); reprinted in *Taiheiyō senka no Chōsen oyobi Taiwan* [Korea and Taiwan during the Pacific War], Kondō Ken'ichi (ed.) (Tokyo, 1961), 32–33.

flow, dragging the finger to form a character until a phrase is composed. The practice is known as *hyŏlso* in Korean and *kessho* in Japanese.

Why did so many young Korean men volunteer to enlist? Why did some of them submit the oath in blood? These are questions worth exploring because they relate directly to Park's later actions. In writing his play for public performance, Park Chung-Hee undoubtedly portrayed the young Korean men as welcoming the opportunity to serve the Japanese emperor, as was expected by the authorities. Some of the recruits may indeed have had such thoughts. But Miyata Setsuko presented three other factors at play in her 1979 study: First, those charged with managing the issue in different localities competed against each other to show that the Koreans in their jurisdiction were more "patriotic" than others. Hence, some may have pressured the young men to volunteer. Second, the authorities offered many economic incentives to the families that produced recruits. Third, the economic condition of the sharecroppers was such that they found the army distinctly preferable to the hardship they had to endure at home.[12] Two-thirds of the volunteers turned out to be from sharecropper families. Added to these factors

---

12 Miyata Setsuko, *Chōsen minshū to "Kōminka seisaku"* [The Korean Masses and the "Policy to Turn Them to Imperial Subjects"] (Tokyo: Miraisha, 1985), 63–71. This portion of the book was first published in article form in 1979. Professor Ch'oe Yŏng-ho wrote about his observation and narrative to me, and his words are very revealing: "There is no doubt that many, if not the most, volunteered willingly for various reasons. One of them was to get out [of] the desperate predicament of dire poverty and the other being the Japanese government exhortations to the point of compelling them to volunteer. And of course the great success in the Japanese propaganda to build up the cult of militarism in Korea is another. I remember the scene of sending off Kim Chong-wŏn (later the infamous Tiger Kim) as a *shiganhei*. He was my next-door neighbor, a bully causing havoc in the neighborhood. His mother ran a street-corner wine-shop (*chumak*), and he (having not even finished elementary school) was restless, going nowhere when he volunteered. There was a big celebratory sendoff for him organized by the police and the officials."

was another: some Koreans argued that their young countrymen should receive whatever military training they could get, because this would be useful when the occasion arose for Korean independence.[13] But what was the significance of the oath in blood? Of course, the oath indicated the eagerness of the person to be accepted. Colonel Umida, charged with the responsibility of training the volunteers, was quite cynical about such an oath. "Anyone can express their passion through petitions or the 'Oath in Blood,' but it should not be encouraged. What is needed is not burning patriotism but deep-rooted, unshakable patriotism."[14] Having been a high-ranking officer in the Chōsen-gun, or the Japanese army in Korea, Umida undoubtedly was familiar with the volunteers' ulterior motives, as described by Miyata. The outward showing of passion could cool down quickly when circumstances changed. Miyata, who quotes Umida's statement, added another reason not to accept the oath in blood at face value. The fact that Koreans had to prove themselves "more Japanese than the Japanese" betrayed their awareness of the discrimination against them. It was a sign of mutual distrust, according to Miyata.[15] Indeed, the Japanese army was very weary of enlisting Korean men into their midst. The whole venture was wrapped in a complex psychological conflict.

Chingbirok

Teacher Park Chung-Hee may have written a play celebrating the Japanese empire, but it is quite certain that while at Munkyŏng, he read

13 Ibid., 88, citing Naimushō Keihokyoku, *Tokkō geppō* (Ministry of Home Affairs, Police and Security Bureau), [Special High Police Monthly Report], September 1941, 80.
14 Ibid., 79.
15 Ibid., 78–79.

Chingbirok (pronounced "zingbirok"),[16] Yu Sŏng-yong's reflections on Hideyoshi's invasion of Korea in 1592 and 1596. This is because Yu was a childhood friend of Admiral Yi Sun-shin, whom Park admired. The manuscript had been published by Yu's descendants in the seventeenth century, but a new edition became available in 1936, just before Park's assignment to Munkyŏng.[17] Park would have been eager for a chance to read the book, not only because Yu Sŏng-yong wrote about Admiral Yi Sun-shin, but also because Yu mentioned both Munkyŏng and Sŏnsan, Park's hometown. Having scaled the rugged and steep mountains around Munkyŏng, which strategists considered to be a natural geographical barrier against invaders, Park would have read *Chingbirok* with an enlightened perspective. What strategy did Katō Kiyomasa and Konishi Yukinaga, the Japanese generals, use to surmount Korean defenses? Why did General Shin Rip, the general commander of the Korean forces, not stop the Japanese forces in the Munkyŏng mountains?

Teacher Park Chung-Hee would have exploded in rage when he found out the answers. The Korean commanding general thought the mountains too rugged for his horses to mount. He thought his Korean soldiers would fight better in Ch'ungju, the town over the mountains. He simply did not wish to make use of the bulwark that nature had provided. Of course, there was no way to counter the waves of Japanese

---

16 Yu Sŏng-yong's *Chingbirok* has been ably translated into English by Choi Byŏnghyŏn as *The Book of Corrections: Reflections on the National Crisis during the Japanese Invasion of Korea, 1592–1598* (Berkeley: Institute of East Asian Studies, University of California, 2002).

17 The Korean History Editorial Committee of the colonial government published the 1936 edition. Yu Sŏng-yong, *Chōbiroku* (Chingbirok), trans. Park Chong-myŏng (or Boku Shō-mei in Japanese) (Tokyo: Heibonsha, 1979), 313 (Tōyō Bunko publications No. 357). This is a Japanese translation of Yu's work. I found this edition particularly valuable because of the translator's annotations. Publication dates are mentioned in the translator's notes at the end of the book.

troops once they passed through the mountains unopposed. The Japanese army was not only larger and better trained, but they also had rifle units. The arrogant Japanese emissary had presented the Koreans a few rifles before the attack started, but Shin Rip had scoffed at them, saying his bows and arrows were far superior. It was very clear that Korea needed better commanders, as well as better rulers.

Reading *Chingbirok* in Munkyŏng, Park Chung-Hee would have wept. The book begins by saying "Alas! The war with Japan was so catastrophic! Within a little more than two months, three major cities collapsed, and soon the entire country."[18] His purpose in writing the book, Yu said, was "to correct the mistakes of the past in order to prevent disasters in the future."[19] While the text of his recollections makes it clear, he could not directly say that King Sŏnjo was a coward and his generals incompetent. A system that had valued book learning and debased military training could not have defended the country, even had the enemy been much less formidable. All the ruling elite wanted was to indulge in the privileges the system provided them. When Yu Sŏng-yong, the prime minister, ordered an inspection of the defenses, his generals toured the towns, enjoying the entertainments provided them and checking bows and arrows. They supposedly checked the books listing the names of the soldiers who had served as a basis for the distribution of grain and cash, winking at the fact that these were no more than fiction. County magistrates protested the order to fortify the towns by arguing that the rivers along the towns provided enough of a defense. Perhaps, in the end, the magistrates served the peasants better that way; they did not have to toil needlessly building fortresses. In fact, many magistrates

18 *Book of Corrections*, 15.
19 Ibid., p. 15

in key towns who doubled as garrison commanders abandoned their fortified cities at the news of the approaching enemy. The people had no choice but to flee to the mountains. No planting in the fields meant no food later, as the war dragged on for years. Yu Sŏng-yong heard the multitudes moaning around him in the evening and found them dead in the morning. The enemy did not even have to use their guns and swords to destroy the people.

In addition to being ill prepared for war, the Korean kingdom ignored the report of their chief diplomat, Hwang Yun-gil, who returned from a ten-month trip to Japan, including a six-month stay at Hideyoshi's castle in Himeji. "All signs indicated that Hideyoshi was getting ready to attack our country," said Hwang. But his deputy, Kim Sŏng-il refuted him. When Kim's friend, Yu Sŏng-yong asked him, "What would you do if it turns out that we are going to have real trouble with the Japanese?" he answered, "How can I be so sure that the Japanese will never invade us? What I was trying to say was that Hwang's words were so extreme that they might raise an alarm and agitation among people across the country."[20] Yu and the court, in any event, sided with the deputy ambassador. There is no indication that the court ever engaged in discussions over the evidence the two envoys presented. To the court, the more important consideration was to which faction each diplomat belonged. Since the chief envoy belonged to the Western faction, his deputy had to oppose him. The deputy belonged to the Eastern faction, which held the dominant position.[21] Kim, it should be noted, supported

---

20 Ibid.., p. 31.

21 See the translator's footnote on p. 31. The Korean public, incidentally, are very well informed about these "incidents." What is truly astonishing is that some Korean "historians" even to this day publish newspaper and magazine articles in support of Kim Sŏng-gil, calling him a "wise man."

his judgment with incredibly absurd evidence, saying, "Hideyoshi has eyes like a mouse; he is not a man capable of attacking us."[22] Seemingly, this was enough evidence to ignore Hwang's urgent calls for preparation. Teacher Kim Yŏng-ki had more than one reason to smash his book down to the floor.

Park Chung-Hee, in any event, could not help but be restless at Munkyŏng. He would have suffered from claustrophobia and a sense of seclusion from the world. Munkyŏng was definitely not a place for a young man bursting with energy to consider as his final destination in life. Being a schoolteacher also had its limits. Many of his classmates at Taegu had gone to Japan to pursue further education after fulfilling their teaching requirements. Park needed a new outlet for his energy.

It was this atmosphere that in 1938 spurred the twenty-one-year-old man to apply for the Manchukuo Military Academy, to be opened in 1939.[23] Having established Manchukuo or the Manchu empire and having started the Manchukuo army in 1932, Kantō-gun officers had been training officers for that army at Fengt'ien (now Shenyang) by providing a twelve-month abbreviated course for the officers. But they needed better-trained men if the army was to grow into a more reliable force. The new military academy was to provide a four-year period of training patterned after its Japanese counterpart. It would be located in the northern city of Ch'angch'un (Long Spring), renamed Sinjing (New Capital) because Manchukuo's new government was located there. Park Chung-Hee would have completed his two years of obligatory teaching by the time the new academy opened, and he sent off an application for

22 Yi Ŏ-ryŏng, p. 36.

23 Manshū Nippō's account, to be presented shortly, indicated that his 1939 application was the repeat of that of the previous year.

admission as soon as details became available. But the new academy's admissions office was not impressed by his plea for them to overlook his age. The academy's age limit for new cadets was set at nineteen, and Park would have exceeded that limit by three years.

V. MANCHURIA AND PARK CHUNG-HEE

Why did Park Chung-Hee decide to cast off his teaching career and opt for the Manchukuo Military Academy? The short answer was because it was the only way for him to fulfill his lifelong desire to become *Rikugun taishō*, or an army general. But what kind of land was Manchuria? How would Park fit in? How would the Manchukuo academy help him in his pursuit of a military career?

Manchuria offered many other attractions other than the Manchukuo Military Academy. Chung-Hee had spent nine days in 1935 in Manchuria as part of a school trip.[1] This was the land of the scarlet sunset and an endless horizon filled with *kaoliang* (sorghum), corn, and soybean fields.[2] The cities the students visited—Dalian, Fengt'ien (now Shenyang), Sinjing (now Changchun), and Antung (now Dandung)—bustled with commerce and industry, rickshaws, and horse carriages crisscrossing each other's paths. It was clearly a land of opportunity, contrasting sharply with the silent world of Munkyŏng. And this land beckoned the Koreans, because the Japanese militarists who conquered Manchuria wanted the Koreans to migrate there. They argued surreptitiously that Manchuria was the traditional homeland of the Korean people and they had the right to be there. A part of Manchuria in fact belonged to the ancient kingdom of Koguryŏ (37 BC to AD 668), whose territory extended from central Manchuria to the middle part of the Korean Peninsula. Now the Japanese empire wanted to populate that land with Japanese and Koreans. Manchuria's inhabitants after the

1 Chŏng Yŏng-jin, *Ch'ŏngnyŏn Park Chŏng-hui* [Young Man Park Chung-Hee], vol. 1 (Seoul: Riburo (Libro) Books, 1997), 203. This was in May 1935, two months before his brother was laid off by the newspaper. The school collected four yen a month from each student to pay for these trips.

2 Kusayanagi Daizō started his two-volume work citing these comments; *Jitsuroku Mantetsu Chōsabu* [Veritable Record: Research Department, South Manchuria Railway Company] (Tokyo: Asahi Shinbunsha, 1979), 11.

collapse of Koguryŏ had been the Manchus, but only a small number of them remained in the twentieth century. Most of them had migrated south of the Great Wall to help rule the Qing (pronounced Ch'ing) Dynasty their chieftains had established in 1644 and gradually were absorbed into the Han majority. The Qing Dynasty regarded Manchuria as their ancestral domain and prohibited the Han Chinese from migrating there until 1887, when they decided that the Han would at least be better than the Russians, who also sought to take over the sparsely populated land. Thus, the Japanese could argue, virtually everyone there were newcomers.[3]

This was the rationale for Manchukuo, the "Manchu empire" headed by Pu Yi. The Revolution of 1911 headed by Sun Yat-sen overthrew the Qing Dynasty of the Manchus and Pu Yi, the last emperor, was out of a job. The Japanese decided to establish Manchukuo, the Manchu state, turning Pu Yi into the head of the new "empire."[4] Manchukuo's motto, in any event, was the "Harmony of Five Races" namely the Japanese, Koreans, Chinese (or the Han race), Manchus, and Mongols. The impoverished Chinese from Shantung and Hobei Provinces poured onto the Manchurian plain in search of land and work after the prohibition was lifted; the Japanese army wanted more Japanese and Koreans to settle there to balance the mixture of the "five races" and to resolve

---

3 I have discussed some of these events in my previous work, *Revolutionary Struggle in Manchuria* (Berkeley: University of California Press, 1983), chapter 1.
4 All this was later made famous, particularly to Western audiences, in the movie *The Last Emperor*.

the problem of overpopulation in Japan and Korea.[5] The Japanese even created special banks to encourage immigration.[6]

While the Manchukuo regime did not announce it explicitly, it offered the Koreans a subtle change in their status. In the binary or the dichotomous system of the conquerors versus the conquered in Korea, the natives could not occupy any other position than that of the subjugated. However, the Manchukuo system placed them in between the Japanese conquerors and the Chinese majority by virtue of the fact that Korea had been under Japanese rule longer. More Koreans spoke the Japanese language than did Chinese, and the Koreans were more attuned to the "Japanese way." Hence, the puppet regime of Manchukuo gave Koreans better access to opportunities in employment, loans, and other services. The Chinese property owners who had long abused the Korean sharecroppers had to alter their behavior toward the Koreans also. The Chinese lost the protection of the Manchurian warlord regime when Japan conquered Manchuria, and the Koreans were in a better position. I find striking analogy in the situation between the Koreans in Manchuria and the Jews in Tunisia, which Albert Memmi described:

> For better or for worse, the Jew found himself one small notch above the Moslem on the pyramid, which is the basis of all colonial societies. His privileges were laughable, but they were enough to make him proud and to make him hope that

5 On the Japanese policy of encouraging Japanese and Korean migration to Manchuria, see *Shisei 30nenshi*, op. cit., 897 ff. Initially, the Kantō-gun wanted at least 10 percent of the population in Manchuria to be Japanese; see also Manshūkokushi Hensan Kankōkai (Editorial and Publication Committee), *Manshūkokushi* [History of Manchukuo], vol. 1 (Tokyo: Manmō dōhō Engokai, 1971), 641–653.

6 For details, see Matsuoka Takao, "The Formation and Development of Immigration and Labor Policies after the Establishment of Manchukuo" [in Japanese] in Manshūshi Kenkyūkai (ed.), *Nihon teikokushugikano Manshū* [Manchuria under Japanese Imperialism] (Tokyo: Ochanomizu Shobō, 1972), 213–314.

> he was not part of the mass of Moslems, which constituted the base of the pyramid. It was enough to make him feel endangered when the structure began to crumble.[7]

There was indeed much danger after the puppet Manchukuo collapsed in August 1945 with the end of the Japanese empire. A large number of Koreans quickly returned to Korea, but some of them became the targets of Chinese bandits and others in such towns as Mutanjiang and Misan in early 1946, which turned the rivers red with blood.[8] The Koreans had been regarded as the running dogs of the colonial regime.

Manchukuo's ration system graphically manifested the pyramidal nature of the "five harmonious races." The ration books for the Japanese had a white cover, the Koreans yellow, and the "Manchurians" blue. The holders of the white books were entitled to rice, sake, sugar, and cookies. Those with yellow books would receive less rice plus millet and little sugar. Those with blue would get kaoliang (sorghum), corn, soybeans, and soybean oil. The white cover holders would get more shoes, socks, underwear, towels, soap, and other necessities than the others. If a Korean worked for the government, either in the military or civilian branch, he would be entitled to the white book. That is why Captain Chŏng Il-gwŏn in Sinjing was able to obtain sake for Cadet Park when he was in the military academy there.[9]

---

7 Albert Memmi, *The Colonizer and the Colonized*, trans. Howard Greenfield, (Boston, Beacon Press, 1965), xiii–xv; preface, xiv.

8 Interview with a historian in Yenji, Jilin Province, in October 1981; he did not wish to be identified.

9 I became an expert of a sort on the ration system, because I served as my family's procurer of rationed goods while idling in Liaoyang between 1943 and 1944. Park Chung-Hee later rewarded Chŏng richly. He served as Park's ambassador to Turkey and France and then as prime minister for six years.

Park Chung-Hee, in any event, had little to lose by resigning his teaching position at Munkyŏng. The Korean communities in Manchuria needed many young teachers like him. By 1940, there were more than a million Koreans scattered in various parts of Manchuria, and virtually every city had an elementary school for Korean children.[10]

Korea in 1939

Manchuria definitely served as a "pull" factor, offering Park Chung-Hee and other Koreans the challenge and opportunity to immigrate there. There were a number of additional factors developing within Korea that also served as "push" factors, encouraging Koreans to forsake their homeland and look elsewhere. One of the strongest for the peasantry of southern Korea was the drought of 1939. Another was the rising inflation and the shortage of goods brought about by the Japanese invasion of China. The war against China also brought ever-tightening police control of the Korean population. For Park Chung-Hee, any factor other than the prospect of becoming an army general may have been immaterial, but his environment nevertheless pressed him to take action.

The 1939 drought was devastating to the area in which Park taught and lived. Words can hardly convey the harshness of the scene. Only such literary giants as John Steinbeck could describe the suffering that was inflicted on the farmers that year.[11] The drought, in any event,

---

10 I attended one of those in Tieling, Liaoning Province, just northeast of Shenyang. It was not a large city then but had a Korean elementary school with a large number of students. I was in the first grade between 1938 and 1939, and my teacher was a Korean named Yi Cha-ha (Ja-ha). Tieling's population in June 1941 was 57,000 according to *Manshūkokushi*, vol. 2, 229.

11 By coincidence, Steinbeck's *Grapes of Wrath* was published in 1939. He depicted the agony of farmers trying to escape from the Dust Bowl in Oklahoma. He won the Pulitzer Prize in 1940 and the Nobel Prize for Literature in 1962.

affected seven of the thirteen provinces in Korea, from the capital area of Seoul down to the southern end of the peninsula, some areas having either no harvest at all or, at best, suffering a decrease of over 70 percent in crop production. This represented 39.4 percent of all rice fields in Korea. Over a million farm households (1,090,000 households) became drifters.[12]

All this suffering was caused by a lack of rain. The last major rains were in mid-May; the northeast region had some rain afterward, but not enough. Unfortunately for Park and his family, they were located in the southern part of the peninsula, which had had no rain whatsoever since spring. The dry winds swept away whatever moisture the soil had contained, and the rising temperatures scorched the land. The severity of the 1939 drought was unprecedented in Korean history, according to Japanese specialists.[13] The result of the drought is shown in table 2. Rice production that year plummeted 40 percent from that of the previous year—from 24,138,000 koku (sŏk or sŏm in Korean) in 1938 to 14,355,000 koku in 1939.

We can only imagine what kinds of conversations the young teacher in Munkyŏng had with the townspeople and his students' parents. Suffering had been commonplace for many of them, but now they had even less on which to survive. Whatever relief programs the colonial government had attempted would have been inadequate. The situation

---

12 Zenkoku Keizai Chōsakikan Rengōkai Chōsen Shibu [The Korea Branch, the Federation of All-Nation Economic Study Organizations], *Chōsen keizai nenpō Shōwa 16–17nen han* [Korea Economic Annual Report, 1941–1942] (Tokyo: Kaizōsha, 1943), 59.

13 Korea had also suffered severe droughts in 1876, 1919, 1924, 1928, and 1929, for example; ibid., 59.

in other parts of the empire was less severe, but Kyūshū and Shikoku in the southern parts of Japan also suffered from a severe crop shortfall.[14]

Additionally, living conditions in Korea deteriorated rapidly as a result of the Japanese war in China. The following is from a secret report filed by the Kyŏnggi Province police in 1939. Police authorities also worried about the effect of the worsening economic conditions in Korea:

> The general masses are deeply trusting of the government and continue to engage in their own lives. But the rapid rise in prices, shortage of goods, discontinuation of peacetime industries and the lagging military supply industries have affected many employees and the public. Farm villages are suffering from drought and in some areas they cannot obtain food. The shortage of rice and staples gave extraordinary shock to public opinion, and the society is in a precarious condition, very susceptible to the recalcitrants' manipulations.[15]

Rapid inflation severely curtailed the purchasing power of salary earners, but the real crisis was the shortage of available food and material. If in 1936, the year before the invasion, the wholesale price index was 100, this index increased to 126.3 by 1938 and to 155.3 in 1939, meaning that prices rose 50 percent in a matter of three years.[16] Living was becoming more and more difficult. The Law on National General Mobilization that the Diet passed in April 1938 had a far-reaching impact on the population. It allowed the military to appropriate any material or human resource it needed for the war effort. The military also took con-

14 Ibid., 58.
15 Keikidō Keisatsubu, *Ch'ian jōkyō* , 1939, 10.
16 Ibid., 85.

trol of all mass media, including newspapers and radio. The Japanese empire, in short, became a totalitarian state ruled by the military.

The Manchukuo Military Academy

If Manchuria looked attractive to Park Chung-Hee, the Manchukuo Military Academy appeared even more so. Not only could Park become an officer in the Manchukuo army after graduation, but there was also a chance to be sent to the Japanese Military Academy. The Manchurian academy dispatched a small number of top cadets each year to the Japanese Academy to finish their third- and fourth-year training there. Park had no chance of being admitted to the Japanese academy directly, but the Manchukuo Military Academy would give him a chance to enter through a side door and receive the best military training available in the Japanese empire. While the Japanese Military Academy was not the Tokyo Imperial University, the most prestigious Japanese academic institution, there was no question about its prestige. If admitted, Park could become a military officer, as he had always wanted, and also receive the higher education he had longed for. The family's financial considerations had prevented him from following his classmates to Japan. Once again, there was a glimmer of hope.

But there was still a major hurdle to overcome. Park had heard about a Captain Kang Chae-ho of the Manchukuo army, who was from Taegu and coming home for a furlough. The captain advised Park to send a letter to the academy with an additional example of his "calligraphy in blood" or "oath in blood," showing his passion for the military.[17] Kang

---

17 Chŏng Yŏng-jin, *Ch'ŏngnyŏn Park Chŏnghui* [Young Man Park Chung-Hee], vol. 1, (Seoul: Riburo (Libro) Books, 1997), 329–330. Cho Kap-je also cited Captain Kang as Park's supporter but did not attribute the "oath in blood" to him; Cho Kap-

planned to use his local connections to get the admissions officers to give Park special consideration.[18]

Park Chung-Hee received the publicity he sought, but to no avail. *Manshū shinbun* [the Manchurian News], published in Sinjing, carried a two-column news item with his photograph on March 31, 1939 (page 7), with the headline "Calligraphy in Blood" (*kessho*) and the subtitle "Desire to be an Army Officer: Young Teacher from the Peninsula."[19] The news story follows:

> On the 29th, the admissions officers at the Military Government Command were deeply moved by a piece of registered mail from Park Chung-Hee, a teacher at Western Munkyŏng Public School in North Kyŏngsang Province of Korea, that contained a passionate letter desiring to be an army officer together with a "Calligraphy in Blood" saying "Will Serve till Death (Isshi motte gohōkō). Park Chung-Hee." Included in the mail were various documents including the "Certificate of Passing Military Training Examination" (Kyōren Kentei Gōkakusho).

The content of Park's letter was indeed passionate.

> The announced requirements for admission for the Japanese candidates indicate that I am disqualified on all grounds. I apologize for daring to ask you to make an exception, but would

je, *Park Chŏnghui ui kyŏljŏngjŏk sun'gandŭl* [Decisive Moments of Park Chung-Hee], (Seoul: Kip'irang, 2009), 67, 70.

18 Cho Kap-je in his 2009 publication quoted Yu Zŭng-sŏn, Park's former colleague at Munkyŏng Elementary School, who says that he suggested the idea while they shared the duty officer's room at the school (Cho Kap-je (2009), 62–65). Yu also remembered Park Chung-Hee saying his brother was the head of the township or Myŏn, but this has not been substantiated by records.

19 The news article was republished in Photostat form in *Han'gyŏre* on November 5, 2009. The peninsula or *Hantō* here was the expression the Japanese used to refer to Korea. Japan, on the other hand, was known as *Naichi* or "the inland."

> it be possible for you to accept me into the National Army? I am determined to serve the public (hōkō) to death with the spirit and fortitude that will not shame the Japanese…As a soldier of the Manchukuo Army I shall do my utmost for the state of Manchukuo and for the fatherland without any consideration for my own glory.

The news article ended by saying that this was the second time Park had sent such a letter. The news article then related, "Becoming an officer, however, is limited to those already in the army; being 23 years old, he exceeded the age limit of 19. Therefore, though regretful, his application was politely rejected."

We do not know how Park Chung-Hee reacted nor what he did afterward, but the admissions office had to reverse its decision. He entered the Manchukuo Military Academy in March 1940. The reason for the admissions office's reversal gave rise to speculation many decades later that Park Chung-Hee had gained admission by joining the Chientao Special Korean Unit, created specifically to destroy the anti-Japanese guerrilla forces. Park was condemned as a Japanese collaborator by some elements in Korea and in Yenbian, Jilin Province, for this alleged act.[20] This charge needs scrutiny, because Park's admission to the Manchukuo academy has become a major political issue in South Korea.

Park and the Chientao Special Korean Paramilitary Unit

The Korean community in Yenbian had reason to be aroused by this issue because Yenbian,[21] at the Korean-Manchurian border, was the region where anti-Japanese guerrillas had been active in the 1930s and early 1940s after the Japanese took over Manchuria.[22] Kim Il-sŏng

---

20 Interview with Chŏng Yŏng-jin (June 6, 2009).

21 This area was known as Chientao in Chinese and Kando in Korean until 1946.

22 Cf. Chong-Sik Lee, *Revolutionary Struggle in Manchuria*.

briefly operated in that region as a guerrilla leader, though most of his career as an anti-Japanese fighter had been west of Yenbian. Those in that region, in any event, firmly believed that Park Chung-Hee voluntarily joined and served in the Special Korean Unit knowing the nature of its mission. Park, in their view, therefore, was an unscrupulous traitor to the Korean and Chinese nations.

The charge is based on two booklets published by Ryu Yŏn-san of Yenbian in 2003 and 2004, which argued that Park had joined the Special Korean Unit because he had to do something extra to overcome his age problem at the Manchukuo Military Academy. Ryu argued that Park joined the Special Unit to prove his patriotism for Japan[23] and produced a witness to prove Park's presence at the Tashaho battle in August 1939, where the Special Unit was decimated by anti-Japanese guerrillas. The witness, Chu Chae-dŏk, claimed that he was a soldier in the Special Unit under Lieutenant Park Chung-Hee in Rehe (or Jehol) in 1943–1944 and knew that Park was at Tashaho in August 1939. To put all this into context, of course, requires some background information.

When the Japanese launched their operation in September 1931 to take over Manchuria, Marshal Chang Hsueh-liang, the warlord there, withdrew his forces to northern China. But the armed groups that were not under the command of Marshal Chang, including former bandits, rose up against the Japanese—their strength at one point reaching three hundred thousand men. The Japanese Kantō-gun engaged in a series of pacification campaigns, and by September 1939, the number of anti-Japanese forces had declined to ten thousand. This is when Kantō-gun

---

23 Ryu Yŏn-san, *Manju Arirang* [Manchuria Arirang] (Seoul: Dolbegae, 2003), 98; *Ilsongjŏng p'urŭn sol e sŏnkuja nŭn ŏpsŏda* [There Were No Forerunners in the Green Field of Ilsongdong], (Seoul: Aifild, 2004), 48, 52, 59.

drew up a master plan to clear out all "recalcitrants." All of the farmers scattered throughout the hinterlands were moved to "defense hamlets" or concentration camps to deny the guerrillas food and information. The army constructed "defense highways" and communication networks to facilitate speedy movement of police and army troops. Special units of "surrendered bandits" were assigned to chase after their former comrades.[24] The Chientao Korean Special Unit was a part of this master plan. In 1941, the Manchukuo Army shot to death Yang Ching-wi, the top guerrilla leader of the Northeast Anti-Japanese Allied Army (*Dongbei Kang-Rih Lien-chün*). The Manchukuo army also celebrated the killing of Kim Il-sŏng, another major guerrilla leader, but the one they killed was not the one they had sought. He managed to flee to the maritime province in the Soviet territory in early 1941 with a dozen or so men under him. The guerrillas in the mountain region became the legendary heroes of resistance against Japan after its capitulation in 1945, and the people in the region became hostile toward anyone who had played a part in the counterguerrilla operations.

Park Chung-Hee would have found the charges against him bewildering and ridiculous. He had never joined the Special Unit, nor had he engaged in any battles against anti-Japanese guerrillas in that region. He was a teacher in Munkyŏng when the Tashaho battle took place. Had he been on trial, Park's defense attorneys would have questioned Ryu Yŏnsan's evidence. The most crucial point was Ryu's source of information. He based his charge on his single interview with Chu Chae-dŏk in July

24 Cf. Chong-Sik Lee, *Counterinsurgency in Manchuria: the Japanese Experience, 1931–1940* (Santa Monica, CA, 1967), and *Revolutionary Struggle in Manchuria*, chapter 9. On the 1939 master plan to destroy the guerrillas, see Ranseikai [Orchid Star Society], *Manshū kokugun* [The Manchukuo Army] (Tokyo, private publication, 1970), 400.

1995, but the information provided by the seventy-six-year-old veteran on events that allegedly transpired five decades earlier was highly questionable. Chu Chae-dŏk, according to Rhu, joined the Special Unit on April 10, 1943, four years after the Tashaho battle, and could not be described as an eyewitness to Park's presence there. If Park's unit was decimated, as Chu argued, Park would not have survived to become an object of speculation. Even if Chu did serve under Park, Park was not a person likely to have talked about his past with a subordinate. The defense attorneys would have told Ryu Yŏn-san, with a copy of a Japanese book on Manchuria in hand, that it was not the Special Korean Unit that the anti-Japanese guerrillas destroyed at Tashaho in August 1939, but a company of Kantō-gun troops from Ming-yueh-kou (*Myŏng-wol-ku* in Korean) in June, not August of 1939. Upon receiving the report that the guerrillas had showed up at Ant'u, the company hurried to the location on four trucks and was ambushed at a point twenty kilometers from Ant'u, according to Japanese scholars on Manchuria.[25] The company did not even have a chance to put up a resistance, and there were no survivors. The Kantō-gun at this time did not have any Korean soldiers in it. It was the same spot where a unit of the Special Unit was destroyed in January of the same year.[26] Park Chung-Hee was not there then, either.

It is quite possible that Ryu's witness actually served under Captain Shin Hyŏn-jun, who served in the same Manchukuo Eighth Regiment as Park Chung-Hee. The witness could easily have confused the two Koreans because neither of them used their Korean names at that time, and it is highly unlikely that either of them told a lowly soldier what their

---

25 Asada and Kobayashi, 190.
26 Ibid., 190.

Korean names were. Being a company commander, Shin had platoons of men under him. Unlike Park Chung-Hee, he grew up in Yenbian and spoke Chinese well. Shin stated in his autobiography that he had been dispatched to the Special Unit from a Manchukuo regiment in 1939 to participate in the founding of the Chientao Korean Special Unit. He was then transferred to the Eighth Regiment in July 1944.[27] While there were two other Korean officers in the same regiment, no one else had served in the Special Unit. Shin in his 1989 book mentioned three other Korean officers in the Special Unit, but Park Chung-Hee was not one of them.[28] The publication date of Shin's book is important here. It was published well before Ryu published his charges in 2003 and 2004, based on unfounded speculation. Had Park been in the Special Unit, Shin would have testified about his reunion with a former comrade in July 1944, but they were total strangers until they met at the front line.

Colonel Arikawa

If Park Chung-Hee was not admitted to the Academy on the basis of his extraordinary display of "patriotism" for Manchukuo through the Special Unit, why did the admissions office reverse their decision? Most likely, this is when Colonel Arikawa Kazuichi intervened. The Manshū Shinbun's news article made no mention of any recommendation letters, and it is clear that the colonel had not written a letter when the young

27 Shin Hyŏn-jun, *No haebyŏng ui hoegorok* [Recollections of an Old Marine] (Seoul, K'at'orik ch'ulp'ansa, 1989), 41–42.

28 There were three others besides Shin; ibid., 44; Park, of course, would not have been an officer of any rank in 1939 had he been in the Special Unit. He was commissioned a lieutenant in 1944.

man first sought admission. But he would have intervened after reading the newspaper article.[29]

The colonel's sponsorship would not have had much effect on the Japanese Military Academy with its over fifty-year tradition, but the situation at the Manchukuo academy was very different. The academy had opened its doors in 1939, and everything was still in the embryonic stages. The academy may have been preparing to use the rules and regulations of their Japanese counterpart, but they had not been implemented at the time of Park's application. Even the entrance examination was perfunctory. The academy did not appear to have been overwhelmed by applicants either. It "imported" 172 Japanese cadets from Japan who were given two years of *yoka* training in the new academy.[30] The Japanese army was in need of more officers than ever before as it was mired on the Chinese front and as it had expanded its front lines into Southeast Asia. Since 1936, Kantō-gun had been preparing for the invasion of Soviet Siberia, and it too needed more officers. The Manchukuo Military Academy could serve a useful purpose by training more officers for the Japanese army.

Colonel Arikawa's recommendation also would have had a strong influence because of the special status of Japanese senior officers in Manchuria. Everyone knew that the state of Manchukuo and its army

---

29 Chŏng Yŏng-jin noted that Arikawa did write the recommendation letter when Park Chung-Hee presented himself in Sinjing. Park is said to have stayed at Arikawa's residence before going to take his entrance examination. I could not verify the information, because the author did not provide the source; Chŏng Yŏng-jin, *Ch'ŏngnyŏn Park Chŏng-hui* [Young Man Park Chung-Hee], vol. 2, (Seoul: Riburo (Libro) Books, 1997), 13.

30 *Manshū kokugun*, 617; according to this source, these cadets had passed the entrance examination at the Japanese Military Academy but were sent to Sinjing for the two-year training program.

were controlled by the Kantō-gun, the Japanese army in Manchuria. While the puppet army had high-ranking generals with Chinese names, actual control was in the hands of the Japanese senior advisor with the rank of major general. The rank of full colonel was just below the senior advisor, since the Japanese army did not have a brigadier general.

While in Taegu, Arikawa had been a lieutenant colonel, but he was now a full colonel in Kantō-gun, commanding an independent garrison unit in the capital city. It is quite possible that Arikawa called Major General Nagumo, the commandant of the academy, on behalf of Park Chung-Hee. Park's gratitude to Nagumo was extraordinary, as I shall relate below.

It should be noted that his age was not the only problem Park had in applying for the academy. Even Colonel Arikawa might not have been able to persuade the Academy to admit Park had his marriage become known. Park not only concealed his marriage; he had a friend produce a document from his hometown government office that did not mention the marriage.[31]

Park Chung-Hee, Yi Sun-shin, and Japan

We should pause here to reflect on the question raised earlier regarding Park Chung-Hee's eagerness to enter the Manchukuo Military Academy in relation to his devotion to Admiral Yi Sun-shin. How could a young man who professed to admire the Admiral serve Japan with a clear conscience? Indeed, much later, South Korea was embroiled in the issue of which prominent figures had collaborated with the Japanese empire: Park Chung-Hee was included, along with 4,388 others, in the *Dictionary of Collaborators* (Ch'in-Il inmyŏng sajŏn) published in November 2009. He was condemned on the grounds that he had voluntarily produced the "oath in blood," swearing his allegiance to the

31 Ibid., vol. 1, 329.

Japanese empire. The implication here was that he was a national traitor. If he had had a chance to explain himself, what would Park have said?

Park would have argued that there was no conflict between his admiration of Admiral Yi Sun-shin and serving his country's Japanese rulers. He would have said that the situation in 1939 was vastly different from 350 years earlier in the 1590s. Admiral Yi Sun-shin fought the Japanese in 1597 because Japan was the mortal enemy who had invaded Korea. The Japanese rule of Korea was brutal, to be sure, but Park did not regard Japan as his enemy. Unless one belonged to the ruling class, the Korean kingdom had not treated its people any better than the Japanese treated them. Park's father's rage against the ruling dynasty had nearly cost him his life, and Park Chung-Hee himself suffered from that legacy. Had the Korean kingdom remained in power, Park could not have dreamed of receiving the education he obtained under the Japanese colonial government. In any event, by the time he was born, Korea by name did not exist on the map, and there was no prospect of the situation changing. In fact, the Japanese empire was becoming stronger by the day and appeared to be ready to swallow China, the giant to which the Korean kingdom had paid homage as its suzerain. This was a situation that a twenty-three-old teacher in a mining town in a Japanese colony could not dream of changing, and Park chose to make the best of the situation he faced. The Korean rulers of the past had sealed Park's fate by wasting opportunities to strengthen Korea, resulting in a foreign power's rule over the country. Park would have been happy to apply to a Korean Military Academy had such an institution existed. Did he deserve to be condemned as a national traitor?

It is very likely that the notion of regarding Japan as an enemy never entered Park's mind. On the contrary, he had been reciting the Oath of

Imperial Subjects (*Kōkoku shinmin no chikai*)[32] with his students every morning ever since he had become a teacher. The Korean Government-General (*Chōsen Sōtokufu*) had decreed in October 1937 that every school should start the day with a schoolyard ceremony where students and faculty would bow to the portraits of the august majesties, Emperor Hirohito and the Empress, stored in a special hut built for that purpose,[33] bow to the east where the majesties resided, and recite the aforementioned oath. The class would then move into the classroom and recite the 126 reign titles of the emperors and the Imperial Rescript on Education.[34] The Oath of Imperial Subjects contained only three items and can be reproduced here.

We are the subjects of the Great Japanese Empire.

We shall be loyal to His Majesty the Emperor with all our hearts.

We shall overcome hardship and fortify ourselves to become strong imperial subjects.

It is difficult to say what effect these ceremonies actually had on Park Chung-Hee, other teachers, and the students. Some may have simply followed the ritual without giving any thought to the content of what was recited. This author can testify that I was one of those students participating in those ceremonies day after day for three years.

---

32 Known as *Kōkoku shinmin seishi* for those above the elementary school level.

33 The huts for the portraits were situated in the front left of every campus; the students lined up in military style. The portraits were taken out only on special occasions by the principal wearing a tuxedo and white gloves; see *Korea of the Japanese* by H. B. Drake, a former English teacher in Korea (London: John Lane the Bodley Head, Ltd., and New York: Dodd, Mead and Co., 1930), ch. 3, the Emperor's Portrait.

34 This was the routine required in all schools. I went through it from the fourth to sixth grades between 1941 and 1944.

Had someone asked me at that time whether I believed in what I recited, I would have given a firm affirmative answer. As these routines were reinforced by a strictly controlled press that reported nothing but Japanese victories, the teachers and pupils would have needed some sort of strong external influence to deviate from the official government message. It should be stressed again that the empire strictly controlled all means of communication. Only those with official permits could listen to shortwave radios. Travel abroad was strictly controlled as a matter of course, and each traveler was subjected to careful surveillance.[35] Severe penalties, including torture and prison terms, were imposed on violators of any of these rules. The question then is whether Park Chung-Hee had any external stimuli; the answer is definitely negative.

Park Chung-Hee's Generation

Some Koreans today may ask why Park Chung-Hee was so different from the Korean nationalists who continued their struggle against Japan in China and the United States.[36] Why did Park Chung-Hee not join the nationalists fighting against Japan? One explanation would be the generational difference. Korea had been a Japanese colony for more than two decades when Park entered secondary school in 1932, and by then,

---

35 A detective "talked to me" for at least twenty minutes on the train from Shinŭiju at the Yalu River to Pyongyang in North Korea either in 1944 or 1945. He was quite friendly to me as a fifth- or sixth-grader but asked detailed questions about my father after he discovered that we spent two years in Hankow, China, very near the battlefront. I discovered much later that my father was investigated by the Japanese Army Military Gendarmerie (*Kenpeitai*) for a number of days. These two events may have been completely coincidental, but I continue to suspect that there was a link. There is no doubt, in any event, about the thoroughness of the surveillance system.

36 For my account of the nationalist movement, see *The Politics of Korean Nationalism* (Berkeley: University of California Press, 1963).

the police allowed no outward expression of nationalism. His family, as noted before, did not encourage him to stray from what the schools taught. The Korean mass media, furthermore, had not been allowed to report on nationalist activities since the mid-1930s. The police censors would force the newspapers and magazines to chisel away the copper-plate in which "subversive" news items were engraved on a daily basis. It was not unusual for Korean newspapers to be printed pockmarked by censored sections.

We have already seen the impact of generational differences among the Japanese teachers with whom Park came into contact. Principal Hirano and Teacher Kishi were of the Taishō democracy generation, as previously noted. Taishō refers to the emperor who reigned between 1911 and 1926. That was the only era in which liberalism dominated the Japanese intellectual and political worlds, and those who received their education and training then behaved differently from later generations of teachers. Perhaps some of Park's more considerate teachers were inherently kindhearted, but there is no doubt that the atmosphere in which they grew up and were educated had an effect. Like the Japanese themselves, the Koreans under Japanese rule had gone through different experiences with different governments at different periods.

Those who grew up in the initial period of Japanese rule, 1905–1919, could not help but be strongly anti-Japanese, because Japan ruled Korea as a conquered territory, just as Hideyoshi had ruled his conquered domains in Japan. In fact, the first governor-general, Terauchi Masatake, copied some of the measures Hideyoshi introduced in the sixteenth century, such as the confiscation of weapons of all kinds and cadastral registration. Even then, most of the Korean elite remained within Korea hoping to continue their educational activities, but Terauchi's suppression of Christian leaders in 1912 under the trumped-up charge of plotting his assassination forced many into exile abroad. Syngman Rhee, Kim Kyu-sik, and Yi Tong-hwi belonged to this generation.[37]

The March First Movement of 1919 led to a change in Japanese policy toward Korea. Governor-General Saitō Makoto under Premier Hara Kei (or Hara Takashi) imposed what was known as the "Cultural Policy." Saitō replaced the military gendarmes with civilian police, allowed much more political freedom, and allowed Koreans to publish their own newspapers and journals. The only prohibition was against open advocacy of independence. While the new policy did not eradicate Korean aspirations for independence, the Koreans did not find it intolerable either, except for the continued discrimination against them. One could call the period "the Era of Moratorium," for both the Japanese rule and the Korean reaction toward it. Had the colonial government continued the cultural policy and improved its treatment of the Koreans, Japan might well have succeeded in assimilating the Koreans. The important point here, in any event, is that the children of the moratorium era in general accepted Japanese rule without much resistance except when they were provoked, as happened in Kwangju in 1929.[38] Park Chung-Hee was a product of this era; he was born in 1917 and attended elementary school between April 1926 and March 1931.

The situation changed in the early 1930s, as militarism in Japan ended the era of moderation, turning Korea into an adjunct of the

---

37 Cf. Chong-Sik Lee, *The Politics of Korean Nationalism*, chapter 6.

38 The Kwangju student uprising of 1929 erupted and expanded into a nationwide student protest movement because of the authority's discriminatory treatment of the Korean students involved in a scuffle. The government punished the Korean students but ignored the Japanese, who had caused the scuffle by insulting a female Korean student.

military depot the Japanese army planned to build in Manchuria. Not only was Korean nationalism suppressed, but the young were actively mobilized for the cause of imperial expansion. Park Chung-Hee, as noted earlier, entered the Taegu Normal School in 1932, the year after the young officers of the Kantō army took over Manchuria. His generation, therefore, was exposed to a very different environment.

Is it not true, however, that some young Korean men deserted the Japanese army on the Chinese front to join the Korean nationalists? Yes, this is in fact true. Some of these heroes even wrote about their experiences. But the number of those reaching the nationalist camps was very small. It seems likely the number did not exceed five hundred, if that many, among the twenty or thirty thousand recruited. This is because one had to be at the very front line to have a chance of escaping from the Japanese army units. A commander who experienced desertions in his unit would take every possible precaution after the first such incidence. Desertion involved a very high level of risk. Those discovered in the act would be shot to death on the spot; those captured in such an act would face an even worse fate. They would be beaten first and then butchered. We do not have any official records of such acts. We only know that virtually nothing could enrage commanders more than desertion at the very front line of combat, face-to-face with the enemy.[39]

Park Chung-Hee may have faced the enemy when he was briefly appointed platoon commander, but he mostly stayed behind the lines at regimental headquarters. He, therefore, did not have opportunities for desertion. But did the thought of deserting his unit ever occur to

39 Chang Chun-ha presented a gripping account of his escape or desertion in "Clean Waters of Chialing Pours into the Muddy Yangtze: My Reflections," *Sasangge* [The World of Thought] (December 1960): 252–267.

him? That's a question we cannot answer. Chu Chae-dŏk, who alleged Park's presence in the Chientao Special Unit, said Park and others in his company did plan to desert the Manchukuo army and join the Chinese Communists in August/September 1944,[40] when they were on the Rehe front, but as we determined earlier, Chu's credibility is very questionable. It is important to note, however, that even those of the same generation as Park Chung-Hee behaved differently depending on their background and circumstances. Each individual was exposed to different opportunities and challenges. Not everyone suffered from the Chosŏn Dynasty as the Park family did, and not everyone was a son of a Tonghak rebel. Nor did everyone wish to eventually become a *rikugun taishō*.

It is important to remember here that Park Chung-Hee was a "Japanese product" as far as his education was concerned. By the time he enrolled in elementary school in 1926, most of the country schoolhouses that taught Chinese classics and often infused Korean nationalism had been replaced by elementary schools where the Japanese language was taught as *kokugo*, or the "national language." Park Chung-Hee's generation and that of Syngman Rhee, Yi Tong-hwi, and Yŏ Un-hyŏng stood in sharp contrast in this respect. By 1931, when Chung-Hee entered the sixth grade, militarism in Japan was in full swing. Everyone expected him to obey the teachers and act according to what the school demanded. Following the instructions of one's teachers without question was a tradition deeply ingrained in the culture. The year 1931 was the first year of the publication of the comic book *Norakuro*, which became a sensation throughout the Japanese empire. In *Norakuro*, a wild black-and-white dog joins the "fierce dogs brigade" (*mōken rentai*) and advances in rank as he moves from one humorous episode to another. The comic

40 Ryu Yŏn-san, *Ilsongjŏng p'urŭn sol e sŏnkuja nŭn ŏpsŏda*, 76.

portrayed army life as not only bearable, but enjoyable. Men and boys alike awaited the next episode, unconcerned or oblivious to the fact that there was a very promilitary message hidden in the story.[41] Park would have read the comics on the long walks back home from school, intensifying his desire to join the army. The Japanese army, one should note here, was the only army he had ever known.

The earlier survey of Japanese teachers at Taegu Normal School also indicated the probability that whatever hostility Park held toward Japan and Japanese teachers was mitigated by the more understanding and compassionate ones. In the vast majority of cases, Korean children's experiences with anything Japanese began in the schools; schoolteachers therefore played a key role in children's developing impressions of Japan and their attitude toward the colonial government. We have no information about Park's elementary school teachers, but he certainly had a number of open-minded Japanese teachers at Taegu Normal School, beginning with Principal Hirayama. Lieutenant Colonel Arikawa could very well have been Park's role model. While Park did have Korean teachers who instilled strong nationalistic feelings in him, this did not translate into his treating Japan as an enemy.

Finally, we should remember that Park Chung-Hee was a cold, calculating realist. Being from a very poor family, he didn't have the luxury of taking chances with his fate. Every step he took had to be deliberate and measured, as he could not expect a second chance. Treating Japan as his enemy would have involved too great a risk.

---

41 *Norakuro* was so popular that *Nihon Keizei Shinbun*, the *Japan Economic News*, serialized the life of Tagawa Suihō, the author, for a long period in the 1970s. He did not indicate any connection between his comic series and the military authorities.

For these reasons, Park Chung-Hee did not direct his enmity toward Japan. In his long essay on modern Korean history, "Trials and Awakening," published in 1971, he did talk about oppressive Japanese colonial policies, but his main criticism was reserved for the degenerate and incompetent Korean regime that had wrapped itself up in the class system, ignorant of what was happening around it.[42] His longtime follower Kim Jae-ch'un said Park Chung-Hee never bad-mouthed Japan in private. Instead, Park used to acknowledge Japan's contribution to awakening the ignorant Koreans. He also believed that the Koreans had much to learn from Japan. Yes, he knew about the Japanese oppression of the Korean people. Japan had caused many Koreans to suffer by forcing them to work as agricultural laborers and even mobilized young men and women for slave labor during the war, using some of the women as sex slaves. Japan forced Koreans to adopt Japanese names, forsaking their original Korean names.[43] For this reason, Park Chung-Hee became "Takagi Masao" during this period. Koreans were made to forget their own language and use Japanese exclusively. Of course, many Koreans hated Japan for these actions and regarded Japan as Korea's enemy. But Park Chung-Hee was not one of them.

Park in the Manchukuo Academy

There were a number of factors in Park's favor, which helped him excel at the military academy. He was not only older than the others, but he also had three years of teaching experience. His Japanese was excellent, exceeding that of most of his non-Japanese classmates. He had

42 Park, *Minjok ui chŏryŏk*, chapter 2, "Trials and Awakening."

43 For a 1940 report on this topic, see "Sōshi no jisseki" [Accomplishment of Creating Names], Kōto Hōin, Kenjikyoku [Korean Government-General, High Court, Prosecutor's Bureau], *Shisō ihō* [Ideological Report Series], no. 25 (December 1940): 47–48 (classified secret).

endured hardship in childhood that few other cadets were likely to have even imagined. He had gone through five years of military drills and excelled at them. He was also experienced in the regimented dormitory life at Taegu Normal School. On top of all this, he did not have to worry about paying for meals, as was the case at Taegu. Above all though, he had the determination to succeed; he was pursuing a dream many years in the making.

But there was much that was new and required adjustment. Park had been used to bilingual life in Korea, speaking Japanese at school and Korean at home, but now he faced a Chinese majority with a smaller but dominant Japanese student body. There were ten other Korean cadets among his 223 Chinese and 107 Japanese classmates,[44] so the Koreans constituted only a tiny minority. With what proficiency the Chinese cadets spoke Japanese we do not know, but Park would have heard Chinese spoken at the dormitory and in the outside world. Furthermore, it was not rare to see Russians in Sinjing; they almost outnumbered the Chinese in Harbin, the largest city north of Sinjing, where Park later spent three months. Russians left their mark throughout Manchuria. Harbin and Dalian (also known as Dairen, which is a Japanese pronunciation of the same name) were distinctly Russian cities. One could see examples of the Russian legacy throughout Manchuria, including railroad stations, cathedrals, mansions, apartment buildings, and government buildings. Tsarist Russia had been intent on taking over Manchuria and had almost succeeded in doing so when the Japanese

---

44 Chŏng Yŏng-jin, vol. 2, 30; earlier, we mentioned the academy "importing" 127 students, but Chŏng's figure is different here. I have no explanation for the discrepancy. Chŏng Un-hyŏn's 2004 book, *Sillok kunin Park Chung-Hui* (Seoul: Kaema Kowon) (p. 86) presents a totally different figure. He said there were 240 Japanese, 228 Chinese, and 12 Korean cadets.

defeated them in 1905. Between 1900 and 1903, the Russians had one hundred thousand troops stationed in that region, with no intention of removing them.[45] For the young man from a mountain village in North Kyŏngsang Province, Manchuria was a new and cosmopolitan world.

Instructors at the Manchukuo Military Academy soon recognized Park's outstanding characteristics, including his command of the Japanese language. One Chinese classmate, Xu Sou-dung, recollected that one of the instructors assigned Park Chung-Hee to help his classmate out because he did not quite grasp the lectures on "operational strategy" and infantry operations. The instructor was Chinese, but evidently the lectures were given in Japanese. Somehow, the fellow became resentful rather than grateful for Park's help. He later hit Park in the face as fiercely as he could when he had an excuse to do so. Perhaps Park had shown his contempt for his slow-witted Chinese classmate. Xu later explained, "What Park said was right and clear, but he hurt my pride." Tension was high on the academy campus. Park Won-ch'ŏl, one year senior to Park Chung-Hee in class status, recollected beating Park one day for being "stiff" with the seniors. The former teacher may have been contemptuous of the seniors who might not have appeared as intelligent as he was. The senior classmate ordered Park Chung-Hee to hold his jaw tight and punched him with all his might. Park Chung-Hee remained standing straight, stoically ready for more.[46]

Xu said Park's Japanese was the best in his class and that Park "learned much better than me."[47] Another Chinese classmate, Kao Qing-in, recollected that Park was an "earnest and prudent man willing

---

45 Cf. O. Edmund Clubb, *China and Russia: the Great Game* (New York: Columbia University Press, 1971), chapters 8 and 9.
46 Chŏng Un-hyŏn, *Sillok kunin Park Chung-Hui*, 90.
47 Ryu Yŏn-san, *Ilsongjong p'urŭn sol-e sŏnkuja ŏpsŏtta*, 71.

to sacrifice his life to attain his goal."[48] In other words, Park Chung-Hee allowed no distractions from his ultimate purpose.

In addition to its cosmopolitan character, Manchuria and the Manchukuo Military Academy were unusual in that they served as a sanctuary for Japanese outcasts. The South Manchuria Railway Company's (SMRC) Research Department (Chōsabu) had long been known as an asylum for left-wing Japanese intellectuals who could not find jobs or safety in Japan proper. Sano Manabu, the famed professor and leader of the Japanese Communist Party, was among these outcasts. Nakanishi Kō, who later became a member of the Japanese upper house, or House of Councilors, as a member of the Japanese Communist Party, was another.[49] Ozaki Hidemi, a colleague of Richard Sorge, the Soviet spy executed in 1944, was another. Many disciples of Yoshino Sakuzō, the liberal professor who founded the Sinjinkai, the New Persons Society, also exiled themselves to the SMRC, known to the Japanese simply as Mantetsu.[50]

Similarly, the right-wing officers of the Kantō-gun used various institutions in Manchuria as a refuge for right-wing mavericks. Army Captain Amakasu Masahiko, for example, had made a sensation in 1923 for murdering the anarchist Ōsugi Sakae and his mistress. But in 1937, Amakasu was working as the effective chief of the Hsüeh-ho-hui (*Kyōwa-kai* in Japanese), the Harmony Society, which was the main Japanese instrument to propagate the idea of harmony among the five

48 Chŏng Un-hyŏn, *Sillok kunin Park Chung-Hui*, 91; the author Chŏng Un-hyŏn interviewed Kao in Las Vegas in 1997. He was seventy-five years old at that time and was operating a motel there.

49 Kusayanagi, *Jitsuroku Mantetsu Chōsabu*, vol. 1, 19.

50 Cf. Itō Takeo, *Mantetsu ni ikite* [Having Lived in South Manchuria Railway Company] (Tokyo: Keisō shobō, 1964).

races in Manchuria.[51] Kōmoto Taisaku, known as the mastermind of the assassination of Chang Tso-lin, the Manchurian warlord, in 1928, was working as a director of the SMRC and the chairman of the Manchurian Coal Mining Company. The latter company controlled all the coal mining in Manchuria except that in Fushun, which was under the SMRC.[52] Mantetsu was the Japanese counterpart of the British India Company, an imperial instrument of colonialism, and owned the steel mill at Anshan. Ōkawa Shūmei, the right-wing intellectual charged as a Class–A criminal at the Tokyo War Crimes trials, at one point headed the Research Department of the East Asia Economic Research Bureau, an arm of Mantetsu.[53]

This atmosphere makes accounts about Captain Kanno Hiroshi, one of Park's instructors at the academy, credible. Kanno allegedly analyzed an abortive attempt at a military coup d'état in 1936.[54] The implication here is that the coup attempt, known as the February 26 (or 2.26) Incident, served as a model for Park's coup of 1961, in that Kanno told Park what to avoid. Park heeded Kanno because, according to Chŏng, Kanno had participated in the coup attempt as a second lieutenant.[55] While the top leaders either committed suicide or were executed, some lower-ranking officers received lighter punishments and were simply dismissed from the army. Evidently, Kanno was one of the latter.[56]

---

51 Mutō Tomio, *Watakushi to Manshūkoku* [I and Manchukuo] (Tokyo: Bungei Shunjū, 1988), 175–192.
52 Ibid., 141–142.
53 See Itō Takeo, 64 ff; for Ōkawa Shūmei in English, please see *Cambridge History of Japan*, vol. 4 (Cambridge, 1988), 729–734.
54 Chŏng Yŏng-jin, vol. 2, 96–98.
55 Ibid., 94.
56 Another lieutenant, Kiyohara Kōhei, a graduate of the forty-seventh class of the Military Academy, participated in the 2.26 coup, and in late 1961, he met with General Park in Seoul. He had changed his name to Yukawa Kōhei and headed a

Kanno had no problem finding employment in Manchuria because most of the officers in Kantō-gun were sympathetic to the 2.26 leaders.[57] He was now a captain of the Manchukuo army and a company commander in the Manchukuo academy.[58] It is interesting that Park Chung-Hee later cited the collusion between politicians and *chaebŏl* as one of the major reasons for his coup d'état of May 1961.[59] It was exactly this collusion that Kita Ikki and the 2.26 leaders had targeted. Jaebŏl in Korean is what the Japanese call *zaibatsu*, the financial conglomerate that the Meiji leaders nurtured as the engine of Japanese economic growth.[60]

The four-year course at the Manchukuo Military Academy was patterned after its Japanese counterpart and was divided into two parts. The first two years were designated as *yoka*, the preparatory course and the latter two, the *honka*, the principal course. None of Park's records at the academy are available, but the list of academy's instructors suggests that *yoka* was devoted to "general studies" subjects very similar to those taken in the freshman and sophomore years at college (e.g., Japanese

---

construction company specializing in chemical engineering, but he did reveal his original name to trigger Park's memory; Yukawa Kōhei, "Boku gichō tono ichijikan" [An Hour with Chairman Park], *Bungei shunjū* (January 1962): 324–335.

57 A group of young officers following Kita Ikki's idea of cleaning up the government rose in revolt in Tokyo, killing a number of cabinet officers and seizing government buildings. The rebels let it be known that they wanted the emperor's direct rule over the government to sweep away the ministers who had served the interests of the zaibatsu.

58 Rikushi Dai 57ki Dōkiseikai, ed., *Chiru sakura: Rikushi 57ki senbotsusha kiroku* [The Falling Cherry Blossoms: A Record of War Casualties among the 57th Class of the Military Academy] (Tokyo, 1999), 24.

59 See the five-volume collection of trial records, *Han'guk Hyŏngmyŏng chaep'ansa* [History of Revolutionary Trials], 1962. (The editor of this collection is noted as the Editorial Committee for the History of Revolutionary Trials.)

60 *Gendai Nihon no shisō* [Contemporary Japanese Thought] by Kuno Osamu and Tsurumi Shunsuke (Tokyo: Iwanami, 1956) provides a succinct summary of the ideology behind the "Showa Ishin" or Showa Reform in part 4. The *Cambridge History of Japan*, vol. 4, 717–722 are devoted to Kita Ikki.

language, economics, mathematics, chemistry, Japanese history, psychology, geography, and so on). The cadets also received instruction on military strategy, weapons systems, swordsmanship, bayonet, and horseback riding.[61] Interestingly, the list includes eight instructors for "*Kokugo*" or the national language, and four instructors of "*Mango*," the Manchurian language.[62] The "Manchurian language," however, should not be construed as the Manchu language. The Japanese in Manchuria at this time referred to the Chinese language as Mango. Presumably, Park Chung-Hee took some Chinese courses. It is also interesting that the Manchukuo Military Academy used the phrase "*national language*" to teach Japanese. That meant that the Japanese language was the "national language" of Manchukuo, or perhaps, one of the national languages. The academy most likely needed multiple instructors to teach the Japanese language to all of the Chinese cadets.

Park Chung-Hee excelled at the Manchukuo Military Academy. The academic courses there were a regurgitation of what he had already learned at Taegu Normal School. His advantages over other cadets have already been noted. It was not surprising that he was one of the five graduating cum laude and was first among the two-hundred-plus non-Japanese graduates. Park was awarded a special citation and a gold watch from Emperor Pu Yi at the commencement in March 1942.[63] This contrasted sharply with what had happened at Taegu Normal School.

---

61 *Manshū kokugun*, 621–622.

62 Ibid., 622.

63 Chŏng Yŏng-jin, vol. 2, 101–103; a photograph shows Park Chung-Hee saluting the dignitaries all alone in front of hundreds of other cadets before receiving his citation. *Manshū nippō* [Manchuria Daily] (March 24, 1942), reprinted in Chŏng Un-hyŏn, *Sillok kunin Park Chung-Hee*, 85.

There is no doubt that Park Chung-Hee cherished his memories of the Manchukuo Academy. He evinced this twenty years later in November 1961, when he visited Tokyo as the head of the military junta and the de facto head of the Republic of Korea. Present at the state dinner given in his honor was the retired Lieutenant General Nagumo Shinichirō, former commandant of the Manchukuo Military Academy.[64] The first thing Park did after the requisite speeches and toasts was walk over to the old gentleman sitting at the end of the table, bow, and pour him a glass of wine. Park then told the General in crisp Japanese that he had personally asked the host to invite him to celebrate this momentous occasion, both for himself and for the two countries. Park then thanked General Nagumo for having been his *onshi*, or honored teacher, and wished him good health. Nagumo stood up and surprised everyone by replying he was enjoying excellent health for having taken the *jinseng* that Park had sent him from time to time.[65]

Park graduated from the Academy and then took a three-month apprenticeship in Kantō-gun's 30th Infantry regiment in Harbin. Park's assigned duty there, according to Chŏng Yŏng-jin, was to maintain a liaison with Manchukuo army units. His first impression of that army was very disappointing.[66] The Manchukuo soldiers fit the old Chinese adage: "Good iron does not become a nail; a good person does not become a soldier." It could not be otherwise. In China, soldiering was interchangeable with banditry and was not a respected profession. Particularly in the case of the Manchukuo army, no one with any kind of skill or education

64 Nagumo Shinichirō was the Academy's commandant between 1939 and 1943; see *Manshū kokugun*, 618–620.

65 *Sillok Park Chung-Hee*, 216.

66 Chŏng Yŏng-jin, vol. 2, 106; Chŏng Un-hyŏng said, on the other hand, that Park Chung-Hee spent the three months at Chichihar with the 635th Army Unit of Kantōgun (*Sillok kunin Park Chung-Hee*, 94).

would have wished to join an army that the conquerors had created. What the soldiers wanted was nothing more than a job that provided food, lodging, and wages. Dedication to duty or loyalty could not be expected from them. Indeed, desertion was commonplace. Illiteracy was high because education had been a luxury that only the rich could afford. Park Chung-Hee would have been glad that he was to become an army officer, but he would not have cherished the thought of commanding these troops.

It should be noted that much had happened in the years Park spent at the Manchukuo Military Academy. The world was in turmoil. In September 1939, Nazi Germany attacked Poland, engulfing Europe in a long and destructive war. Japan signed a pact with Hitler and Mussolini in September 1940 to form a tripartite Axis, as well as a neutrality pact with the Soviet Union, ratified in April 1941. Germany attacked Russia in June 1941, and Japan occupied French Indochina in July 1941. Then, on December 7 1941, the Japanese navy attacked Pearl Harbor, opening an entirely new venue for the war. The Japanese empire was on the march, and, to those within the empire, it appeared to be invincible. Park Chung-Hee was probably glad that he was on the winning side. He appeared to have made the right choice.

It was at the end of Park's first year at the Academy that he changed his name from Park Chung-Hee to Takagi Masao. Changing Korean names was a key part of Governor-General Minami's program to "Japanize" the Koreans, or to transform the Koreans into Japanese. Even though it was supposed to have been voluntary, everyone was expected to accept the "generous opportunity" to change their names into Japanese ones. Adopting new names was a phenomenon that caused much anguish among most of the Korean population, because ancestry and lineage occupied an important part of their tradition. Minami decided that every subject of Emperor Hirohito should use the Japanese language as a matter of course. Henceforth, the Koreans should stop using their native language. Students who used the Korean language were to be disciplined. Japanese was to be spoken even at home, regardless of the fact that most parents and other relatives spoke no Japanese.[67] Park's biographers made it appear that Park chose Takagi, meaning "High Tree," as his new surname, but he would have had to consult his brothers, as the change applied to the entire family. (Park's father was no longer alive, having died in 1938.)

The choice of Takagi Masao as his new name tells much about Park's mentality at this time, in that there was no trace of Korean in it. It was not unusual for Koreans to choose very Japanese-sounding last names, but most Korean families left their first names unchanged. If Park had followed the norm, his name would have been Takagi Seiki.[68] Park Chung-Hee did retain the character "Chŏng" in his new name, whose Chinese character is pronounced "Masa" in Japanese, but Masao was distinctly Japanese. Park evidently decided at some point that he was going to become a Japanese officer—perhaps Japan's Napoleon—and thought it wiser to choose a genuinely Japanese name.

Kantō-gun and the Development of Manchuria

Much happened in Manchuria while Park Chung-Hee was at the military academy; what he saw and heard affected him as much as the training he received. He would have learned soon enough that the Kantō-gun, or Japanese army in Manchuria, was the driving force behind the

67 I have discussed these events in *The Politics of Korean Nationalism*, 265, and *Japan and Korea: the Political Dimension* (Stanford: Hoover Institution Press, 1985), 9–10.
68 The two Chinese characters for Chung-Hee are pronounced *seiki* in Japanese.

region. The Kantō-gun had assassinated the Manchurian warlord Chang Tso-lin in 1928 and driven out his son Chang Hsueh-ling in 1931 in defiance of the civilian government in Tokyo, and they were determined to create a promised land of their own.[69] In time, the army headquarters in Tokyo and other branches of the government came to share in governing Manchuria, but the staff officers at Kantō-gun headquarters, particularly those at the Fourth Section, never loosened their control. Manchukuo, headed by the puppet emperor Pu Yi, was a state within the Japanese empire controlled by Japanese army officers. Mutō Tomio, who spent nine years in Manchuria in the highest echelon of political power, called himself a "hired hand of Kantō-gun."[70] The Fourth Section, he said, was "the crucible (*motoshime*) of Manchukuo; all major policies, whether they originated in the Japanese or Manchukuo government would not be translated into action without that section's approval."[71] What Kantō-gun leaders wanted was an economy based on the capitalist system, wherein the *zaibatsu*, the financial and industrial conglomerates, would not be allowed to use their monopoly power to exploit others. The conglomerates would operate under strict supervision, their profits limited to five percent of their investment. In short, Manchukuo was to have a regulated capitalist economy that "utilized the best brains, technology, and capital that the Japanese nation could muster."[72]

---

69 Cf. Sadako Ogata, *Defiance in Manchuria* (Berkeley: University of California Press, 1963).

70 Mutō Tomio, 414.

71 Ibid., 414.

72 The quotation is a rough translation of what Ishihara Kanji wrote in his manuscript "On the Development of Manchuria and Mongolia," dated February 1932; quoted in Asada and Kobayashi, 135 (chapter 3). A complete and direct translation would be: "Ideally the economic developmental plan of Manchuria and Mongolia should be accomplished through the assembly and unification of the best intelligence that the Japanese people possess."

In purely economic terms, the results were phenomenal. Even though there were many twists and turns in planning and execution, industrial development in Manchuria proceeded at an unprecedented speed and scale. The Kantō-gun initially relied on the personnel of the South Manchuria Railway Research Department, but the dispatch of Hoshino Naoki and six others from the Ministry of Finance (*Ōkurashō*) in June 1932 made Manchukuo the mecca for the best and the brightest. In a country run by bureaucrats, the prestige of the Ōkurashō was unmatched. Soon the Ministry of Trade and Industry (*Shōkō-shō*) dispatched Kishi Nobusuke, the future prime minister of Japan, and Shiina Etsusaburō, his deputy, to run the Manchukuo government. In addition to the glamour of running a new colony, Kantō-gun paid well. Mutō Tomio, a thirty-year-old aspiring judge in Tokyo, was hired to help run the new Ministry of Justice in Sinjing and was paid 6,500 yen a year, the salary of the chief justice of the Supreme Court in Tokyo (*Daishinen*).[73] An ordinary schoolteacher in Japan or Korea made approximately 500 yen. The *zaikai*, or the business and financial world, was reluctant at first because of Kantō-gun's control over capital, but they could not resist the opportunity to build new factories, explore mines, and reap profits. Manchuria had an abundance of resources and labor. It was a capitalist paradise.

The end result was to turn a predominantly agricultural society that had been known for its soybeans, corn, millet, and kaoliang into a major industrial center that could effectively compete against the Osaka-Kobe or the Tokyo-Yokohama industrial complexes. They did so very quickly, well within a decade, through massive mobilization of

---

73 Mutō, *Watakushi to Manshūkoku*, 17.

personnel and resources.[74] Park Chung-Hee would not have known the behind-the-scenes stories, but he did witness a part of what was taking place and would have read what the newspapers and journals reported daily. He was witnessing extraordinary events.

74 Cf. Manshikai (Association for the History of Manchuria), ed., *Manshū kai-hatsu yonjūnen shi* [Forty-Year History of the Development of Manchuria], (Tokyo: Kenkōsha, 1964).

VI. THE JAPANESE MILITARY ACADEMY

Having completed the two-year preparatory course at the Manchukuo Military Academy, Park Chung-Hee went to Zama, Japan, to complete his military training at the Japanese Military Academy. With him were three other Koreans, seventy Chinese, whom the Japanese called *Manjin* or "the Manchurians," and 240 Japanese who had finished the two-year *yoka* (preparatory) course at Sinjing.[1] Zama offered a much better environment for Park than the Manchurian academy. Sinjing (now Changchun) was located not very far from Siberia and was severely cold in the winter and steaming hot in the summer. Zama, where the Japanese academy was located, could get chilly, but the temperature would not fall below the freezing point as frequently. Sinjing was still under development as Manchukuo's capital and didn't offer much culture or entertainment for cadets on furlough. In contrast, the Japanese Academy was located only twenty-five miles southwest of Tokyo and fifteen miles directly west of Yokohama, both of which had everything that Sinjing lacked. Above all, Tokyo had publishing houses, such as Iwanami and Kōdansha. Iwanami's paperback books had long been the staple of college students and intellectuals. Kōdansha published numerous titles on Japanese history and Japanese heroes. Park, the aspiring intellectual, had been deprived of intellectual nourishment. Financial problems had kept him from studying during the last half of his time at the Taegu Normal School and had prevented him from joining Taegu classmates at Japanese colleges and universities. Munkyŏng and Sinjing were both intellectual deserts. There is no doubt that Cadet Takagi frequented bookstores whenever he had a chance to do so.

---

1 Chŏng Un-hyŏn, *Sillok kunin Park Chung-Hee* [Veritable Record of the Soldier Park Chung-Hee] (Seoul: Kaema, 2004), 92; as noted earlier, not all accounts agree on the number of Japanese cadets at the Manchukuo academy.

Kim Jae-ch'un, who spent most of his adult life in close contact with Park Chung-Hee, told me recently: "He was a Japanese soldier through and through, from the way he sat and stood, to his actions," referring to Park's thought process and behavior.[2] Yukawa Kōhei, who met Park in late 1961, characterized him as "a pristine Imperial Army soldier (Namassui no teikoku rikugun gunjin) of the Meiji era."[3] Teacher Kishi agreed by noting Park's accuracy, speed, decisiveness, and his action-orientation based on his fifty-minute interview with Park in 1977 at the presidential palace.[4] How did Park come to have such characteristics?

One could attribute these traits to his upbringing and his training at the elementary school and Taegu Normal School, but the four years he spent at the military academies, particularly the twenty months at Zama between 1942 and 1944, had the most significant impact. The Japanese empire aimed to shape its future leaders, just as a blacksmith would pound on a piece of hot iron until satisfied with its shape. The iron had to be pounded to acquire the necessary strength and shape to serve a designated function. Similarly, a young man had to be pounded to acquire physical strength, resilience, and mental toughness; his spirit also had to

---

2 Interview with Kim Jae-ch'un, May 4, 2009; Kim was Park Chung-Hee's student at the Republic of Korea Military Academy in the 1940s and was Park's very frequent drinking partner. He claims to have introduced Miss Yuk Young-soo to Park Chung-Hee; they later married. He served as Park's Korean Central Intelligence Agency director.

3 Yukawa differentiated "the soldier of the Meiji era" from the later ones "who glittered with (blood thirstiness) to cut down an opponent in one slash from the head down." His impression of Chairman Park was "truly refreshing" (*makotoni sawayaka datta*). Interestingly, Yukawa characterized Park as a combination of Field Marshall Ōyama Iwao and General Nogi Maresuke, the two heroes of the Japanese Army (Yukawa, "Boku gichō tono ichijikan" (An Hour with Chairman Park), *Bungei shunjū*, January 1962, 324–335. The quotation here is from page 325).

4 Kishi Yonesuke, *Ryūten kyōiku rokujū nen* [Sixty Years of Meandering Education] (Kawasaki, 1982, private publication), 242.

be fortified to lead others and to serve the empire. The academy worked on these aims through regimented training programs, lectures, and recitations and through constant indoctrination sessions.

The effect of this intense indoctrination program upon the young should not be minimized. We have seen enough examples from far and wide in the twentieth century—the Nazi SS, Kamikaze pilots, the Red Guard, and even the Mujahedeen in our era. Much is known about the "brainwashing" process. "Wash out" the impure and rotten thoughts, pour in "the truth," and solidify the ideas into conviction and belief. When this process is repeated in a confined environment for a prolonged period among a group of peers, the young emerge in most cases as fighters willing to sacrifice the "little self" for "the greater cause," whatever the cause may be. It would take a shock of great magnitude to shake such a person into deviating from his or her "programming."

As at the Manchukuo Military Academy, Takagi Masao was an exemplary cadet at Zama. Unlike many of his classmates, whose initial enthusiasm waned under the strict discipline, harshness of the routine, homesickness, and fatigue brought on by rigorous training,[5] Park thrived in his new environment. The Japanese Military Academy, after all, was the place he had aspired to since childhood. This was the very place where Japanese military giants had been trained. But above all, Takagi Masao did not have the luxury to fail at anything; he had to give his all for the only chance he would be given.

---

5 Various instructors recorded these phenomena in their records; Takano Kunio (ed.), *Kindai Nihon guntai kyōiku shiryo shūsei* [Collection of Historical Materials on Modern Japanese Military Education], vol. 6 (Tokyo: Kashiwa Shobō, 2004), section on "Actuality of Cadet Education." This is a reprint of a booklet issued by the academy for instructors.

Park's work experience and age again served him well. He did not have to be reminded about the importance of the subjects taught at the academy and the training he was receiving. Another of his Chinese classmates, Pan I-zing, who was with Park both at Sinjing and Zama, said the following about him:

> He held his immobile straight posture with his lips firmly closed even during general studies lectures and at military training exercises, making it difficult for others to approach him. Even during break times he had few words and refrained from contacting others. He would sometimes talk to Kazumi (Yi Han-lim) in Korean. He and I were in the same Infantry Unit at the Japanese Military Academy, but he concentrated on studying and training there too, limiting contact with others. He never revealed his inner thoughts. So we remained superficial classmates.[6]

Why was Park seemingly so distant, taciturn, and aloof? Perhaps the young man found lectures on military strategy, military tactics, and military history more engrossing than socializing. The academy's booklet *Bukyō Nyūmon* (Introduction to Martial Learning) called these the key elements of *heigaku*, or martial studies, to which the cadets would be devoting their entire lives. While the history of *heigaku* goes back to the ancient period, it is not a science but an art. The art of warfare, however, has certain principles that need to be followed. The warriors of the past applied those principles in so many different and ingenious ways that each case required thorough study in order to learn the lessons. These episodes and anecdotes on military history covered not only the battles among Japanese warriors but those of Western countries as well. The booklet discussed the failures of the Russian, French, and German

---

6 Chŏng Un-hyŏng, 92; Pan was seventy-three years old in 1997 when he was interviewed.

generals during various campaigns. Cadets in the Japanese Military Academy needed to know not only about Japan, but also Western countries. One never knows who tomorrow's enemy will be.

"*Bukyō Nyūmon*" reveals much about the academy's orientation. The use of the word *bukyō* in its title invites special attention, because the Chinese character (or *kanji*, as the Japanese would call it) used for "*kyō*" in "Bukyō" make it sound as though martial learning was a religion, as in *bukkyō* (Buddhism). The author or the academy's authorities could have used either "*budō*" (the martial way) or "*bugaku*" (martial learning), but it appears that the author(s) deliberately used the ambiguous word *kyō* to connote a spiritual element in the Japanese learning of martial arts. Indeed, the booklet emphasized Nippon *seishin* or the Japanese spirit.

The cadets had to learn, nay believe, that the Japanese Imperial Army was unique among all others because the Japanese imperial state was no ordinary state. In this sense, the cadets were fortunate to be born in a nation headed by an emperor who was the direct descendant of the august goddess who founded the empire at the creation of the human world. All Japanese under the emperor were his children, who formed a huge family, with the emperor as their head.[7] Love (*jyō*) and a sense of duty (*gi*) tie them together, while other armies are bound either by self-interest, power, or the law. How could they ever match the Japanese army, which was backed by divine power?

---

7 For an explanation of the Japanese notion of the divine nation, how and why the Japanese overcame the notion of filial piety (kō) for the cause of the emperor, and their identification of militarism and imperialism as the extension of the divine cause, see Marius B. Jansen, *the Emergence of Meiji Japan (*Cambridge and New York, Cambridge University Press, 1995), chapter 3, p. 148-150.

Cadet Takagi, of course, was familiar with these arguments, as they had been drummed into children at schools of various levels. We cannot know how much of this doctrine he internalized, although any schoolteacher could deliver a fine speech about the Japanese *kokutai* (state) at the drop of a hat. But he would not have found it difficult to accept other points in "*Bukyō Nyūmon*," such as the importance of the personal quality (*shishitsu*) of the commander. A commander must constantly cultivate and polish himself in order to lead other men. He must be loyal; he must be courteous, respectful of superiors, and benevolent to those under him. He must be brave, frugal, insightful, and decisive. These points were expounded at length in the booklet, with historical illustrations of their importance. Undoubtedly, many lectures were devoted to these points.

In view of the simple and Spartan life Park led even after becoming the president of the Republic of Korea in the 1960s, it is interesting to note the illustrations provided in the "*Bukyō Nyūmon*" on the importance of frugality. In Japanese history, it argued, the Taira (or Heishi) family had vanquished the Minamoto (or Genji) family in battles. But the winning family forgot their roots as warriors and tried to imitate the lifestyle of the imperial house. Having lost martial spirit in the process, the Tairas lost everything to the Minamoto family. The booklet also cited examples in the West: how the French officers competed among themselves in pursuit of ever more luxurious lifestyles until they were beaten by Prussia.

Park Chung-Hee and others who had taken an interest in Korean history would have attached special meaning to these teachings. Had General Yi Sŏng-gye maintained a martial spirit in the Chosŏn Dynasty he had founded, it would not have suffered the humiliation Hideyoshi inflicted in the sixteenth century. Had Korean leaders maintained the quality the Japanese Military Academy demanded of their officers, Park would have attended a Korean military academy, rather than a Japanese academy. It is quite possible that Cadet Takagi thought about Yu Sŏng-yong's *Chingbirok* and Yi Kwang-su's account of Yi Sun-shin. He was now training to be a Japanese officer to serve the Japanese empire.

Along with such principles as loyalty and frugality, the academy emphasized the importance of negating the self and the fear of death. The commandant of the academy summed up the issue succinctly when he told the new cadets that the academy's mission was to teach them "how to die."[8] A professor from Tokyo reached the same conclusion after touring the academy.[9] Indeed, all schoolchildren in the Japanese empire were indoctrinated to give up their lives gladly for the emperor. They may not have pondered the meaning of the words they sang every day, but "*Umi Yukaba*" (When I Go to the Sea) contained a message of sacrificing oneself for the emperor without regret. The words were taken from an old Japanese classic, but the tune was composed in 1937 to be played in classrooms, at public ceremonies, and at soldiers' send-offs virtually every day in the Japanese empire. What came to be known as the second national anthem can be translated as follows:

When I go to the sea,
I shall be a corpse soaked in water.
When I go to the mountain,
I shall be a corpse with the grass grown over me.

---

8 Chŏng Yŏng-jin, II, p. 113.

9 *Seito kun'iku no zissai* (Actuality of Cadet Nurturing), (n.p., March 1942), pp. 103-105. This booklet is included in Takano Kunio (ed.), *Kindai Nihon guntai kyōiku shiryō shūsei*, vol. 6, Rikugun shikan gakkō (The Military Academy).

But if I died for the Emperor,
I shall not look back.[10]

How was loyalty and frugality related to the notion of overcoming death? Life is ephemeral; death comes to everyone sooner or later. Therefore, one could spend his short life searching for sensual pleasures or accumulating wealth, but these would not serve any purpose after death. The alternative would be to die for a cause, and there could be no greater cause than serving the emperor. A person willing to sacrifice himself for a great cause would not absorb himself in material wealth or sensual pleasures because such acts would betray his insincerity. Similarly, Zen masters have taught meditation and discipline so that one can reach the stage of enlightenment where virtue, discernment, and wisdom become an innate part of the self.

Did Park Chung-Hee "transcend" death? He told his former teacher Kishi in 1977 that he was prepared to die, "kakugo wa shite orimasu." He explained that he had taken power by violence, dashing into the presidential palace in 1961 with a submachine gun in his hand. Fortunately, no one was there when he broke in, but he was prepared to kill anyone who challenged him. Park felt strange that he now lived in the palace as its master. He could be killed in the same manner someday, he said, and was prepared for it.[11] He was referring to the coup of May 1961, and his meeting with Kishi took place on September 25, 1977. It is significant that Park dealt with such a matter in his conversation with his old teacher, whom he had not met for nearly four decades. Park, it should be added, had lost his wife to an assassin three years earlier in 1974. Mun Se-gwang, a third generation Korean living in Japan, had intended

10 My translation.
11 Kishi, *Ryūten kyoiku rokujūnen*, p. 247.

the bullets for Park Chung-Hee but killed his wife instead. So, Park had every reason to contemplate death by assassination.

Park's speech of August 30, 1963, the "Farewell Address" he delivered upon retiring from the Army of the Republic of Korea, deserves another look in this context. He said the following with tears in his eyes:

> I have never thought of my life as my own since I donned the military uniform that the nation had bestowed upon me. I only wanted to do my duty to the fullest and sought to find the meaning of life within the confines of life as a soldier… The right to life can be guaranteed only through the sacrifice of other sacred lives. To overcome death between the extremes of life and death, and to abandon the little self for the sake of the greater cause of justice and truth: these are the acme of sacrificial spirit and the glorious and sacred privilege only the soldiers can have. Only a nation that guarantees the rights of human beings on the basis of justice and truth is worthy of such deaths.[12]

Any graduate of the Japanese Military Academy, and for that matter any Japanese person who grew up in the 1930s and 1940s, would recognize the tenets of *bushidō* in the above paragraph. There is little doubt that Park Chung-Hee absorbed and internalized bushidō's teachings on overcoming death. This statement, of course, gives Park's justification for the coup d'état he led. Park found that the nation had failed at guaranteeing "the rights of human beings on the basis of justice and truth."

---

12 "The Farewell Address" August 30, 1963, Shin Pŏm-sik (ed.), *Park Chŏnghui taet'ongryŏng sŏnjip* (Selected Works of President Park Chung-Hee), (Seoul: Chimunkak, 1969), vol. 3, pp. 321-328. (at p. 321).

Bushidō and Park Chung-Hee

Some Koreans today may argue that Park's statement had nothing to do with bushidō: he simply articulated the essence of native Korean teachings. Did Admiral Yi Sun-shin not "abandon the self for the cause of the nation"? Were there not many others among his contemporaries who fought to their deaths defending the nation against invaders? Why mention bushidō at all? Such retorts, of course, are reasonable. Confucius and his disciples did emphasize the importance of loyalty to the sovereign and of filial piety, but their teachings did not include the notion of death or transcending death. Nowhere in the lexicon of Korean Confucian teachings could one find such ideas codified as they were in Japan. The Japanese borrowed the notion of transcending death from Buddhism, particularly Zen Buddhism (or *Chan* Buddhism in Chinese). While Zen Buddhism had been transmitted to Japan through Korea at some point in history, the Chosŏn Dynasty's suppression of Buddhism had its effects in Korea.

Other Koreans may find the whole discussion of bushidō in relation to Park Chung-Hee irrelevant and repugnant. How could Koreans accept the notion of explaining the beliefs of a Korean leader through bushidō, which is of Japanese origin? Is it not an attempt to add fuel to the charge that Park Chung-Hee had sold his soul to the Japanese? Would it not implicitly subjugate the Korean nation under the Japanese by acknowledging Park Chung-Hee's debt to Japanese bushidō?

Discussion of Park Chung-Hee's mind-set is filled with so many emotional traps that it is very difficult to engage in dispassionate analysis. Some Japanese intellectuals of the past have exhibited similar emotional traps as they defended the "purity" of Japanese culture; they rejected all suggestions that Japan imported much of its culture from such Korean kingdoms as Paekje and Silla. They would acknowledge Japan's indebtedness to the Tang or Sung Dynasties of China, but not to the Korean ones.[13] Korea was too inferior to Japan, in their minds, for Japan to acknowledge its debt to it. In the same vein, Koreans of the eighteenth and nineteen centuries rejected all forms of Western learning, simply because it came through the Qing Dynasty of the despised and hated Manchus. Contemporary Koreans, on the other hand, find it hard to stomach the idea that a Korean like Park Chung-Hee learned anything useful from Japan. These Koreans may grudgingly acknowledge Japanese superiority in science and technology but definitely not in the intellectual, philosophical, or spiritual realm.

But how "Japanese" was bushidō? Was it truly of Japanese origin? Some Japanese would find such questions offensive, but bushidō's components were of continental origin. The Japanese contribution lay only in the manner of blending Confucianism with Buddhism. It is time for both the Japanese and Koreans, in any event, to remove national labels from the debate. Neither Confucianism nor Buddhism originated in Japan or Korea. The old masters who introduced Buddhism to China, Korea, or Japan long ago transcended the notion of national origin.

The birth of the notion of bushidō is interesting in this connection. Recent scholarship has shown that Japanese *samurai* of the classical period did not know such a code of conduct existed.[14] Nor was it concocted by Japanese officialdom. It was codified and published by an

---

13 I have examined this issue in my *Japan and Korea: The Political Dimension* (Stanford: Hoover Institution Press, 1985), pp. 151-163.

14 See G. Cameron Hurst, "Death, Loyalty and the Bushido Ideal," in *Philosophy East and West,* 40.4 (1990); and Karl Friday, "Bushido or Bull? A Medieval Historian's Perspective on the Pacific War & the Japanese Military Tradition," in *The History Teacher,* 27, no. 3 (1994). I am indebted to Frederick Dickinson, my colleague at the University of Pennsylvania, for bringing these important articles to my attention.

agricultural economist, Nitobe Inazō (1862–1933), in 1900, in response to a question posed by his host in Belgium about how the Japanese provided moral education to the young.[15] Nitobe stated in the first chapter of his work that it was not something written by anyone, nor was it based on the life of any individual leader. It was more like the British constitution—a conglomeration of tradition, convention, and custom.[16] Since it was intended to satisfy the curiosity of foreign readers, Nitobe wrote an idealized version of the samurai, rather than a description of how they actually behaved. Nitobe Inazō, incidentally, was born the son of a samurai but had never been a samurai himself. In fact, Cameron Hurst, who researched the origins of bushidō, noted that "Nitobe was the least qualified Japanese man of his age to inform anyone of Japan's history and culture."[17] More of Hurst's commentary follows:

> Here was a man [Nitobe] far more familiar with the themes and metaphors of classical Western literature than those of his native Japan, far more certain of the dates and events in Western than in Japanese history, who nonetheless set out to present to the West a view of the ethics of pre-modern Japan that has been accepted rather uncritically ever since.[18]

But Nitobe's work soon caught the attention of Japanese rulers, who found his synthesis of the ways of the Samurai valuable. Nitobe's attempt at explaining the content of Japanese moral education thus became a guidebook for generations of the Japanese, including cadets at the military academy. The irony is that Nitobe joined the Society of Friends (the

---

15 Nitobe Inazō, *Bushidō* (trans. Yanaihara Tadao) (Tokyo: Iwanami Shoten, 2004), 11 (preface to the first edition). The Iwanami edition was first published in 1938 and revised in 1974. It went through scores of reprints.

16 Ibid., 27–28.

17 Hurst, 512.

18 Ibid.

Quakers) in the 1880s in the United States (in Philadelphia) and became a pacifist. But his work became a primer for Japanese warriors.

Some additional knowledge about Nitobe's work is essential to understanding Park Chung-Hee because bushidō, at least Nitobe's version, taught not only how to die, but also how to live. Nitobe's Bushidō table of contents illustrates this point. If we exclude the introductory chapters (the first and second) and concluding chapters (fifteen to seventeen), we have the following chapter titles:

- Rectitude or Justice
- Courage
- Benevolence
- The Feeling of Distress
- Politeness
- Veracity and Sincerity
- Honor
- The Duty of Loyalty
- The Education and Training of a *Samurai*
- Self-Control
- The Institutions of Suicide and Redress
- The Sword, the Soul of the *Samurai*
- The Training and Position of Woman.

Nitobe was not writing Machiavelli's *The Prince* or Sun Tze's *Art of War*. What he taught were universal values transcending nationality or time. It is no accident that his chapters bear a strong resemblance to Judeo-Christian ideas. Nitobe converted to Christianity at the Sapporo Agricultural College (now Hokkaido University) in 1878 under an American Methodist Episcopal missionary; Nitobe's classmates who converted to Christianity at the same time included Uchimura Kanzō

(1861–1930), who later became the most influential Christian and pacifist intellectual Japan has ever produced.

Seen in this light, bushidō was neither parochially Japanese, nor were its teachings relevant only for the warrior. This explains in part why Li Teng-hui, a contemporary of Park Chung-Hee who later served as the president of the Republic of China (Taiwan),[19] wrote and published a book on bushidō in Japanese in 2003. Li was born a Japanese subject in Taiwan when the island was a Japanese colony, but became a Chinese citizen after Japan ceded the island back to China in the wake of the Second World War. Subsequently, he served as president of the Republic of China. Li's purpose in writing the book was to urge the younger generations in Japan to live by bushidō. His intended audience, one should note, was the Japanese. One of the questions that Li and his generation of students in Japan had constantly pondered, he said, was how one should live. He read Suzuki Daisetsu and Nitobe Inazō, authorities on bushidō, and Nishida Kitarō, who synthesized the essence of Zen Buddhism and Confucianism in his classic work, *Inquiry into the Good* or "*Zen no kenkyū*."[20] Li, in any event, spent his student years grappling with the questions of life and death, the meaning of life, and the way to live. He came to comprehend Japanese culture and values through the teachings of bushidō. Park Chung-Hee may have gone through the same thought processes as Li when he was at Zama in the early 1940s.

Park, in any event, was mentally prepared for death, and he put everything in order so that his death would not cause confusion to those

---

19 Li Teng-hui was born in 1923, six years after Park Chung-Hee, who was born in 1917. Li served as the Republic of China's president between 1988 and 2000.

20 Li Teng-hui, *Bushidō kaidai* [Exposition of *Bushidō*] (Tokyo: Shōgakukan, 2003), 17–111; the "*zen*" in "*Zen no kenkyū*" refers to "good." *Zen* in *Zen* Buddhism is a different Chinese character from *zen* in good.

around him, according to his daughter, Kŭn-hae.[21] "Not because he particularly felt threatened," but being the supreme authority, he paid attention to what the situation would be after he was gone," Kŭn-hae said. "In implementing various decisions, he knew he had to take final responsibility. Therefore, when he made decisions he prepared for the worst possible outcomes."[22]

Frugality was another important element of *bushidō*, and in the early 1940s, it was not merely a value that was taught, but a real necessity. All consumer goods and food were rationed in portions that were barely enough to sustain life. A black market existed in pockets of the empire, but the government created "Economic Police" departments to control them. The government also propagated the slogan "Hoshigari masen, katsu madewa," meaning "I will not covet it, until we win." A Spartan existence, therefore, became a habit and lifestyle for many. Most of the people abandoned that lifestyle as soon as they could at the end of the war, but evidently Park Chung-Hee did not. His wife was of a similar mind. She is known to have worn mended skirts even when she was living in the presidential palace, and this was not for political display.

The tenets of bushidō, in any event, were the ideals that the Meiji leaders wanted the younger generations to follow, but the seeds were sown on rocky soil or among thorns and could not produce good crops. Many high-ranking Japanese officers, presumably indoctrinated in bushidō, succumbed to corruption and debauchery, proving themselves no better than the chieftains of the Manchurian bandit groups they despised. Major General Tanaka Ryūkichi, the head of the Military

21 He told his daughter about this about a year before he was assassinated. Sono Ayako, "Waga chichi Boku Seiki" [My Father Park Chŏng-Hui], interview of Park Kŭn-hae by Sono Ayuko, *Bungei shunjū* (April 1980), 114–128 (at p. 124).
22 Ibid.

Affairs Bureau (Heimu-kyoku) in the Ministry of the Army vividly recorded such events in his personal memoir.

> A certain head of the garrison unit killed a pro-Japanese overseas Chinese man to rob him of a vast amount of gold. A certain head of army gendarmerie unit gave his mistress the money he received as a bribe to run a geisha house to earn even more money. A certain head of a special agency gave the father of his mistress the right to run a coal mine. A certain company commander on furlough raped the wife of a soldier in his company who carried the photograph of his pretty wife. He even gave her venereal disease. [23]

Tanaka recorded a private letter from Lieutenant General Endō Saburō in Hankow, China, that "the war cannot be won unless the high ranking officers reformed their ways.'"[24] These events occurred between 1939 and 1945, during the period when the Japanese army occupied Hankow, which is now a part of Wuhan.

General Endō's statement shows that misbehavior was not uncommon. Not all Japanese officers were devoted enough to give up their lives, let alone obey the expected codes of behavior to serve the emperor. How do we then explain Park Chung-Hee's exemplary "Japanese-soldier-like" behavior? How was it that Li Teng-hui, the Taiwanese-Chinese leader, believed in bushidō to the extent of daring to publish a book on it many decades after he ceased to be a Japanese subject? Was it because both of them became true believers in the "Japanese teaching"? Or was it because they were rebelling against their ancestors, who had preached all those high-sounding universal values but had

23 Quoted in Kamada Sawaichirō, *Chōsen shinwa* [New Stories on Korea] (Tokyo: Sōgensha, 1950), 226–227.
24 Quoted in ibid., 226–227.

not practiced them? Confucius, after all, stressed such principles as justice, benevolence, politeness, truthfulness, sincerity, honor, loyalty, and self-control, as had Nitobe. As Li stressed in his book, the only problem with his ancestors was they did not practice what they preached. Li Teng-hui and Park Chung-Hee appear to have pursued the ideals the Japanese empire instilled into their soldiers and subjects, but we now know that few in China, Japan, or Korea actually practiced what they were taught.

Another aspect of Park's lifestyle deserves to be noted. The leader who ruled Korea for eighteen years and supervised the transactions of billions of U.S. dollars did not leave his heirs any inheritance worth mentioning. The efforts of the muckraking press after his death led nowhere, and a consensus emerged that Park was a "clean man."[25] This was in stark contrast to his five successors as Korean president, who were either imprisoned for corruption or saw their sons, brothers, or underlings sent to prison for the same reason. One of them even committed suicide when he could not escape the hands of investigators. How was Park Chung-Hee, who grew up in stark poverty, not tempted like the others?

Park Chung-Hee not only eschewed corruption himself but denounced it in the strongest terms. During his time in the military, he had even lambasted his immediate superior before his subordinates when he had a drink or two.[26] When Park became president, his dinner

---

25 Park's junta regime (1961–1963) and his government (1963–1979) were involved in a number of scandals. But there was no indication that Park himself was directly involved or enriched himself through any of them.

26 Dr. Kim Ilhoon, an MD in Chicago, wrote the author about his encounter with Park in the summer of 1957 when he was the deputy commander of the Sixth Army Corps. The commanding officer operated a large-scale bean sprout factory on the

tables were no different than those of simple peasants, with a few vegetable dishes and rice mixed with barley.[27] His separation of private and public affairs was so stringent that he severely scolded his sixth-grade daughter for riding in his official car to school on a snowy day, even though it was his chauffeur who had urged her to take the ride.[28] Park's behavior was definitely "un-Korean." His education at Zama had much to do with this.

Park Chung-Hee and Japanese History

Japanese history was one of Park Chung-Hee's best subjects in elementary school and at the Taegu Normal School. He also mentioned in his autobiographical notes that while in elementary school he admired the heroes[29] in Japanese history. Park further pursued his study of Japanese history at Zama, where it was a required subject.[30] Kim Chŏng-ryŏm, who served as Park's chief of staff for nine years, told a

---

side, which supplied the units under the Corps. Park knew about it and denounced the general in front of those under him on the front line.

27 Interview with Choe P'illip, May 5, 2009. Choe served in Park Chŏng-Hee's secretariat for many years before he was sent out as ambassador to New Zealand, Sweden, Libya and other countries. Choe was shocked at the simplicity of the dinner served him on the first evening of becoming the duty-officer in the presidential compound. It had a few dishes of vegetables but no meat. Upon protest, the chef showed him the presidential family table that had just been withdrawn to the kitchen which was identical to what he was served. Choe ended up ordering hamburgers from a nearby hotel every time his turn of duty-officer came around.

28 Park's classmate, Kim Pyŏng-hui, mentioned this in his long autobiography on internet. See http://home.megapass.co.kr/~gimbyngh/hoigorog00.html.

29 Park, "My Childhood Days," 23.

30 The teaching of Japanese history at the Military Academy went through remarkable changes through the years. Since 1941, history teaching focused on Shintoism and the spiritual foundation of Japanese polity (*kokutai*) centered on the imperial household (see Suzuki Kenichi, "Rikugun Shikangakkō ni okeru kokushi kyōikuno suii" [Transition in Teaching National History at the Military Academy], *Kinki daigaku kyōiku ronsō* [Kinki University Education Essays], vol. 11, no. 2 (January 2000), 33–52 (particularly 48–50).

reporter later that "[the president] was profoundly knowledgeable or well-versed (haebak) in Japanese history and the history of wars that he learned at Japanese Military Academy."[31]

It is interesting to note Park's basic attitude toward learning history. It was not the facts or principles that were important to him, but the lessons they imparted that could be applied in reality. The following story was recorded by his teacher Kishi in 1977:

> President Park told me that Korean Confucianism has become nothing but a form and a shell. Its content has disappeared and only the rituals remain. In contrast, Confucianism succeeded in Japan. Park could not forget what he learned at Taegu Normal School—that Yamazaki Ansai (1619–1682) asked his students at Edo school (*juku*), "What would you do if Confucius and Mencius led an army to attack Japan?" The students did not know how to answer. Yamazaki said he would face their army and capture both leaders. That is what he taught. Scholarship must be alive. Confucius and Mencius have achieved greatness in Japan being alive.[32]

The key word here, of course, is *alive*, and it can be subject to different interpretations. My conjecture is that Ansai was not content to impart the masters' teachings; he wanted his students to apply them in real life. He also wanted his students not to follow blindly what was written, but to apply their knowledge for their own purposes. Many students might have chosen to surrender if Confucius and Mencius led an

---

31 Chungang Ilbosa, *Sillok Park Chŏng-hui*, 118.

32 Kishi, *Ryūten kyōiku rokujūnen*, 245; Yamazaki Ansai's exchange with his students is repeated in Matsumoto Sannosuke's, *Kindai nihon no chiteki jyōkyō* [Intellectual Condition of Modern Japan], (Tokyo: Chūō Kōronsha, 1974), 86; Pak Ch'ung-sŏk quoted the relevant paragraph in Pak Yŏng-jae, Pak Ch'ung-sŏk, Kim Yong-dŏk, *19segi ilbon ui kŭundaehwa* [Modernization of Japan in the 19th Century] (Seoul National University Press, 1996), 69.

army to attack Japan, but Ansai would confront the masters as his adversaries. Such talk, of course, was unthinkable in the old Korean kingdom. Most Korean Confucians spent their entire lives memorizing and reciting the masters' writings or feuded over the meaning of the masters' teachings. Yamazaki Ansai, the great admirer and first scholar to introduce the writings of the Korean Neo-Confucian scholar Yi T'ogeye to Japan, was also a Japanese nationalist.[33]

Meiji Ishin or Meiji Revolution

Park Chung-Hee's discussion of Ansai with his former teacher Kishi reveals that he delved deeper into Japanese history than just reading about a few heroes. The topics in Japanese history that the academy at Zama taught were more specialized.[34] We can be certain that Park found the history of the Meiji Revolution (1868) particularly important, because he devoted several pages of his 1963 work to that topic. He discussed it in the context of comparing revolutions in China, Turkey, and Egypt, but his coverage of the Meiji Revolution is more sophisticated than his discussion of the others.[35] Park mentioned only one or two of the principal figures for the other countries' revolutions, but it was different in the Japanese case. There is no doubt about his command of his subject material, which included Sun Yat-sen's revolution in China and

33 See Abe Yoshio, *Nihon shushi-gaku to Chōsen* [Japanese Study of Zhu Xi and Korea] (Tokyo University Press, 1975), 231–251; Mary Evelyn Tucker, "Religious Dimensions of Confucianism: Cosmology and Cultivation," *Philosophy East and West*, vol. 48, no. 1, (January 1998), 23.

34 See Suzuki, "Transition in Teaching National History."

35 His coverage of revolutions in Turkey and Egypt were even more detailed than his coverage of those in China and Japan, but I had the distinct feeling that he had not digested the information on the first two countries.

the Meiji Revolution in Japan.[36] Instead of simply describing the events, he analyzed the collapse of the Tokugawa regime, the emergence of the supporting forces for the restoration, and the reasons for the success of the reform.

Park's writing also shows the extent of his admiration for the Meiji Revolution. The following paragraph epitomizes his views.

> In a country consisting of three small islands, sixty eight separate local fiefs have been engaged in internecine struggles. A country that claims to have had two thousand years of history engaged in perverse feudalistic life being proud of their isolation and their rejection of alien thoughts. But within ten years or so after going through the revolutionary process called the Meiji Revolution, it has suddenly emerged as a strong power of the Far East. This was the real astonishment of Asia, a miracle.[37]

How did Japan manage such a transformation?

I believe Park's answer to that question and his analysis of the Meiji Revolution deserve close attention, because Park at this time was grasping for ideas for his own course in the future. It should be noted that Park published the booklet in 1963, just before he launched his reform efforts. Since the date of printing is given as August 25, most likely he wrote these lines sometime between 1962 and early 1963. These dates are important because at that time, Park was still in the process of exploring or plotting the future course of his junta regime.

Park started with the ideological foundation of the Meiji Revolution. He characterized it as "emperor-centered ultra-nationalistic patriotism,"

---

36 Park, *Kukka wa hyŏngmyŏng kwa na*, 156–220; on the Meiji Revolution, see pp. 167–172.

37 Ibid., 167.

but Japan's strong ideological foundation enabled it to domesticate (or Japanize) the flood of foreign ideologies and prevent the meddling of foreign forces. The new leaders replaced the feudalistic sociopolitical system with a new ideology by establishing a direct link between the emperor and the energetic middle layer of the social forces. Finally, the revolutionary leaders put big business, which had taken leadership in the revolution, at the center of the political and economic platform so as to nurture state capitalism and consolidate the imperial system.[38] In conclusion, Park attributed the success of the Meiji Revolution to Japan's solid national identity.[39] Thus, Park considered the establishment of an ideological foundation the key element to rebuilding Japan, and he made efforts in later years to buttress Korean nationalism. Among the many things that Park learned from studying Japan, this was probably the most important.

38 Ibid., 171.
39 Ibid., 172.

VII. THE JAPANESE EMPIRE IN CRISIS

In April 1942 when Park Chung-Hee entered the Japanese Military Academy, the Japanese empire had reason to be euphoric. Its navy had destroyed most of American Pacific fleet and its army had marched to Southeast Asia without encountering much resistance. Japan now had access to the Dutch East Indies' oil and Malaya's rubber and tin. By May, Japan even controlled the Philippines and Burma. East Asia was free of the British, American, French, and Dutch imperialists, and the Japanese empire was seemingly beyond challenge. Even the American bombing of Tokyo, Yokohama, Kobe, and Nagoya on April 18, 1942, would not have dampened Japanese spirits. We do not know what Cadet Takagi felt when he saw the sixteen B-25s flying overhead, but they did not inflict much physical damage.[1]

The euphoria did not last long, however, and the mood in Japan began to change. The hope of dominating the Pacific Ocean by decimating the U.S. Pacific fleet faded after the Japanese navy lost four large aircraft carriers at the battle of Midway Island in June 1942.[2] Naval and marine battles at Guadalcanal and the Solomon Islands proved to be very costly to the Japanese, even though they sank three U.S. cruisers near the Solomon Islands. It was not only American resources and technology that crippled the Japanese navy. Americans had broken the Japanese naval code before the Midway battle, and they were reading every communication transmitted to and from Japanese vessels.

---

1 By coincidence, Yŏ Un-hyŏng happened to be in Tokyo that day. He predicted to his friends later that Japan would lose the war because the American airplanes were much more powerful than the Japanese ones. If the war is prolonged, he said, Japan could not match American resources. This remark subjected him to torture by the infamous *kenpeitai* (Army Gendarmes) and a year of imprisonment.

2 The four carriers were *Akagi*, *Kaga*, *Sōryū*, and *Hiryū*, the pride of the Japanese navy. I have consulted the chronology provided in Thomas M. Leonard (ed.), *Day by Day: the Forties* (New York: Facts on File, 1977).

Americans knew exactly which ship was going where and for what purpose, while the Japanese had to rely on their instincts. The war planners had assumed a steady supply of essential commodities from Southeast Asia, but the supplies dwindled sharply as the Pacific became a graveyard for Japanese ships.[3] To make the situation worse, Americans shot down the bomber carrying Admiral Yamamoto Isoroku, the commander in chief of the Japanese Combined Fleet, in Bougainville, Solomon Islands, on April 18, 1943.[4] By August, Japan was clearly on the defensive. Emperor Hirohito told the Imperial Diet in October that the war situation was "truly grave."[5] Prime Minister Tojō Hideki described Japan as an "invincible fortification against invasion,"[6] meaning imperial expansion was no longer a part of the agenda. It was unfortunate that bushidō had no provisions for surrendering.

Park Chung-Hee graduated from the academy at Zama on April 22, 1944, with 1,267 others in the fifty-seventh class[7] and was sent back to Sinjing in Manchuria, where he was commissioned as a second lieutenant of the Manchukuo army. Whatever his thoughts were at this time,

---

3 See Nakamura Takafusa, *Shōwa keizaishi* [Economic History of Showa Era] (Tokyo: Iwanami, 1986), 135; Japan's total ship tonnage declined from 6,376,000 metric tons in December 1941 to 1,527,000 tons in August 1945. The Japanese navy's loss increased from 1,096,000 tons in 1942 to 2,066,000 tons in 1943 and 4,115,000 tons in 1944.

4 The Wikipedia entry for "Isoroku Yamamoto" provides a very good account of these events. A Japanese source, Kusayanagi, *Jitsuroku Mantetsu Chōsabu,* vol. 1, p. 19, reported that Yamamoto told a private gathering in Shanghai in 1940 that "They can talk about fighting America because they don't know America's strength. Their productive power is bottomless; naval officers and men are sharp. I am a soldier and will fight even America if the Emperor orders us but we won't last more than six months even if we went wild." Yamamoto spent two years at Harvard (1919–1921) and later served as a naval attaché in Washington D.C.

5 *Day by Day*, 340.

6 Ibid., 342.

7 Japanese edition of Wikipedia.

he was fortunate not to have been appointed an officer of the Japanese army. Casualties among his classmates in the army were extremely high.

When the twenty-seven-year-old Takagi Masao returned to Sinjing, the atmosphere was very different than it had been two years earlier—and not only because of the changing tide in the Pacific war. While the eyes of Tokyo were riveted on the Pacific, Kantō-gun had been concentrating on the target in the north, the Soviet Far East. The conquest of Siberia had become the primary concern of Kantō-gun ever since November 1936, when Japan signed the "Anti-Communist Pact" with Germany against the Soviet Union.[8] When Germany began its attack on the Soviet Union on June 22, 1941, Kantō-gun followed it four days later on June 26 by putting its war plan into action. Activation of Kantō-gun Special Exercise (Kan-toku-en or Kantō-gun *Tokushu Dai Enshū*) meant the increase of its forces from 300,000 men to 850,000 men, from twelve divisions to twenty-four divisions. The attack would begin as soon as Stalin transferred half of his Far Eastern forces to meet the German attack.[9] The Soviet-Manchurian border was thrown into frenzy; Kantō-gun worked to build railroads, highways, storage facilities, and barracks to accommodate the plan. Workers produced ships and railroads, working overtime to transport vast numbers of men, horses, and equipment to the front line from Japan and Korea. By August 1941, 750,000 men, 140,000 horses, and 600 airplanes were actually assembled in northern Manchuria, and food and supplies for them were piled

8 Asada Kyōji and Kobayashi Sadao (eds.), *Nihon teikoku shugi no Manshū shihai: 15nen sensōki o chūshin ni* [Control of Manchuria by Japanese Imperialism: Centered on the 15-Year War Period) (Tokyo: Jichōsha, 1986), 202.
9 Shimada Toshihiko, *Kantō-gun* (Tokyo: Chūō Kōronsha, 1965), 156–157.

up.[10] The Japanese had mobilized 200,000 Chinese workers[11] and 10,000 Korean women for the task.[12] But the attack was forestalled when the Soviets effectively resisted German attack and only a small portion of Soviet forces were transferred out of the Far East.[13] Stalin was obviously aware of the Japanese threat and did not wish to further weaken his overall position by opening another front. But a large number of Japanese forces remained in Manchuria until the latter part of 1943, when the war in the Pacific demanded more troops.[14]

Thus Kantō-gun was on the ascendant when Takagi left Sinjing for Zama, but it was in the process of dismantling itself when he returned in the spring of 1944. Starting in February, Kantō-gun sent half of its air force to where they were more urgently needed in the Pacific and dispatched a number of army divisions to the Solomon Islands, New Guinea, and China. Between June and August of the same year, it sent out its best divisions to the Pacific region. Park may not have known it, but Colonel Arikawa, his drill master from Taegu, was one of those shipped to Okinawa. The Japanese Imperial Army began hemorrhaging its brightest stars from this point to the end of the war.[15] Kantō-gun organized fourteen new divisions by February 1945, by recruiting every remaining veteran and many young Koreans in Manchuria; three divi-

---

10 Ibid., 175.

11 Manshūkokushi Hensan Kankōkai [Editorial and Publication Committee], *Manshūkokushi* [History of Manchukuo], vol. 2 (Tokyo: Manmō Dōhō Engokai, 1971), 261.

12 The army mobilized 10,000 Korean women to fulfill the soldiers' sexual needs. The plan was to mobilize 20,000 women, who would be paid by individual soldiers for the service rendered (Shimada, *Kantō-gun*, 176). The author did not provide the source for his provocative information.

13 Ibid., 138–167.

14 Asada and Kobayashi, 238.

15 Ibid., 242–244.

sions were quickly dispatched to the southern end of Korea to face the anticipated American attack.[16] By necessity, therefore, Kantō-gun had to change its posture from offensive to defensive by the time Takagi returned in 1944.

This was the context in which the Manchukuo army was operating. Having been created as a supplementary force to maintain the internal security of Manchuria, its role had not changed much. By November 1936, it operated independently in mopping up the anti-Japanese forces in Manchuria; it soon had a sufficient number of Japanese officers to conduct operations on its own.[17]

By the time Takagi returned to Manchuria, however, most of the anti-Japanese guerrilla forces had either been destroyed or, as in the case of Kim Il-sŏng's contingent, escaped to Soviet territory in the Maritime Provinces. On the other hand, the Chinese Communist forces had become active in harassing the western border regions of the Japanese-occupied area. By 1935, Mao Zedong's forces had moved from southern China in an epic called the Long March and were engaging the Japanese in north-western China. Most of the Chinese forces were set against the Japanese army, but guerrilla units carried out forays against Rehe Province in the westernmost part of Manchukuo territory.[18] That region had been an integral part of China proper before the Japanese takeover in 1935 and was administered as either part of the Zhili or Hebei Provinces.[19] Kantō-gun considered the guerrilla operations grave enough to dispatch half of

---

16 Ibid., 244; I attended a send-off party for the young Korean men in Liaoyang, Liaoning Province, sometime in 1945.

17 Ibid., 183–185.

18 Rehe is in the Pinyin form of transliteration. It was known as Jeho or Jehol in the past using the Wade-Giles form.

19 Ibid., 185.

the entire Manchukuo army to the region. The Fifth Military District[20] responsible for that region had an original force of some forty thousand men, but fourteen units were dispatched to more than double the total strength.[21]

It is therefore not surprising that in 1944, army headquarters dispatched the fresh graduate of the Japanese Military Academy to the Fifth Military District, with its headquarters in Chengde (formerly known as Rehe). Still, one wonders why Park Chung-Hee was sent to the remotest part of the district, at the northwest corner very near Inner Mongolia. The assignment may have been routine, but it would not be surprising if those in charge of distributing new officers at Chengde, out of envy and revenge, wanted to "punish" the recipient of Emperor Pu Yi's gold watch. An assignment to Banbishan (Half Wall Mountain), a small village on the Xiao Luan River northwest of a town called Guojiatun (Guo Family Hamlet), was akin to punishment. It was about 250 kilometers northwest of Chengde, accessible only by horse or donkey. The roads were not suitable for military trucks transporting supplies; the roads and trucks often tumbled down the mountain cliffs together. The headquarters of the Eighth Infantry Regiment were located in Banbishan, with Second Lieutenant Takagi Masao serving as a platoon commander; he was then made one of the adjutants to the regiment commander.[22]

---

20 The Fifth Military District had its headquarters in Chengde. The first was in Fengtien, the second in Jilin, the third in Chichihar, the fourth in Harbin, and the sixth in Mudanjiang; Shin Hyŏn-jun, *No haebyŏng ui hoegorok* [Recollections of an Old Marine] (Seoul: K'at'orik ch'ulp'ansa, 1989), 41–42.

21 Ranseikai [Orchid Star Society], *Manshū kokugun* [The Manchukuo Army] (Tokyo: private publication, 1970), 839.

22 Shin Hyŏn-jun, 65; Shin was then a captain in the Manchukuo army. He was appointed company commander in the Eighth Infantry Regiment where he met Park Chung-Hee on July 28, 1944.

Chengde, the provincial capital of Rehe in Manchukuo, is famous for its vast imperial garden, which was used by Qing emperors as a summer retreat. There were, however, reasons why Emperor Chin and his successors did not include the region within the Great Wall. The vast area outside of the Great Wall is mountainous and desolate, with little area for cultivation. More Manchus than Han Chinese lived there, and the Mongols were just above the border in the north. Park Chung-Hee would have found Banbishan even more remote and desolate than Munkyŏng, where he had been a teacher.

How did Lieutenant Takagi spend his long nights in the deserted and windy corner of the earth known as Banbishan? What preparations did Takagi make when he learned that his first assignment as a Manchukuo army officer was to be in the Fifth Military District, with its headquarters in Rehe near Mongolia? Park Chung-Hee did not leave us any clues to the answers of these questions, but they are not difficult to find for anyone familiar with the intellectual scene in Korea. This is because the Chinese word *Rehe* does not evoke anything but *Rehe Diary* or *Yŏlha Ilgi* to the Koreans. No Korean besides Pak Chi-won (1737–1805) has ever written anything about Rehe; nor did anyone have any kind of dealings involving Rehe, other than an ambassadorial mission dispatched there ten years after Pak's journey. Pak Chi-won had traveled in 1780 from Seoul to Uiju on the Yalu River and then to Ch'engzing (later Shenyang), Liaoyang, Shanhaiguan, and Beijing as a part of the Korean mission to celebrate the seventieth birthday of the Qing emperor Qianlong (1711–1799).[23] It took the retinue of 281 men forty days to reach Beijing on August 1, 1780. But being informed that the emperor had gone to his summer retreat in Rehe, the ambassadors and a smaller retinue of seventy-four men headed

23 Reigned between 1735 and 1796.

northeast to Miwin, Kubeik'ou, Luanp'ing, and Rehe, traveling for five days without nightly stops.[24]

Pak's writings have been universally recognized as a Korean classic, not only because Pak Chi-won wrote about the unknown world, but also because he was a well-read man of insatiable curiosity who roamed the neighborhoods wherever his ambassadorial train took him. Pak's verbal skill in Chinese was limited, but he had the assistance of an interpreter. He also carried a writing set that included the grindstone, ink stick, writing brush, and a roll of paper. His uniquely Korean outfit, gregarious personality, and highbrow learning in Chinese classics attracted his Chinese counterparts, who opened their minds and homes to him. Pak Chi-won used the written exchanges in Chinese script as a source for his later writings, even though some of his counterparts quickly burned the "conversational sheets" or smeared the words and sentences that could cause them trouble with the Manchu Dynasty. The Chinese, or Han race, were not at all happy under Manchu rule, particularly because the Manchu conquerors forced the Chinese to wear Manchu costumes and hairstyles. Pak Chi-won narrated these and other events so vividly and in such detail that one could easily become spellbound.

Pak Chi-won's writings were circulated in hand-copied versions in his day, but a number of printed editions have become available since

24 For Pak Chi-won's life and the writings, I depended on Kang Chae-ŏn, *Kindai Chōsen no henkaku shishō* (Tokyo, Nihon Hyōronsha, 1973), 7–54, and Imamura Yoshio (trans. with annotations), *Nekka nikki* [Rehe Diary] (Tokyo, Heibonsha, 1978), 2 volumes. Imamura made a valuable contribution through his book-end commentaries in the two volumes and text annotations. With his background as a scholar of modern China, he added much to our understanding of Pak Chi-won and his work. The entries on the number of the retinue and the dates are from vol. 2, pp. 334–335.

then, the latest edition being published in 1932.[25] It was inconceivable, therefore, for any Korean headed for Rehe in the 1940s not to look for a copy of Pak Chi-won's works before he embarked on his trip. If Park Chung-Hee failed to acquire Pak's writings in Sinjing before his departure, he surely would have asked a friend mail a copy through the military mail system. Like Yu Sŏng-yong's *Chingbirok*, which Park read at Munkyŏng, Pak Chi-won's works were written in Chinese, but Park Chung-Hee would not have had any difficulty with them.

Why does it matter whether Lt. Takagi or Park Chung-Hee read Pak Chi-won's work or not? Why do I attach so much importance to Park Chung-Hee's reading of the *Rehe Diary*? The simple answer is because Pak Chi-won could very well have contributed to Park Chung-Hee's historical perspective of Korea's past. The similarities between Park's views and those of Pak Chi-won and his group are so striking that one cannot attribute this to mere coincidence. But more on Pak Chi-won first.

In addition to being a poet, novelist, and satirist, Pak Chi-won was a highly regarded social critic and reformer, who left a deep imprint on Korean intellectual history. Indeed, he has been acknowledged as the leader of a reformist group known as Pukhakp'a, or the Northern Learning group. Pukhakp'a advocated that Koreans should learn from all available sources, including Qing China, so as to improve the welfare of their people. This was a startling argument in eighteenth-century Korea, because the ruling elite regarded the Manchus with unmitigated hatred and contempt, therefore rejecting all learning from China. The Manchus had invaded Korea twice, in 1627 and 1636, devastating the nation. Worse still, the Manchus, who were, from a Korean perspective,

25 Printed editions were published in 1900–1901, 1911, 1916 (in Shanghai), and 1932; Imamura, vol. 2, 348–349, 353.

nothing but savages from the Manchurian hills, vanquished the Ming Dynasty in 1644 and replaced it with the Qing Dynasty. Since the Mings had rescued the Korean kingdom from Hideyoshi's invasions, the Manchus were a double enemy to the Korean kingdom. The Manchus were, therefore, a target to attack and destroy rather than a source from which to learn. It was humiliating enough for the Chosŏn Dynasty to send tributary and congratulatory missions to the Qing Empire. The Chosŏn kingdom was now the only true inheritor of the Confucian civilization that the Ming had represented, and it took pride in being "Little China," or *Xiao Chunghwa*. Such a kingdom could not condescend itself to learn from such barbarians.

Pak Chi-won rejected the binary division between Chunghwa, the civilized country, and the savages.[26] Holders of such a view, in Pak's opinion, were no more than frogs in a well, unable to see beyond the deep confines of a narrow space. The yangban elites took pride in the rectification of the self or the refinement of the individual as required by Confucius and Mencius, but ignored the teachings concerning the improvement of people's welfare, which was essential for refining the people. Virtue could not be attained through rote memory of Confucian texts or writing treatises on abstract principles, Pak argued. The Koreans must learn from China, even when it was ruled by the despised Manchu race.

Pak Chi-won produced a few writings explicitly criticizing Korean norms and practices of his time,[27] but he imbedded much of his criticism in his *Rehe Diary* or *Yŏlha ilgi*, his best known work. He would, for

---

26 Kang Chae-on, 17.

27 Including such works as the "Tale of the Yangban" [Yangban-jŏn], "The Life of Hŏ Saeng" [Hŏsaengjŏn], or "Tiger's Admonition" [Hojil].

example, describe a Chinese boy on horseback herding a large number of cows, horses, and sheep to the field, followed by other families opening up their fences to let their animals out. Pak Chi-won would then produce a long treatise on horses in Korea.[28] The entire country bred no more than four or five horses a year, importing all its needs from Manchuria. There were state-run relay stations at various localities that somehow kept good horses, but they collapsed quickly when dignitaries rode them because the saddles were too heavy, and the two stabilizers for the rider held by four slaves on both sides of the horse made the load even heavier. Any trotting would make it impossible for the horses to bear the load.[29] Even army officers in the front line moved about in this manner. In 1592, two Japanese soldiers beheaded a Korean officer dispatched by General Yi Il (1538–1601) to investigate possible Japanese movement in the front; the Korean officer's horse had been held by slaves on both sides endeavoring to reduce the saddle's sway.[30] All that the Japanese soldiers had to do to bring down the officer was to thrust a sword into the horse's belly. Park Chung-Hee would have been amused that Pak Chi-won cited Yu Sŏng-yong's *Chingbirok* to narrate this event.

Pak Chi-won also used allegory to denounce the strictures the government placed on the Korean people. The Korean horses were always driven by a man walking at the horse's side, taking the more comfortable points on the road. No attempts were made to build a bond between the horse and his driver, who relied on whips and fists to force the horse, which resulted in the horse's resistance and rebellion. Such a manner of driving a horse is most dangerous, particularly in crossing deep and swift rivers, as he himself had done. Pak Chi-won, however, crossed the

---

28 Ibid., 113–120.
29 Ibid., 115–116.
30 Ibid., 37.

river by loosening his rein, holding onto the saddle, and letting the horse use his senses.[31] His message was clear. The horse driver represented the Chosŏn Dynasty, which applied so many strictures that the petrified people could not be productive.

Lieutenant Takagi's duty as adjutant was to communicate with the various units under the regiment commander, who was Chinese. While the regiment had thirteen Japanese officers and four Koreans scattered through various units, the remainder of the regiment consisted of Chinese soldiers. One wonders how Takagi spent thirteen months in that remote village. He visited Chengde once, according to Captain Shin Hyŏn-jun, but it was his only known trip outside of the valley. Winter in northern China is long and brutally cold and even more so at its northern edge. It would reach 20 degrees below zero centigrade (-4 Fahrenheit), according to residents in the village.[32] Winds from Siberia would sweep down the valley, making the cold intolerable. We do not know whether the regiment had access to shortwave radios, the only possible means of learning about the outside world in such a territory. Shin Hyŏn-jun recollected that the news about the bombs on Hiroshima and Nagasaki did not reach him until ten days later, indicating that he had no access to a radio. He heard about the Japanese surrender only on September 17, when his unit reached Xinglong in the south.[33]

The remoteness and inaccessibility may have been the very reasons why the Palu-chün, or the Eighth Route Army, targeted the Eighth Regiment for a concentrated attack. At least five Chinese Communist regi-

31 Ibid., 35–37.

32 I wish to thank Professor Kim Yong-ho of Inha University for accompanying me in visiting Chengde and Banbishan in September 2009.

33 Shin Hyŏn-jun, 72.

ments confronted the Manchukuo forces from the south.[34] Shin Hyŏn-jun, one of the company commanders in the Eighth Regiment, has provided a long account of a battle his battalion engaged in in September 1944, soon after his arrival.[35] *Manshūkokugun* (Manchukuo Army), a book compiled by the Manchukuo army's Japanese veterans, provides a report with a large map that recounts the infiltration of two thousand Communist guerrillas on July 20, 1945, less than a month before Japanese capitulation. The guerrillas thrust upward from the south along the wide valley toward Banbishan, causing the district commander to dispatch guerrilla units of his own to counter them. The operation lasted until August 6, the day the atomic bomb was dropped on Hiroshima.[36] While it does not appear that First Lieutenant Takagi (promoted on July 1, 1945)[37] engaged in these battles himself, much action surrounded him.

The Japanese surrender on August 15 was like a bolt of lightning in a blue sky for the Eighth Regiment. It was totally unexpected in the hinterland of China. But the news changed everything for the Koreans. The Chinese officers and soldiers in the Manchukuo army now assumed the role of victors against the Japanese empire and disarmed the Japanese and Korean officers, even though no one knew what their own future would be. Captain Shin, the company commander, said he could not describe his feelings on that day; it was simply too overwhelming. It was like his wings were clipped when he had to surrender his long Japanese sword, his pistol, and the binoculars that had been a part of him ever since he became a commissioned lieutenant in the Manchukuo army, he

34 Ranseikai [Orchid Star Society], *Manshū kokugun* [The Manchukuo Army] (Tokyo, private publication, 1970), 838, provides a full-page map of the region and shows where the Communist regiments were located.

35 Shin Hyŏn-jun, 67–69.

36 *Manshū kokugun*, 836, 838.

37 Chŏng Yŏng-jin, vol. 2, 154.

said.[38] Shin probably summed up the feelings of many Korean officers, including Park Chung-Hee. He had barely begun to climb the ladder of success when the ladder was taken away without warning. He faced nothing but a void. The officers in the puppet army were not alone.[39] The entire Japanese empire was thrown into chaos and uncertainty. Park did not know it then, but an even worse fate awaited him.

* * *

The unceremonious and anticlimactic denouement of Park's career in the Manchukuo army gives us an opportunity to reflect on Park Chung-Hee's growth as a man up to this time. His only concern until his graduation from the Normal School had been to escape from the poverty that his father had imposed on him. He paid no attention to political questions and did his best to climb up the ladder. He was rewarded with a teacher's position in Munkyŏng, but he had grander dreams. He made the jump to Manchuria and became an officer in the Manchukuo army, but now he was stripped of that position. Had he made the wrong decision when he abandoned his teaching career and gone to Manchuria? Had all the hardship at the Manchurian and Japanese academies been worth the trouble? Was not the year spent at Rehe a waste of time? Had he stayed at Munkyŏng rather than venturing into Manchuria, he might have had a steady and respectable job, even after Japanese capitulation.

---

38 Shin Hyŏn-jun, 72.

39 Professor Ch'oi Yŏng-Ho wrote me about his reaction to the Japanese surrender. "I remember that day very clearly in Taegu. Upon learning the Japanese surrender, my immediate reaction was: 'O, My God. Am I going to lose my testicles?' As you know, the Japanese teachers constantly told us that the first thing 'the beastly American and British devils (kichiku Bei-Ei)' would do was to cut off testicles of all Japanese and Korean boys if Japan were to lose the war. I was certainly at a loss. But within a few hours, when I saw one of my Korean high school teachers attired in Korean traditional dress waving the Korean flag, instantly I recognized my own Korean identity. I believe most Koreans experienced a similar reaction."

He might even have become the school principal after the Japanese defeat. But now, at twenty-eight, he was an unemployed former officer of a puppet army with no useful skills to offer.

When Park recovered from the shock of the bewildering end to his career, he would have concluded that he had taken the right road. Remaining at Munkyŏng would have severely limited his future, because a person with only a secondary education had no future in a society where many young men and women graduated from college and university. The Manchurian and Japanese academies gave him what he needed most, in that they put him on equal footing with the graduates of higher institutions of learning, a position that had been far out of his reach. Even though his education was specialized, it was a postsecondary education of the highest quality. No one patronized graduates of the Japanese Military Academy as uneducated bumpkins. In fact, alumni of that academy ruled Japan for many years. This fact alone would have justified his career switch.

The Manchurian academy was important to him also because it enabled him to win back his confidence. Without that, Park would have had to live with his dismal record at Taegu Normal School—the last or penultimate student in his class. But the Manchukuo academy gave him an opportunity to prove his ability and to show his indomitable spirit. Perhaps this was what he wanted to say when he greeted General Nagumo in 1961. His gesture transcended nationality and history; that is, it did not matter why the academy was established and what the Japanese were doing there. Had Park not been to the Manchukuo Military Academy, he would have spent his whole life as a frustrated and unknown school principal somewhere in the Korean countryside.

The most valuable aspect of these experiences, in the long run, was Park's exposure to the outside world. Except for the school trips to Japan and Manchuria at the Normal School, all Park knew when he left Munkyŏng in 1940 was the world between Kumi, Taegu, and Munkyŏng, a radius of not more than one hundred kilometers. Park was no more than a mountain-town boy who had spent five years in the provincial town of Taegu, before moving on to teach the impoverished children in yet another mountain town. But since then, he had spent two years in Japan and three years in Manchuria. While he had to spend much of that time on campus grounds, he had also had time to travel and observe those societies firsthand. Japanese and Manchurian ways of life were vastly different from each other and from Korean. Each had much to teach the young Korean man, both positive and negative. In short, Park was exposed to very different cultures, broadening his outlook.

Park's exposure to different languages also merits attention. We do not know with what proficiency he spoke Chinese, but he did spend a significant amount of time at the Manchukuo and Japanese academies learning the language. He also spent at least three years among the Chinese in Manchuria. Regardless of his level of language skill, Park would have come to a better understanding of the feelings of the people. More important, however, was his training in the Japanese language. As noted earlier, Park's entire education was under the tutelage of the Japanese, and he continued reading Japanese publications even after Korea's liberation from Japan. This has been the case for most of those who grew up under Japanese rule, and Park was no exception. This enabled them to escape from the narrow perspective of the postliberation press in Korea, but at the same time, such reading prolonged the influence of the Japanese perspective on many matters in Korea, including lifestyle and politics.

Park's career change also enabled him to see the realities of Japanese imperialism. Being at the front line of Japanese aggression against China and having seen the struggle of the Chinese people against the aggressors, Park would have begun to question his identity. Why should a Korean like himself die for the cause of Japanese aggression against China? He may or may not have reflected on Japan's role in Korea before he was sent to the remotest corner of the earth, but those questions would have become real as he witnessed the daily carnage at the front line. Many Chinese officers and troops in Park's regiment evidently asked these questions. Some of them answered them by defecting to the Chinese side. If Park Chung-Hee had not been at the front line, he could have set aside such questions as abstractions that served no real purpose. But the situation at Banbishan was different. His pursuit of success exposed him to questions that he could not ignore. If I were allowed to present only one question to him, I would present this paragraph and seek his reaction.

VIII. POSTWAR CHINA AND PARK CHUNG-HEE

Park and two other Korean officers, Captain Shin Hyŏn-jun and Lieutenant Yi Chu-il (Joo Il Lee) were stripped of their insignia and other paraphernalia from the Manchukuo army, but their former Chinese colleagues in the Eighth Regiment continued to treat them with civility.[1] So they followed the regiment southwest to Miwin, a city northeast of Beijing. The terrain the regiment had to traverse was near the Great Wall and extremely rugged. The summer downpour had washed some of the roads away, and the regiment had to move very slowly. Only in late September did they reach Miwin. There, the regiment was to meet the Chinese army to await instructions. The Koreans bid farewell to the regiment on September 21 and proceeded to Beijing by train.[2] The three could have left the regiment much earlier, taken the Tientsin-Shenyang railway to Shenyang, then to Andung (now Dandong), and across the Yalu River to return home, but the group decided this would be too risky. Parts of the railroad were damaged and travel was uncertain. In addition, local mobs or bandits might attack them, or the Soviet forces could capture them as prisoners of war.[3] A large number of Soviet forces had moved into Manchuria in early August and had occupied many key cities. Therefore, the three men decided to join the fifteen thousand Koreans living in the Beijing area[4] and try their luck. Their

---

1 Shin Hyŏn-jun, *No haebyŏng ui hoegorok* [Recollections of an Old Marine] (Seoul: K'at'orik ch'ulp'ansa, 1989), 69; I have not encountered any record of Korean officers being mistreated by the "Manchurian" soldiers, but the Japanese officers were not so lucky.

2 Ibid., 69, 75.

3 The Soviet army took tens of thousands of officers and men from the Fifth Military District with its headquarters in Chengde and sent them to Siberia, according to Ranseikai [Orchid Star Society], *Manshū kokugun* [The Manchukuo Army] (Tokyo, private publication, 1970), 845; this included not only the Japanese officers but the Chinese.

4 Yŏm In-ho, "The Korean Independence Party's Movement to Expand the Kwangbok Army South of the Great Wall after Liberation" [in Korean], *Yŏksa munje yŏn'gu*

best hope was to find ship transportation to the American occupation zone in South Korea, but in the meantime, they had to find lodging and the means to sustain them. The wait for transportation turned out to be a long one—seven and a half months to be exact, from September 21 to May 6 of the following year.

The main problem was that the men could not find ships bound for home. There had never been a shipping company handling routes between north China and any part of Korea. China had been engulfed in war against Japan, and such needs had not arisen before. The railroads had been sufficient. Now in September 1945, the Chinese recovered Beijing from the Japanese, but their government was in disarray. The Chinese could not assist the stranded Koreans because they did not have any ships. The Japanese took away all seaworthy vessels as soon as they heard Emperor Hirohito's surrender message on August 15. It would have been most convenient if the U.S. occupation forces in Korea had sent ships for the Koreans stranded in north China, but the Americans were in no better shape than the Chinese; they too had no spare ships to transport people. The 24th U.S. Army Corps arrived in South Korea in early September, but it was too preoccupied with the problem of repatriating the Japanese from Korea and handling the thousands of Koreans returning from Japan, Manchuria, and other overseas areas. There was also the overwhelming problem of governing the Koreans, who expected nothing short of a paradise now that the Japanese oppressors had been defeated. No one in the U.S. Military Government in Seoul was responsible for the protection or repatriation of the Koreans stranded in northern China.

[Studies on Historical Problems], vol. 9, no. 1 (1996), 163–313 (the citation is from 280). This is a valuable work based mostly on Chinese documents.

The Korean Kwangbok Army

The three ex-Manchukuo officers, however, did not have to join the rank of drifters in Beijing. They found a Korean organization eager to accommodate them. It was the second brigade of the Korean Restoration Army, known in Korean as Kwangbok-kun. It does not appear that the three were enchanted by their association with the Kwangbok-kun, but it provided them food and lodging. It also provided Park Chung-Hee valuable insight into the character of the Korean exiles in China. But who were these "Samaritans" who took in the three Korean officers?

The Kwangbok-kun was an arm of the Korean Provisional Government (KPG) in Chungking, whose history goes back to 1919 when the March First Movement erupted in Korea. Many of the exiles, who had been scattered throughout China, Manchuria, and Siberia, gathered in Shanghai and organized it in April 1919 as a vehicle to carry on the movement for Korean independence. For a short period, until 1921, the group became the center for the nationalists in exile everywhere, but financial difficulty and internal discord turned it into a nominal organization without much activity.[5] But for Kim Ku's bombing of Japanese leaders celebrating their conquest of Shanghai in April 1932, the Provisional Government would have long ceased to exist even in name. The bombing was a turning point, because it avenged the Chinese humiliation for losing Shanghai to Japanese marines. To add insult to injury, the Japanese marines had paraded through the city and announced the celebration of Emperor Hirohito's birthday on April 29 at Hungkou Park. All Japanese residents were invited. Kim Ku dispatched a young

5 See Chong-Sik Lee, *The Politics of Korean Nationalism* (Berkeley: University of California Press, 1963), chapter 8.

Korean man, Yun Pong-gil, in a casual Japanese-looking outfit with two bombs shaped like Japanese bentō. When the singing of the national anthem was about to conclude, Yi threw the bombs in rapid succession onto the dais where the dignitaries were standing, seriously wounding the leaders.[6] Nothing could have pleased the Chinese more. The Chinese government from that point forward became consistent supporters of the Korean nationalists, which enabled them to organize the Kwangbok-kun, the Restoration Army, in Chungking in September 1940. The city of Chungking at the upstream of the Yangtze River had become China's wartime capital, and the Chinese government offered Koreans accommodation there. But since the number of young Korean men in the Chinese-controlled regions was not very large, the Kwangbok-kun had only some two hundred men. As some of the Korean men who had been drafted into the Japanese army defected at the front line, the size of the Kwangbok-kun gradually increased, but it was far from what could be called an "army." The Kwangbok-kun did gain momentum in 1944 or 1945, however, when the United States OSS (Office of Strategic Services) unit in China under Major Clyde Sargent decided to train the Second Brigade in Xian to be sent behind enemy lines in Korea for intelligence gathering and sabotage activities. Thus, American officers and men also worked with the Kwangbok army. It was natural for the Koreans to use this connection to open an office in Beijing as soon as the Chinese government established its authority there.[7]

---

6 Ibid., 184–185; two of the wounded, Kawabata Teiji, chairman of the Japanese Residents Association, which had called the troops into Shanghai, and General Shirakawa Yoshinori, commander of the Japanese forces in Shanghai, died of their wounds.

7 These events are related in Yŏm In-ho, "The Korean Independence Party's Movement," op. cit., 278–279.

Now that Korea had been liberated, the Korean exile leaders in Chungking were dreaming of the future, and they needed men like Park Chung-Hee. The hope was to gather and organize all the young Korean soldiers in the defeated Japanese army to create the basis of a new Korean army. There was a political incentive for the Provisional Government leaders too. The exiled government had a long history dating from 1919, but had nothing to show to the public in 1945. A large army "returning from China" under the command of the Provisional Government would impress the public enormously and provide the legitimacy it needed to compete against any group that might challenge its authority.[8] The news that a group of men in Seoul had organized the Korean People's Republic in early September had aroused the Korean Provisional Government's concern.

Park Chung-Hee at that time may not have realized it, but he and his comrade Yi Chu-il were extremely important in the scheme for the Provisional Government because they were among the few who had received four years of rigorous military training. The head of Kwangbok-kun and that of the Second Brigade were graduates of Chinese military academies, but their training was shorter, as Captain Shin Hyŏn-jun had received at Shenyang. Even though Shin outranked Park and Yi in the Manchukuo army, the younger men clearly had superior training.

It is no wonder that the man from Xian asked Park Chung-Hee to serve as the battalion commander of the Beijing unit of Kwangbok-kun, officially known as the P'ing-Jin Brigade. Beijing at this time was called Beip'ing and the unit was to cover the nearby city of T'ienjin also. But Park declined the offer on the grounds of propriety. Shin was not only older than he was but outranked him in the army. Ignoring rank

8 See Yŏm In-ho, 269–273; Shin Hyŏn-jun, 77.

would violate the sense of propriety and hinder the task of maintaining discipline.[9] Shin Hyŏn-jun was appointed the battalion commander, Park Chung-Hee the commander of the first company, and Yi Chu-il the second company.[10]

It is important to note that the "higher authorities" bypassed Yi Chu-il when they chose Park as their man to lead the Beijing unit. Although Yi was also a graduate of the Japanese Military Academy and had the same rank as Park in the Manchukuo army, he was ahead of Park both at Sinjing and Zama by a year.[11] Whoever was in charge of these matters saw something special in Park Chung-Hee. The short, tight-faced, and laconic man outshone others.

The Implications of the Kwangbok Army Appointment

The Kwangbok army's appointment of the three Manchukuo officers as commanders of the Beijing unit had very significant implications, particularly in view of later charges that Park Chung-Hee was a pro-Japanese collaborator. But in Beijing, those on the winning side not only accepted the three men, but also assigned them to very important leadership positions. The leaders of the Kwangbok army did not regard the graduates of the Manchukuo and Japanese military academies as traitors. On the contrary, they embraced them for their training and experience. This need prevailed over all other concerns. The Kwangbok army's judgment and attitude toward the three stands in sharp contrast to the attitude of today's twenty-first century Koreans, who "convicted" Park and others as traitors. The exiled nationalists not only took the men

---

9 See Shin Hyŏn-jun, *Nohaebyŏng ui hoegorok*, 76–77.

10 Yŏm In-ho, "The Korean Independence Party's Movement," op. cit., p. 279.

11 See Chŏng Yŏng-jin, *Ch'ŏngnyŏn Park Chŏng-hui hui* [Young Man Park Chung-Hee], vol. 2 (Seoul: Riburo (Libro) Books, 1997), 118.

in but also kept them together in the Beijing unit, rather than dispersing them. If the Beijing unit had expanded itself to a division force, Captain Shin would presumably have become the division commander and the other two regimental commanders.

There was a psychological factor at work here. The quality and ranking of schools and institutions one attends play important roles in any society, often serving as the sole criterion in determining the status of a person, and Korea was no exception. From the perspective of the military men in China at this time, the Japanese Military Academy was at the top of all military schools. Generalissimo Chiang Kai-shek, the head of the Chinese government, was one of the very few Chinese to graduate from there. He rose in Chinese politics by serving as the commandant of the Hwangpao Military Academy, which trained most of the Chinese officers. Seen from this perspective, Park Chung-Hee was a valuable officer.

Life in Beijing

In spite of his new station in life, Park's existence at the Beijing unit was uncomfortable in many ways. Although Generalissimo Chiang had promised Kim Ku, the premier of the Korean Provisional Government, to help the latter's Kwangbok army, no measures were taken to supply the food, transport, and cash necessary to operate the camp. In December 1945, the Beijing unit had about two hundred men,[12] but by February, this number had reached 1,300.[13] The army was accommodated at a former paper mill owned by a Korean proprietor in the northeast of the city, known as Beishinchiao (North New Bridge), but there was no steady source of food. Ch'oe Yong-dŏk, the Kwangbok army

12 Shin Hyŏn-jun, 78.
13 Yŏm In-ho, 280.

man in charge of Beijing operations, should have been responsible for the procurement of food, but evidently the Generalissimo's agreement to help the Koreans had not translated into orders for his men in Beijing. Commander Shin complained in his memoir that he had to make the rounds to Korean businessmen in town to beg for funds.[14] The exiled leaders are said to have dreamed of an army of one hundred thousand, but one wonders whether they had even thought of a way to feed the recruits. The paper mill had ceased to operate at the end of the war, but it was not equipped for the large number of men. Even the officers had to stand around a long table at mealtimes. The others probably had to eat without the luxury of even a table.

U.S. Recognition of the Korean Provisional Government

Another more serious problem was the uncertainty surrounding the Kwangbok army and, indeed, the Provisional Government behind it. The basic problem for both entities was that neither had any power to exercise. Their very existence in the foreign land depended on the support and good will of the Chinese government. And they had no means to return to Korea. Given its long history and its record of attempts at winning Korean independence, the KPG might have been able to win approval of the majority in the American zone of occupation, but no means was available to return to Korea without American support. And all those involved in the exiled government were fully aware that the United States was firmly opposed to the recognition of the KPG as the legitimate government of the Korean people. Representatives of that government, including Syngman Rhee in the United States, had redoubled their efforts to win American recognition after Pearl Harbor

14 Shin Hyŏn-jun, 80.

without avail. The United States would allow the leaders of the exiled government to return to Korea only if they promised to return as individuals, rather than as a political body. (The KPG has had no contact with the Soviet Union up to this point because Soviet participation in Korean affairs had not been anticipated. As it turned out, it was dead set against the Korean Provisional Government, and there was no prospect of winning Soviet support.)

Why did the United States refuse to recognize the Korean Provisional Government? The fundamental reason was that KPG was not an entity elected by the people in Korea. It might have embodied the will and spirit of the Korean people, but that was not enough for the United States. The KPG was an entity "elected" by no more than a few dozen Korean exiles in China. They had been "electing" themselves for quite some time. In fact, the number of the "electorate" or the popularity of the KPG within Korea were of little concern to the United States. The U.S. State Department's European Division, for example, had the following to say about the recognition of the Polish government in exile headed by General Władysław Sikorski, the hero of the Battle of Warsaw against the Soviet army:

> Of all the Polish leaders, Sikorski undoubtedly has preeminence in his potentialities as an individual, and he is generally regarded as representing sufficiently the majority of Polish opinion to assure his continued leadership during the interim.
>
> It should be borne in mind, however, that any special considerations shown the Sikorski Government will be taken as a pattern for our relations with other Governments-in-exile. The European Division strongly believes we should not at this time make any formal commitments or declarations which in

> any way indicate that the American government is committed to a policy of *imposing upon the people of occupied countries a government now in exile.*
>
> This Government has with considerable success impressed on the various governments that we will not negotiate on questions of European frontiers at this stage of the war. Any weakening on this line—which still seems to have such great practical utility that it would be unfortunate to abandon it—*will bring nearly all of the United Nations to us with their claims. In many cases these claims are those of allies against each other or each other's pretensions.* Therefore the European Division does not recommend any direct communication to the head of any exiled government that in any way indicates commitments at this time.[15] (Italics added.)

This was not just the opinion of the European Division. It reflected the policy of President Franklin D. Roosevelt. An unsigned memo dated December 24, 1942, said the following:

> *The sovereignty of France rests with the French people.* Only its expression was suspended by German occupation. The indispensable element for the restoration of France is the assurance of conditions making that expression possible when the time comes.
>
> *No French political authority can exist or be allowed to attempt to create itself outside of France.* It is the duty of the United States and Great Britain to preserve for the people of France the right and opportunity to determine for themselves what government they will have, and the French people as

15 U.S. State Department, *Foreign Relations of the United* States, vol. 3 (1942) (Europe), 206–207.

> well as the world must receive that solemn assurance.[16] (Italics added.)

The United States set up that principle because it received appeals for recognition not only from the Korean exiles, but also from fifteen other exiled "governments," including Poland, Lithuania, Latvia, Estonia, and France. This principle, incidentally, was published in the State Department Bulletin and was well known to all those concerned.

There was another, perhaps even more important reason not to recognize the Korean Provisional Government, namely, the United States had not determined the status of Korea, the former Japanese colony. In November 1943 at Cairo, President Roosevelt had declared with Prime Minister Churchill and Generalissimo Chiang Kai-shek that "mindful of the enslavement of the people of Korea, [we] are determined that in due course Korea shall become free and independent," but no other decisions had been made by the time Japan surrendered. The decision on Korea had to be delayed because of the involvement of the Soviet Union in the war against Japan. The Soviet forces, as noted earlier, quickly occupied Manchuria and a corner of North Korea as soon as Moscow declared war against Japan on August 9, 1945. The United States, therefore, had to consult Marshall Stalin before deciding Korea's fate.

The death of Roosevelt in April 1944 made the situation more complicated. He had been very accommodating of the Soviet Union, but his successor Harry Truman decided on a more "realistic" or hard-line policy, ushering in the Cold War era. It was only in December 1945 that the two powers issued a joint communiqué at Moscow, announcing a decision to place Korea under a five-year international trusteeship.

---

16 Robert E. Sherwood, *Roosevelt and Hopkins: An Intimate History*, rev. ed. (New York: Grosset and Dunlap, 1950), 681.

The Koreans were to establish a "provisional government" of their own under international supervision. Under this scheme, the Chungking Provisional Government was counted as only one political group among many, rather than a "government" that could rule the liberated country.

The Return of Exiled Leaders

By November 1945, three months after the Japanese surrender, the exiled Korean leaders gave up their efforts to win U.S. recognition and returned to Seoul en masse as individuals. The KPG left a liaison office to take care of remaining business, but that office had no means to help the troops in Beijing. The way the leaders returned to Korea severely demoralized those involved in the Kwangbok army. If KPG was denied recognition and its chiefs could not return to Korea in their official capacity, it was obvious that the Kwangbok army would not be recognized either. The dream of the Kwangbok army troops marching triumphantly through the streets of Seoul with crowds of people on both sides waving flags to welcome them would not come to pass. Battalion Commander Shin Hyŏn-jun dissolved the unit in April 1946, marking the occasion with a brief ceremony. One wonders how he and the officers managed to feed their troops in the meantime. By then, the Korean store owners of Beijing would run for cover as soon as they saw men in tattered uniforms approaching their neighborhood. They were having enough hardship feeding their families in the postwar chaos. Inflation became rampant as the government kept printing money to cover its expenses. The Chinese may have recovered their territory, but the mechanism to collect taxes or tariffs was yet to be established. The government had no other means of supporting its vast army and other expenses, other than printing money. The price of goods doubled and redoubled as a result, while the producers increasingly became more reluctant to sell what they had produced. The market required more than a few months to adjust to the sudden collapse of the Japanese occupation, which had imposed strict control over the economy. A vicious cycle of hyperinflation affected everyone's life.

Thus, Park Chung-Hee learned that the Kwangbok army was an army built on dreams rather than reality. He and hundreds of other young men had been mobilized under lofty slogans, but they were discarded once the dreams dissipated. Additionally, Park's unit became the object of political wrangling among some of the Kwangbok army leaders, and he and other officers had to suffer the humiliation of being disarmed and jailed by the local Chinese army. A unit of Chinese soldiers raided the battalion while they were training, the sound of machine guns shattering the air. They disarmed the troops of whatever rifles they had and put the officers in the battalion's jail.[17] No one offered any explanation for what happened. Nor did they know exactly who the Chinese were. Captain Shin attributed the incident to left-wing Koreans with links to the Chinese Communists who wanted to take over the battalion,[18] but he was probably in error. No one appears to have taken the troops away after the event. The left-wing Korean army he referred to, the Korean Volunteers' Army (Chosŏn Uiyong-kun), had moved with the Chinese Communists to Manchuria, where they had no problem recruiting young Korean men.[19] Yŏm In-ho's account is more credible. He concluded after consulting a number of different sources that the incident

17 Yŏm In-ho, 278–280; Shin Hyŏn-jun, 78–79.
18 Shin Hyŏn-jun, 78–79.
19 For the origins of the Korean Volunteers' Army, see Chong-Sik Lee, "The Korean Communists and Yenan," *China Quarterly* (January–March, 1962), 182–192; on that army's activities in Manchuria, see Shin Sang-ch'o, "The Escape from the Chinese Communists," (in Korean) *Shin-Dong'a* (New East Asia), (March 1965), 318–345 (particularly 356–343).

was the result of a personal feud between two Kwangbok army officers from Xian and Chungking. In any event, whoever perpetrated the incident was clearly not interested in maintaining the integrity of the army or winning the trust or loyalty of either the officers or the men. Using the Chinese troops to disarm the Korean military unit was the most reprehensible crime a Korean could commit. If Kwangbok army officers committed this crime without being aware of the gravity of their act, it clearly showed their depravity.

The new recruits, therefore, would have rejected the organizers of the Kwangbok army in Beijing, even if they had been provided with a steady supply of food. In all likelihood, Park Chung-Hee became disillusioned by the Kwangbok army. General Yi Pŏm-sŏk, the head of the Second Brigade in Xian, later mobilized thousands of young men in South Korea and organized them as the National Youth Corps (*Minjok ch'ŏngnyŏn-dan*) under the auspices of the U.S. occupation forces, but Park did not join it.

Unfortunately, the experience Park encountered in Beijing was not unique. Another former Japanese soldier, Han Sŭng-dong, reported his experience with the Shanghai brigade in the following manner:

> The first thing we noticed was the disorderliness of the Kwangbok Army. There was no line of command or organization.[20]
>
> The next thing we deeply regretted was the ugly discord and conflict among the compatriots. The Three Brigades have been fighting against each other since the Army was established. There was a great conflict between the First Brigade headed

20 Han Sŭng-dong, "The Days with the Kwangbok Army" (in Korean), *Shinch'ŏnji* [The New World] (May 1948): 116–119; the quotation is from p. 116.

> by Kim Won-bong and the Third headed by Kim Ku and Yi Ch'ŏng-ch'ŏn surrounding the question of who should enlist the great number of Korean troops in the Japanese Army. The 1,300 troops in Shanghai had the worst difficulty of maintaining their subsistence. There were no funds for food, clothing, and medical care. But the Kwangbok Army's intention was to absorb all the Korean troops in the Japanese Army that numbered about 30,000 and return to Korea with weapons and grandeur. But this was impossible either for international or economic reasons. Finally the 1,300 troops gained the freedom of speech and organized a committee to promote our quick return to Korea.[21]

The long wait ended on May 6, 1946, when the men of the Beijing battalion were able to board an LST in T'angku. (LSTs, or "Landing Ship, Tanks," were ships built during the Second World War to transport tanks and other heavy equipment.) The KPG representatives probably used all their connections with the U.S. forces in China to facilitate the return of the Koreans stranded in northern China. The LST, a 328-foot- or 100-meter-long ship with a displacement of 3,640 tons, had enough space on various decks to carry thousands, although it had sleeping quarters for only 130 troops, who were packed on board as though on Noah's ark. Fortunately, the refugees needed only a space to squat or lie down, some drinking water, and a minimum amount of food. They would have endured any hardship inflicted upon them if they could only reach Korea. Traveling at a maximum speed of twelve knots, the ship arrived in Pusan two days later, on May 8. The landing required two more days. Thus Park landed in Pusan on May 10.[22] Another passenger was Shin Yong-ho, who later recollected seeing a young officer stripped of his epaulets, standing alone on the deck all day without speaking

21 Ibid., 117.
22 Shin Hyŏn-jun, 89.

a word to anyone.[23] We do not know whether the author of Shin's biography heard the story from Shin Yong-ho or imagined the scene as such, but it does fit the established image of Park. What was he thinking as he stood on the deck in a contemplative mood? While languishing in Beijing? Again, these are questions I wish I could ask Park Chung-Hee.

The Effect of the Beijing Days

Park had experienced Japanese colonialism in Korea as well as the Japanese attempt at creating a puppet state in Manchuria. In 1946, the Chinese were attempting to forge a new nation. The Chinese Nationalist and Communist parties may have agreed on the ultimate goal of building a new nation, but they had been fighting each other for decades because of diametrically opposing views about the details.

Witnessing the Chinese conflict was valuable for Park, because he could see the U.S. government in action. In the wake of the allied victory and concern about the future of China in turmoil, President Harry Truman sent his most prestigious representative, General George Marshall, to intercede between the two parties in hopes of creating a stable China. The first fruit of Marshall's efforts after his arrival in Beijing in January 1946 was the convening of the Chinese People's Consultative Conference, and there were reasons then to be optimistic. Marshall brought together not only the Nationalist and Communist

---

23 Yi Kyu-t'ae, *P'yŏngjŏn Taesan Shin Yong-ho* [Biography of Taesan Shin Yong-ho] (Seoul: Kyobo Mun'go, 2004), 65; this biography contains many inaccuracies. On the same page, he claimed that Park had his Japanese *guntō*, the military sword on his belt, but it was one of the items taken away immediately after the Japanese surrender. Nor would the ship have taken fifteen days to cross the Yellow Sea. It was two days, according to Shin. The refugees' wait in Beijing was far less than a year, as the author claimed. I would, therefore, disregard the author's claim that the refugees landed in Pusan on May 25. Shin Hyŏn-jun said it was May 10.

parties, but also the numerous minor parties of diverse views. They engaged in heated debates and arrived at a formula to establish a new unified Chinese government. The civil war that had started in the 1920s and had torn the nation apart for so long appeared to be at an end.[24] The show of unity, however, turned out to be an illusion. Not even George Marshall, who had virtually directed the Allied war against the Axis powers, could reconcile the irreconcilable. Generalissimo Chiang Kai-shek simply could not accept the Communists as equal partners, even if they were willing to accept a minority status in the coalition government. Chairman Mao Zedong, on the other hand, did not wish to accept the minority position because he was confident of vanquishing Chiang's forces in battle. The two forces, therefore, resumed their confrontation as soon as Marshall took his eyes off China and returned to Washington for consultation in March 1946. The Chinese fighting resumed in April.[25]

Park and his colleagues were aware that fierce ideological battles raged in Korea; while they were in China, they would have watched these events closely, because what was happening in China was similar in character to the events unfolding in Korea. The foreign ministers' conference in December 1945 produced an agreement to let the commanders of Soviet and American occupation forces consult with one another and to establish a new Korean government. The Soviet-American Joint Commission met in Seoul in March 1946 as a follow-up, but the meeting broke up as soon as it started. Since the Moscow conference had given the U.S. and Soviet commanders full authority over the Korean issue, the Koreans had nowhere else to turn for solutions. The issues in Korea were not exactly the same as in China, but there were enough

---

24 Tang Tsou provides a detailed account of this period in his *America's Failure in China* (University of Chicago Press, 1963).
25 See ibid., 412–421.

similarities for the Koreans in Beijing to pay keen attention. We do not know how Park Chung-Hee reacted to the events in China, nor do we know whom he blamed for the failure of the Marshall mission, but the Chinese were engaged in a fierce civil war by the time Park left for Korea in May 1946.

IX. THE TRAUMA OF LIBERATION

His wings clipped, a dispirited and exhausted Park Chung-Hee returned to Korea in May 1946—only to face further hardship. In time, it became clear that Park was extremely lucky to have escaped execution by firing squad, a fate which befell many of his army colleagues, but the same South Korean military court had sentenced Park to life imprisonment. Had Kim Il-sŏng and Joseph Stalin not intervened in the form of the Korean War, the world would never have heard of Park Chung-Hee. Why Park had to endure such tribulations and how he survived them is a gripping story in itself, but more important for us are the lessons Park Chung-Hee learned. How did these events affect Park's outlook on life? How did his experiences affect Korea's history? These questions will be addressed as we trace Park's life through the gates of hell.

The Cold War

While his LST was moored in the port of Pusan for two days waiting for approval from the quarantine officers to disembark, Park Chung-Hee would have noticed a new problem his country was facing. Pusan had been the busiest port in Korea, ferrying cargo between Japan and Korea. Ships carried away rice, fruits, farm animals, and other agricultural products Korea exported. Korea, in turn, imported manufactured products from Japan. Korea had also served as the land bridge between Japan, Manchuria, and China. While Dalian, Yingk'ou, and other ports in Manchuria served as major trading ports, Pusan had also fulfilled some of that function. But in 1946, there was no trace of such traffic. All Park could see were the ships and LSTs loading the last of the Japanese returning to Japan and unloading the Koreans returning from Japan and elsewhere. The demise of the Japanese empire had drastically changed Japanese-Korean economic relations, which in turn severely affected the character of Korea's economy.

The city of Pusan had changed too. The trading port had suddenly been converted into a vast refugee camp. Japanese refugees were still pouring in from Manchuria and North Korea, waiting to be loaded on the ships and LSTs bound for Japan. There were countless numbers of Koreans returning from Japan, Southeast Asia, or the South Pacific. The young Korean men had been drafted into the Japanese army. The older ones had been conscripted to work as laborers in Japanese factories, mines, or on the front lines beyond Japan. Many others had been living abroad for one reason or another. These men had their families with them, but Korea was no longer their true home. They had been away from Korea too long and had no relatives to receive them. All of these refugees had to be fed, sheltered, and transported to other parts of the country. One can easily imagine the noise and stench of a port city that had been thrust into this new role.

The chaos in Pusan more or less epitomized the situation in postwar South Korea as a whole. The Japanese had imposed tight control on Korea since 1905, but the system collapsed with Emperor Hirohito's broadcast of August 15, 1945. The Koreans themselves quickly built a system of their own to replace it, but they soon discovered that they could not be their own masters because they had played no role in liberating their own country. Unbeknownst to the Koreans themselves, the liberators, the United States and the Soviet Union, had decided to divide the country into two parts, and South Korea was placed under American occupation. Americans in Washington had hoped to place Korea under an international trusteeship to prepare Korea for self-government, but they had no other plans for Korea.[1]

---

1 A number of works have been published on this period in English, Japanese, and Korean. I have presented my analysis in "The Road to the Korean War: The United States Policy in Korea, 1945–48," G. Krebs and C. Oberlander (eds.), *1945 in Europe and Asia* (Munchen, Germany: Iudicium, 1997), 195–212.

Since the division of Korea had been predicated on the continuation of an amicable relationship between the Soviet Union and the United States, and since their relationship quickly deteriorated after the disappearance of their common enemies, the long-term question of Korea had to be placed on hold. South Korea, as a result, drifted into confusion, its economy deteriorating daily and frustration and anger rising proportionately. The situation did not augur well for the young man returning from China.

South Korea's food shortages reflected the uncertainties of the time and the ignorance of the U.S. Military Government. Koreans had been suffering for many years from the diminishing food rations the colonial government had provided, and they wanted the ration system abolished. They argued that Korea should have an ample supply of rice now that it had ceased to be Japan's food basket. Korea could consume all the rice it produced, rather than exporting it to Japan. The U.S. Military Government was easily persuaded, and the Koreans celebrated liberation from rations by consuming as much rice as they possibly could. They also brewed rice wines and made rice cakes. Restaurants and bars rose like mushrooms after a rain. But Koreans soon discovered the rice supply was dwindling and the price of food skyrocketing. General John Hodge, Commanding General of the U.S. Forces in Korea, was forced to restore the ration system, which required the restoration of the compulsory purchase of rice and barley from the farmers, leaving the local clerks and the police to administer the system. That system, unfortunately, was the one that the farmers had resented most of all, because the Japanese colonial government had used it to squeeze out every last grain of rice and barley. The officials often broke into the farmers' properties to search for these "grains"—whether the farmers had them or not—beating or abusing the farmers in the process. To the farmers, therefore, the ration system meant nothing other than the restoration of an oppressive system. Nor did the restoration of the ration system please consumers. Rationing meant hunger, because people could barely survive on what the government allowed them. As the food shortage grew worse and food prices skyrocketed, angry citizens vented their frustration by joining street demonstrations. They had welcomed Americans as their liberators, but they soon found the liberators wanting.

At that moment, few Koreans were aware that Korea's agricultural production had steadily declined during the war years because of a shortage of fertilizers. The introduction of chemical fertilizers had increased agricultural productivity before the war, but this had made the depleted soil highly dependent upon fertilization. And once the Japanese military had diverted the production of fertilizers to produce explosives, they became very scarce. As the bombings in Oklahoma City (1995) and Oslo, Norway (2011), showed, nitrogen and phosphoric acid could be used either for explosives or fertilizers, and there was nothing more important for the Japanese military than the production of gunpowder. As a result, the fertilizer supply rapidly declined as the war continued. Tables 4 and 5 show the extent of this reduction. We do not have the data for 1944 and 1945 (for the period from May to November, when fertilizer was used) but the supply undoubtedly diminished further. The situation was even worse in 1946, as the Soviet command in the north refused to deliver what Hungnam Chemical Plant produced to the American command in the south.

Table 4: Percentage of Fertilizer Requirement Supplied for Rice Production[2]

	Nitrogen	Phosphate
1939	105.3	95.7
1940	72.7	78.9
1941	71.4	74.2
1942	82.7	45.5
1943	59.8	21.6

Table 5: Percentage of Fertilizer Requirement Supplied for Barley Production

	Nitrogen	Phosphate
1939	51.7	36.3
1940	46.4	39.8
1941	49.8	38.4
1942	43.0	16.5
1943	35.2	9.2

Table 4 shows that the supply of nitrogen for rice production declined from 105 percent of what was required in 1939 to 59.8 percent; by 1943, there was a cumulative decline of 40 percent. The supply of phosphate, an essential nutrient for plant growth and health, declined from 95.7 percent in 1939 to 21.6 percent in 1943. The supply of fertilizers for barley was even worse; supplies were already very low in 1939 (52 percent of nitrogen and 36 percent of phosphate), but the situation in 1943 was

2 Source for tables 4 and 5: calculated from tables in Chōsen Sōtokufu Nōrinkyokuchō, "Hanbai hiryō shōhi jisseki ni kansuru ken" [Chief, Agr. and Forest Bureau, Korean Government-General, On the Actual Consumption of Fertilizers Sold], (August 26, 1943), a document of Naimusho Kanrikyoku, the Ministry of Interior, Control Bureau. Percentage figures were obtained by dividing the total tonnage of fertilizers supplied by area of cultivation and required amount.

disastrous. We do have the figures for rice and barley production in those years, but it will be redundant for our purpose, since our interest lies in determining the reasons for the food shortage in 1945 and 1946. The farmers could have switched to traditional fertilizers using vegetation, animal, and human wastes, but they no longer had the manpower needed to make such fertilizers. The young men had been drafted into the army; older men had been drafted to serve in Japanese factories and mines.

Those returning from abroad could readily see the signs of poverty in the faces and appearances of those around them. Life was hard for everyone. An episode Chŏng Yŏng-jin recorded makes a poignant illustration of this. In Miryang, Park Chung-Hee and his cohorts encountered three families boarding the northern-bound train from Pusan to Seoul. Their tattered clothing, darkened faces, and everything about them broadcast their suffering. These families had been refugees from Mudanjiang in northern Manchuria. They had returned to their native villages near Miryang several months before, but they found no way to survive there. They decided, therefore, to board the train and return to the land they had abandoned. They knew they would not be welcomed in the old homestead, but they had no other choice.[3] Park Chung-Hee had been to Mudanjiang. That is where he took the entrance examination for the Manchukuo Military Academy.

The situation in Seoul was not much better than in Pusan. The city that had served as Korea's capital since General Yi Sŏng-gye founded the Chosŏn Dynasty in 1392 was embroiled in political turmoil. The Soviet-American Joint Commission was charged with the task of reuniting Korea and establishing an independent government,

3 Chŏng Yŏng-jin, *Ch'ŏngnyŏn Pak Chŏng-hui* [Young Man Park Chung-Hee], vol. 2 (Seoul, 1998), 185–188.

but as noted earlier, the Soviet and American representatives adjourned their meetings on May 11 without reaching any agreement. The major powers might consider the stalemate a minor glitch and move on to more weighty matters, but the situation was different for Koreans. The adjournment signified an indefinite postponement of Korea's independence, as the Commission had not even set a date for the next session. That stalemate put everything in Korea in limbo, particularly in South Korea. Stalin had issued a secret order on September 20, 1945, to establish a "democratic regime" in the Soviet-occupied area, and the Soviet command in Pyongyang systematically implemented political and economic plans for North Korea.[4] However, General John Hodge, the American commander in Seoul, did not receive similar instructions. His military government was thus obliged to continue drifting aimlessly while the various factions of Korean politicians clamored for solutions.

The left wing, centered on the People's National Front, blamed the right-wing groups for the stalemate. Had they not opposed the Moscow decision of December 1945, to install trusteeship in Korea? Was it not natural for the Soviet Union to reject them? The right wing charged the left for selling out Korea's independence by supporting the Soviet position at the Commission. How could the Korean left support the Soviet position to exclude all opponents of the trusteeship in the future Korean government, when the entire people opposed trusteeship? Had not the Communists themselves opposed it until they were compelled by their

4 For Stalin's reasons for this instruction, see "Stalin's Korea Policy, 1945" (in Korean), chapter 5 of Yi Chŏng-sik, *Taehan min'guk ui kiwon* [The Origins of the Republic of Korea] (Seoul: Iljogak, 2006); it was his reaction against the confrontational attitude of the United States at the London Conference of Foreign Ministers that started on September 12.

foreign masters to change their position? Why should the Korean people be forced to wait another five years for their own government? Each side held mass rallies and demonstrations denouncing the other side. Mobs attacked newspapers of the left and right. Added to the political discontent was the police announcement of May 16, 1945, that the Korean Communist Party (KCP) had engaged in producing counterfeit money. The KCP countered by denouncing this as an attempt by the U.S. Military Government to suppress the party. Seoul was in turmoil.

Park Chung-Hee managed to find some of his old friends. One of them was now in the new Constabulary Academy established by the U.S. Military Government. Yi Pyŏng-ju, his old Sinjing classmate, urged Park to join him in the South Korean Constabulary. In a few months, there would be an entrance examination for the second class of the Academy. The Constabulary needed Park Chung-Hee's training and experience.[5] Many of their *sŏnbae*—those who had preceded them in the military academy—were now senior officers in the constabulary.

The reception at home in Sŏnsan was mixed. The Park family was happy to see that Chung-Hee had survived the war, but his older brothers did not hide their disgust and disdain that Park Chung-Hee had abandoned the comfortable teaching job he was trained for, run away seeking glory, and returned home in rags. The third brother Sang-Hee, the person he adored the most, shared the same attitude.[6] He had strongly opposed Chung-Hee's adventure from the very beginning. Park Chung-Hee found his wife and daughter living near Sang-Hee and also

5 Ibid., 188–190.

6 Cho Kap-je, "Pak Chŏng-hui wa kŭui shidae" [Park Chung-Hee and His Era] 1, *Wŏlgan Chosŏn* [Monthly Chosŏn], January 1987, 222–254 (at p. 254).

his sister Chae-Hee and her husband. Park decided to stay at his sister's house, rather than to return to his wife. Chae-Hee would have been the youngest child in the family had Chung-Hee not been born three years later. The two had been close since childhood, and her husband did not object to Chung-Hee's staying with them. Chung-Hee idled away his time, visiting friends occasionally and reading the newspapers, but did not have much else to do. His home village had not changed much and offered no entertainment for him. Here is what Chae-Hee told Cho Kap-je:

> He spent many days at our house rather than going to the mother's or to his wife. He loved his daughter; her mother would send her for him to come to eat, but he would not budge. It was summer. He idled away the days using our home as his base. It was pitiful. When I returned home from visiting the town, I would find him napping on the floor covering his face with the newspaper. Tears would swell up in my eyes looking at such scenes. Even our brother Sang-Hee, who cared about him more than anyone else, shunned him; he would not ask him to join him at meal time even though we lived right next to his house.[7]

Was Park Chung-Hee simply waiting for the time for the entrance examination at the Constabulary Academy? Was he engaged in deep contemplation? In either case, Chŏng Yŏng-jin recorded a dialogue Park Chung-Hee had with his brother Sang-Hee around this time. It is noteworthy because Sang-Hee was deeply involved in politics. Chung-Hee, naturally, was very much interested in his brother's ideological stand, and the author reveals to us Sang-Hee's political identity through the dialogue.

---

7 Ibid., 254.

Park Sang-Hee and Yŏ Un-hyŏng in 1946

Chŏng Yŏng-jin portrayed Park Sang-Hee as a follower of Yŏ Un-hyŏng, or Lyuh Woon Hyung as he spelled his name, which is credible. Sang-Hee had worked in the Taegu branch of Yŏ's newspaper, *Chosŏn Chungang Ilbo*, between 1934 and 1935. It should be recalled that this was the only time Sang-Hee was gainfully employed with a steady salary. Yŏ had been a dashing nationalist leader engaged in the Korean independence movement since 1919, taking part in the establishment of the Korean Provisional Government in Shanghai and making speeches on behalf of the exiled movement in Tokyo, Moscow, and various places in China. His encounters abroad included meeting Lenin, Sun Yat-san, Mao Zedong, Ho Chi-min, Yoshino Sakuzō, Ugaki Kazushige, and Ōkawa Shūmei. Yŏ worked for a few years for Mikhail Borodin, the Soviet advisor to Sun Yat-sen in China, and worked closely with Wang Ching-wei, Sun's immediate successor. Yŏ Un-hyŏng then spent three years in prison in Seoul, having been arrested by the Japanese police in Shanghai in 1929. His record earned him great admiration and respect from much of the Korean public, and he was asked to run the *Chosŏn Chungang Ilbo* in 1933 as president upon his release from prison. This was also the reason Yŏ became the head of the Korean People's Party (Chosŏn Inmindang) in 1946.[8]

Although Yŏ had joined the Koryŏ (Korean) Communist Party in 1923, he was not a Bolshevik. That party was a variant of the nationalist movement of the time and had not even adopted an ideological platform at the time he joined. The party disappeared before long, in

8 Much of Yŏ's career has been covered in volume 1 of *Communism in Korea*, coauthored by Robert A. Scalapino and Chong-Sik Lee. For my longer biography in Korean, see *Yŏ Un-hyŏng* (Seoul: Seoul National University Press, 2008).

any event. Yŏ later told his Japanese interrogators that his Christian background prevented him from accepting the tenets of Communism, such as dialectical materialism or violent revolution. He had been a missionary's assistant in Seoul for seven years before he went to China in 1913 for further education and served as a lay preacher for the Koreans in Shanghai for a few additional years. Yŏ could best be described as a Fabian Socialist wishing to bring about an egalitarian society through democratic means. His "harmonist" personality and his moderately left-wing orientation, however, became a severe handicap in postwar Korean politics, where extremism prevailed. The right wing rejected him as a Communist sympathizer, while the Korean Communist Party regarded him as a convenient tool to mobilize the progressive young men he attracted.

On August 16, 1945, Yŏ Un-hyŏng organized the Committee for the Establishment of the National Government, known in Korean as Kŏn-Jun, immediately after the Japanese surrender, but it was soon taken over by the Communists he had enlisted in the organization. Yŏ then organized the People's Party on his own in November, but it was again infiltrated by Communist Party agents. In fact, Kim Se-yong, the head of Yŏ's propaganda department, was a member of the KCP. Yŏ's speeches on critical issues were moderate in tone, but his party's propaganda department would issue statements that mimicked those of the Communist Party.[9] The public, therefore, treated the People's Party as a fringe organization of the KCP, and Yŏ made no effort to dispel the impression. While Yŏ was deeply involved in the Left-Right Coalition Committee that the U.S. Military Government promoted, he also joined

9 See my *Yŏ Un-hyŏng*, 578–585 on the discrepancy between Yŏ's speeches and the People's Party's pronouncements.

the KCP-led Democratic National Front, leading to the charge that he was an opportunist. Yŏ believed, however, that the new nation needed the collaboration of both the right and the left, although he did not hide his distaste for the right-wing extremists. What is important from our standpoint is that Yŏ was the man Park Sang-Hee supported, and Sang-Hee was a member of Yŏ's Inmindang or the People's Party.

Yŏ Un-hyŏng may have been able to maintain his integrity as a man walking a fine line between the left and right, but the People's Party members at the local level could not. Park Sang-Hee, for example, had been active in establishing the People's Committee in Sŏnsan around the time Kŏn-Jun was established in Seoul, and he continued to hold on to his title as head of the local security department within the committee. That title was equivalent to police chief, the committee being a new name for the Sŏnsan prefectural or county government. The U.S. Military Government denounced the people's committees as unauthorized and illegal organizations, but this had no effect on Sang-Hee and others at the local level. Those participating in the People's Committees concurrently worked as a part of the Democratic National Front, protesting the Military Government's suppression of the People's Committees and its misgovernment of the country as a whole. Thus Sang-Hee became a part of the movement against the U.S. Military Government, while Yŏ Un-hyŏng collaborated with it.

The Conflict between the USMG and the KCP

Why did the U.S. Military Government (USMG) suppress the People's Committees? It was because United States government did not recognize the People's Committees as a legitimate body to govern the country. The United States had declared its intention to let the Korean people govern their own country "in due course" at the Cairo conference of 1943, but the Allied powers fighting against Japan since then had not decided on the time or manner of establishing an independent government in Korea. The situation would have been different had the Koreans liberated their country from Japan on their own, but such was not the case. The United States dispatched its military forces to South Korea in September 1945, and the United States was to govern that territory until the Allied powers agreed on Korea's future. In the meantime, the USMG was the sole government power in South Korea, and it could not accept the authority of the People's Committees.

Some Koreans understood and accepted the explanation the U.S. commander Major General Hodge provided, but many did not. They insisted on the right to self-government, regardless of the circumstances. They argued that the committees derived their authority from the Korean People's Republic, proclaimed by a "national conference of the Korean people" on September 6, 1945, and hence the USMG had no right to suppress them. It did not matter to them that the "national conference" did not represent anyone other than a crowd that had been gathered.[10] The conflict between the USMG and the KCP escalated in May 1946 when the USMG discovered a counterfeit operation at the KCP headquarters building in Seoul, which had previously been a government printing facility. The military government ordered the arrest of KCP leaders, who quickly went underground or fled to North Korea, but the fight was on. These events were followed by KCP's new strategy that virtually turned South Korea into a battleground between the KCP and the USMG. The Communists blamed "U.S. imperialism"

10 Cf. Yi Chŏng-sik, "The People's Republic and the Post-Liberation Politics" [in Korean], *Han'guksa shimin kangjwa* [Citizen's Lectures on Korean History], no. 12 (1993), 15–45.

for the clash, but the suppression of Communism was not part of the American agenda at this time. What happened in Japan then can be cited for comparison. The Communist Party there maintained cordial relations with U.S. occupation forces, even thriving under them.[11] General Hodge in Seoul, it should be added, was subordinate to General Douglas MacArthur in Tokyo, who was the general commander of the Allied forces in the Far East. Hodge had been known as "the soldier of soldiers" and had no ax of his own to grind.

The New Moscow Strategy of July 1946

Neither the Americans nor the Koreans realized it, but the KCP's new hard-line strategy resulted from developments to the north of the Yalu and Tumen Rivers, on the border between Manchuria and Korea. What mattered to Joseph Stalin, the supreme leader of the international Communist camp at this time, were not the borderlines, but the struggle against the United States. Manchuria and Korea constituted the same front line in his eyes, and all resources had to be mustered to defeat the Americans. The problem for him at this time was that Chiang Kai-shek's forces were demolishing the Communist army in Manchuria. If Chiang Kai-shek succeeded in defeating the Communists there, all the assistance the Soviet Union had provided the Chinese Communist Party (CCP) since August 1945 would be wasted. The CCP's future would look bleak indeed, if the situation deteriorated further. The CCP had dispatched most of its crack troops there in the hope of squashing Chiang Kai-shek's forces, but they were nonetheless outmatched.

---

11 See Robert A. Scalapino, *The Japanese Communist Movement, 1920–1966* (Berkeley: University of California Press, 1967), chapter 2: "Making Communism Lovable." Instead of clashing with the U.S. occupation, the Japanese Communist Party concentrated on making Communism lovable.

For Stalin, the events in Manchuria meant more than a match between the Chinese Communists and Chinese nationalists, because he could easily see the hand of the United States behind the successes of the nationalist forces. General Marshall had been in China since December 1945, deeply involved in Chinese domestic politics. Even though Marshall's official role was that of a neutral mediator, the CCP believed he was aiding the Nationalist Party.[12] What made it worse from Stalin's viewpoint was that the American-equipped New First and New Sixth Armies had overwhelmed the Communist forces.[13]

Stalin was in a convenient position to help the Chinese Communists because North Korea was under Soviet occupation; hence, he was the de facto ruler there. He permitted the Chinese Communist forces to use North Korea as a sanctuary, supply depot, and transportation route between eastern and western Manchuria. Manchuria and North Korea, it should be remembered, are separated only by the Tumen (Tuman in Korean) River to the east of Changpai (Paektu in Korean) Mountain and the Yalu (or Amnok in Korean) River on the west. The emaciated CCP forces could cross the Tumen from eastern Manchuria, move through the railways and roads in North Korea, and exit into southwestern Manchuria across the Yalu. The material transported through North Korea reached 300,000 metric tons by 1948. Stalin provided the CCP forces not only an opportunity to recuperate and regroup in North Korea, but also munitions and other essentials from North Korea. The CCP obtained more than 2,000 railway cars of war materials.[14] Chiang's

12 Tsou, *America's Failure in China*, 420.

13 Ibid., 419.

14 Chen Jian, *China's Road to the Korean War* (New York: Columbia University Press, 1994), 107–109; North Korea at this time was under Soviet occupation as

Guomindang forces pursuing the CCP, however, could not go beyond the Korean border.

Thus, the new strategy of July 1946 for the Korean Communists was an extension of the war in Manchuria. Stalin summoned the two Korean Communist leaders, Kim Il-sŏng and Pak Hŏn-yŏng, to Moscow in July 1946 and issued new marching orders.[15] It was time, he said, for the Korean Communists to consolidate their forces and display their power not only in North Korea but in South Korea as well. Fomenting disturbances in the American zone would divert attention from what was happening in the north. It would also help to persuade the Americans of the futility of their efforts to control the Asian continent.

The first requirement for this strategy was to integrate all the left-wing elements in North and South Korea, respectively, into one integrated unit. Thus, in August the North Korean Communist Party absorbed the more moderate New People's Party, led by returnees from northern China, and created a new entity known as the North Korean Workers' Party. The Soviet Command in Pyongyang then ordered the KCP in South Korea to absorb the two left-wing parties, including the People's Party, headed by Yŏ Un-hyŏng. Yŏ's refusal to follow the merger plan delayed the establishment of the South Korean Workers' Party (SKWP) until November, but it did not stop the KCP from moving toward the next stage of disrupting South Korea's economy. The KCP already had a strong grip over the labor and farmer movements there, and it could order a general strike.

South Korea was under American occupation. Stalin, therefore, had full authority and power over the North Korean territory. Kim Il-sŏng was the chairman of the North Korean People's Committee and hence the head of the North Korean government, but Stalin had the supreme legal authority there.

15 Chungang Ilbosa, *Pirok Chosŏn minjujuiui inmin konghwaguk* [Democratic People's Republic of Korea, the Secret Records] (Seoul: Chungang Ilbosa), 1992, 326–330.

The Strikes as a Prelude to the October Riot

All forces thus converged for the final clash between the USMG and the Communists. Unfortunately, the USMG unwittingly provided the KCP the momentum to launch a general strike at least a month ahead of schedule. Seeing the state-owned railroad company continuing to run a deficit, the USMG's transportation department announced on August 20 its plan to reduce its labor force by 25 percent and to turn all of its employees into daily workers.[16] This was a measure virtually designed to enrage all employees. The railroad labor union submitted a demand to retract the announcement, and when it was ignored, a strike was ordered. Beginning with the work stoppage at Pusan on the twenty-third, the entire railroad with its forty thousand workers screeched to a halt. The Korean economy had depended on the railways because trucks were few in number and Korea had no gasoline supply of its own. Nor was there any private railroad to rely on. Printers' unions followed suit on September 26, which halted the production of newspapers. Postal and telephone workers in Seoul also joined in by the twenty-eighth.[17] No one doubted these strikes were coordinated from the center. Yŏ Un-hyŏng had been informed about it and tried to persuade the KCP leadership to abandon its plan, but in vain.[18]

While there were some violent incidents in the Seoul rail yard at Yongsan between the strikers, police, and right-wing youth and labor organizations, the conflict there was localized. But such was not the

---

16 Kim Nam-Sik, *Sillok Namnodang* [Veritable Record of the South Korean Workers' Party], (Seoul: Shin Hyŏnsil-sa, 1975), 279.

17 See ibid., 278–281.

18 Yŏ Un-hyŏng reported this to the Americans on October 1, after his brief visit to Pyongyang where he talked to Soviet and North Korean leaders; see U.S. XXIV Corps, G-2 Summary, October, 1946; for a detailed account of Yŏ's trip, see Major General Romanenko to Colonel General Schitikov, dated September 28, 1946; Jeon Hyeon-su (ed. and trans.), *Switikof ilgi, 1946–1948* [Diary of Terenty F. Shitikov, 1946–1948] (Seoul: Kuksa py'ŏnch'an Wiwŏnhoe, 2004), 174–179.

case in Taegu, where Park had attended school. The strikes led to massive demonstrations, which in turn escalated into a riot. The rioters then spread out to the towns and villages, burning police stations and killing policemen and other USMG collaborators. These events, collectively known as the October Uprising or the Taegu Riot, require our attention because Park Sang-Hee became one of its victims.

The Taegu Uprising

Kim Nam-sik provided a fairly detailed and credible account of these events,[19] but we cannot be certain whether the KCP leadership in Seoul or even the provincial leaders in Taegu had planned to fan the strikes into violent confrontations. This is an important question because the Taegu Riot became a harbinger of massive and vicious violence between the left- and right-wing forces in South Korea. The local leaders or subleaders at various levels could easily incite the masses to violence, with or without instructions from the central leadership. The USMG's lack of effective governance and the overall indifference of the United States created a situation in which the frustrated masses were willing to follow almost anyone who offered an alternative. Ironically, the USMG's mismanagement of the national police was a tinderbox that kindled an explosion.

The police were a favorite target of the left because they had been at the front line against the People's Committees. The police symbolized the continuation of Japanese colonial rule, particularly because the USMG decided to utilize all of the vicious interrogators notorious for their cruelty against the enemies of the Japanese empire. The national police under the USMG now contained those who had served

19 Kim Nam-sik, 283–289.

the Japanese rulers in South Korea and in the north as well. They had all moved to the south as they found the Soviet-occupied zone inhospitable. Additionally, the USMG used the police and town clerks to collect food for city dwellers, a situation that did not sit well with farmers. Nothing had changed from the colonial era, as far as the farmers were concerned.

This explains why the police station in Taegu became the first target of the rioters there and how the violence spread like a wildfire to nearby communities. The second targets were the township officers. The following story depicts the atmosphere in which Park Chung-Hee's older brother was killed. The "*myŏn*" in the story refers to the township. The "taxes-in-kind" refer to the food collected by the government.

> The people of our hamlet live near the city of Taegu. One morning we were awakened early by the ringing of the town's alarm bell. Going outside, I saw some fifty men passing our house, carrying shovels, picks, and clubs. They were farmers from a nearby hamlet. Some were old, some young, and there were even boys who had barely finished elementary school. They were shouting, "Let's go to the myŏn (township) office!"
>
> I joined them, and off we went to the myŏn office, about one kilometer away. There, two young men in Western clothes were making speeches. "Taegu has been occupied by the People's Committee," they shouted. "The police have been disarmed. Now we must destroy all running dogs of the Japs. We must have a world where there are no more taxes in kind…"
>
> Our life at that time was miserable. Commodity prices were rising every day. "Liberation," moreover, was a sham. The rascals who had been *myŏn* office clerk under the Japanese were still there, behaving as arrogantly as ever. If a farmer fell into arrears in paying his taxes, he would make that farmer kneel on the ground, even if it was a rainy day, and berate him. He

> himself was a farmer who had gotten rich under the Japanese. Hence, the farmers marching to the *myŏn* office were really seeking revenge for the evil tax-in-kind system, and on the arrogant bastards. That was all.
>
> But the leadership—and the agitation that provoked us to action—came from those young men who claimed to represent the People's Committee. Of course, at that time, the People's Committees were everywhere. If a person had a sixth grade education, he almost automatically became a member of the local People's Committee. In any case, the farmers rushed to the *myŏn* office, destroying everything in it and burning all of the documents. The police fled, as did the clerks. But the farmers followed them, burned their houses down, and even built a special fire for the book containing their ancestral records. That night, in celebration, the farmers had a big feast and everyone got drunk. We all believed that a world without taxes or clerks had arrived.[20]

The local police were not ready for such events and were easily overpowered. Reinforcements sent from Seoul, including American troops, quelled the riots in the cities, but they were too late in most towns. Police casualties included 33 killed and 135 wounded.[21] In many towns, daredevil young men exchanged fire with the police with the rifles they had taken from police stations.

The grievances related above were real. To their credit, the Americans had abolished the universally condemned "taxes-in-kind" program when they landed in Korea, but finding a shortage of food,

---

20 Yi Mok-u, "Taegu sip-il p'oktong sakŏn" [The Taegu October First Riot Incident], *Sedae* (Generation), October 1965, 226–233, quoted from pp. 230–231; the English translation is from Scalapino and Lee, *Communism in Korea*, 262.

21 Ch'oe Yŏng-hui, *Kyŏkdong ui haebang 3nyŏn* [The Turbulent 3 Years after the Liberation] (Ch'unch'ŏn: Hallim University, 1996), 274.

soon restored it and left the same rascals to administer it. That, however, did not solve the problem of food shortages. The colonial government in the past would have imported food grains from Manchuria to relieve the food shortage, but that option was no longer available. Clashes with the police expanded to other regions of South Korea until the end of the month.[22] The Americans did not appear to know what they were doing; All they brought, as far as the farmers were concerned, was chaos, confrontation, and continued suffering.

How did all this affect Park Sang-Hee? What role did he play in the uprising, and how was he killed? Park, it should be remembered, was only a minor actor seen from the national or provincial perspective, and no one in an official position bothered to record what happened to him. But according to Chŏng Yŏng-jin, Park Sang-Hee was shot by a police unit from a neighboring province, which had arrived to restore police authority in Sŏnsan. Local men had raided and occupied the police station, and some of the hotheads wanted to execute the police chief and a few others known to have been malicious under the military government. Park Sang-Hee, according to our author, placated the crowd and succeeded not only in preventing the violence but in dispersing the crowd. The grateful police chief would have protected Sang-Hee, but he started to run when the police unit from another town arrived. Seeing him and others fleeing through the rice field, the out-of-towners aimed and shot the three men down.[23]

22 Demonstrations and riots occurred in Seoul and other cities on October 22; ibid., 281.

23 Chŏng Yŏng-jin, vol. 2, 304–305; he put the story down in the form of Park Sang-Hee's old friend Hwang T'ae-sŏng telling it to Park Chung-Hee, but we cannot establish the veracity of the information.

Whether one believes the story or not, there is no doubt that Park Sang-Hee was killed, and in all probability, it was the police bullets that killed him. He probably went to the police station because he was in charge of the Security Section under the People's Committee system. If the townspeople believed the story about the People's Committee replacing the U.S. Military Government, as the story above suggested, Park Sang-Hee would have become the new police chief. Since he was a well-known figure in Sŏnsan starting in the late 1920s, the police chief would have readily turned over his authority. That may explain the fact that he and his cohort remained at the police station until the police unit from a neighboring town arrived. He and others would not have been shot to death had they not attempted to flee the scene.

X. THE SOUTH KOREAN WORKERS' PARTY

I have traced the events leading to Park Sang-Hee's death in considerable detail because they directly affected Park Chung-Hee's life. All the sources agree that Park Chung-Hee joined the South Korean Workers' Party (Namnodang) in anger and thus "became a Communist" soon after his brother's death. But that proposition raises important questions about the future president of the Republic of Korea. Is it plausible that he got angry about his brother's death even when it was due to "an accident" caused by a "misunderstanding," as we have been told? Or did his brother die in some different way? One must ask these questions because we do not know for certain Park Chung-Hee's motivations in joining the Workers' Party. It is important to emphasize here that the party he joined was not the Communist Party, as I shall present in the following.

All accounts suggest that a Reverend Yi Chae-bok, a friend of Park Sang-Hee, persuaded Park Chung-Hee to join the *Namnodang*, the South Korean Workers' Party. Kim An-il, who was then a major in charge of the Constabulary's Special Investigation Corps, remembered reading Park's "Confessions," submitted to Major Kim Chang-yong, the investigator. Park said in his statement that he had joined the party after meeting Yi Chae-bok, who was at his brother's house helping his grief-stricken widow. Yi was at that time a Christian minister, but was also in charge of organizing the officers in the Constabulary for Namnodang.[1] He subsequently brought Park propaganda material, including *The Communist Manifesto*, and urged him to join the party to avenge his brother's murder. Kim An-il got the impression from Park's confession that he was not an ideologue but someone drawn to the party for emotional reasons.[2]

---

1 Cho Kap-je, *Nae mudŏm e ch'im ŭl paett'ŏra* [Spit on My Grave], vol. 2 (Seoul: Chosŏn Ilbosa, 1998), 218, 224.
2 Ibid., loc. cit.

According to Chŏng Yŏng-jin, however, Yi Chae-bok asked Park to join the party when he was at the Eighth Regiment located at Ch'unch'ŏn, some seventy-five kilometers northeast of Seoul. Yi had visited Park twice before, but the talks were centered on his brother and the socio-political conditions in general. Then, on the third visit, Yi asked Park to be introduced to his superiors in the regiment because he wanted to treat them to show his appreciation. Yi wanted to be introduced as a business-man and his maternal uncle. Park thought such a gesture appropriate and arranged a dinner at a restaurant where the regiment commander and others were invited. It was after the dinner that Yi Chae-bok revealed his identity as a Namnodang organizer who wanted Park to join the party. Yi wanted Park's occasional advice and introductions to various officers in the constabulary.[3]

Much later, after the coup in 1961, Park told another story to one of his subordinates who was curious about the escapade. Kim Chong-shin had just talked to General Chŏng Kang, Park's classmate at the Constabulary Military Academy, who was certain that Park was a Communist.[4] This was Park's response:

> It was when I was a Captain serving as instructor at the Military Academy. One day, Yi Chae-bok, a good friend of my brother, came from Taegu and told me there would be a gathering of the friends from my hometown that Sunday and I should be there. It was a little boring at the Academy and having been told it was for my honor I did go to the gathering. I found out later that all my brother's friends at that gathering were Reds. I did not sign any application or put a seal to any document, but

3 Chŏng Yŏng-jin, *Ch'ŏngnyŏn Pak Chŏng-hui*, vol. 3, 15–22.
4 Chungang Ilbo, *Sillok Pak Chŏng-hui*, 67.

> the event caused me to suffer severe torture and face the Court Martial.[5]

There is a discrepancy in these stories about the timing and place of Park's admission to Namnodang. Had it taken place soon after his brother's death (November 11, 1946), it would have been late 1946 or early 1947, the period when he was in Ch'unch'ŏn. He was there between December 1946 and September 1947. If Park Chung-Hee's recollection was accurate, it would have taken place later, after September, because he was appointed as the military academy's instructor that month. I am inclined to believe he joined Namnodang while he was in Ch'unch'on. Yi Chae-bok would not have brought up Namnodang before the end of 1946, as Park was still under deep emotional stress until then.

Park was in Ch'unch'ŏn when Namnodang was engaged in a frenzied campaign to expand its membership, aiming not just to double its membership, but to expand it five times over. This was because the Soviet-American Joint Commission had resumed its meetings on May 1, 1947, and there was the prospect of the Commission's consulting Korean sociopolitical organizations to establish the "Korean Provisional Government." The party, therefore, launched a massive propaganda campaign to discredit right-wing leaders and organizations and, at the same time, expand its membership. The party wanted to prove beyond any doubt that it alone had "the absolute support of the people."[6] Park Chung-Hee was no ordinary person from the party's perspective, so having him join it was important for the membership drive as well.

---

5 Ibid., 68.

6 Kim Nam-sik, *Sillok Namnodang* [Veritable Record of the South Korean Workers' Party] (Seoul: Shin Hyŏnsil-sa, 1975), 341–342.

All versions of the story agree, in any event, that Reverend Yi Chae-bok played the key role in persuading Park to join. Each version also identifies Yi as the Party's man in charge of organizing officers in the constabulary. We do not know the circumstances of Yi's joining the party, but he had become active in the local people's committee, and then established himself as the head of the Security Department (*Bo-an-bu*) of the North Kyŏngsang Province. Yi thus became Park Sang-Hee's immediate superior in the SKWP's chain of command. Yi was the security chief of the province while Park Sang-Hee was of the Sŏnsan County. Yi Chae-bok told Park Chung-Hee that he had been a good friend of his brother, Sang-Hee, for a long time. Yi was a handsome and gregarious man who easily established a rapport with persons from all walks of life.[7] There is no doubt that Yi held an important position in the party. He was promoted to the position of the Chief of the Military Department in the party headquarters, although we do not know when that happened.[8]

Park Chung-Hee told Kim Chong-shin that he did not sign any application, nor did he put his seal on any document, but Park did affirm his membership in Namnodang. But what did joining the South Korean Workers' Party mean to Park Chung-Hee? Was he aware of the magnitude of his action at that time? Furthermore, did he in fact become a Communist by joining Namnodang? If he did, what did "becoming a Communist" mean at this time?

Park and Namnodang

Normally, joining the Communist Party would automatically signify the person's identity as a Communist. The Communist Party would

7 Chŏng Yŏng-jin, vol. 3, 15–16; Kim Nam-sik, *Sillok Namnodang*, 287.
8 Kim Nam-sik, 287.

require and train all candidates to follow Communist ideology, beginning with dialectical materialism, labor theory of values, surplus value, and so on, and make certain that (s)he would dedicate her/himself to the cause of destroying the Capitalist system. But the party Park joined in 1947 was not a "Communist Party." It was rather the Workers' Party, an amalgamation of the KCP and the two left-wing parties that had significantly different ideologies. The Communist plan was to merge the heterogeneous elements under one rubric, hoping to forge a disciplined corps of fighters against the United States. This was something Yŏ Un-hyŏng, the head of the People's Party, could not accept. As noted earlier, he was a Fabian Socialist, opposed to the use of violence to attain power. The KCP members who had infiltrated the People's Party leadership maneuvered the situation to let that party join Namnodang, but Yŏ adamantly opposed the idea. Yŏ established another party of his own and declared its mission was to work with the U.S. Military Government. Yŏ Un-hyŏng enraged the KCP to the extent that he suffered a number of physical attacks and a kidnapping.[9] This was the man Park Chung-Hee's brother Sang-Hee followed. We do not know how much attention Park had paid to these complicated events, but it would be wrong to cite Park's membership in Namnodang as prima facie evidence of him being a Communist.

Nor is there evidence that Park wanted to be a "Communist." Many young Korean men became Communists under colonial rule through their readings of Marxist literature, but this is not a route Park would have taken. His background, in fact, made it impossible for him to become a Communist. He had been trained by the Japanese as an anti-Communist

9 For details on the Communist attack against Yŏ Un-hyŏng, see my *Yŏ Un-hyŏng*, 619, 621–622.

soldier. The Japanese empire severely suppressed Communism and forced every Communist and proto-Communist to abandon it. The Japanese empire even joined Nazi Germany and fascist Italy in 1940 and formed the Anti-Communist Axis. The major task of Japan's Kantō-gun (the Kwantung army) in Manchuria, moreover, was to attack the Soviet Union. Park's own regiment was engaged in battles against the Chinese Communist army just before the Japanese Empire collapsed. Park also had personal reasons to fear the Soviet Union. Having been a part of the puppet Manchukuo army, he was afraid that the Soviet Army would send him away to a Siberian work camp, as it had many of his former comrades. This is why Park chose not to return to Korea through Soviet-occupied Manchuria after the Japanese surrender in August 1945. He had heard many horrendous stories about Soviet occupation in North Korea, and many of his former classmates at Sinjing had told him about their bitter experiences in the Soviet-occupied territory.[10]

The timing of Park's admission to the party also suggests that it would not have been necessary for him to go through an ideological conversion. Reverend Yi Chae-bok did not need to indoctrinate Park in the principles of Communism. The story about Yi handing Park a copy of *The Communist Manifesto* was more likely conjecture than fact. All Yi needed was to persuade Park to oppose American rule, to eliminate injustice, and to work toward the establishment of an egalitarian society. Cho Kap-je argued that Namnodang simply fit Park's character. Park had always found his existing surroundings wanting, and he longed for a change. Resistance against the establishment was in his blood. It was Namnodang's resistance against American forces and its call for

10 Yi Ki-gŏn, a graduate of the first class of the Manchukuo Military Academy, served in the North Korean Army and told Park about his bitter experience there (Cho Kap-je (1992), 166–167).

progressive reforms that Park found attractive, rather than its underlying ideology.[11]

It is also likely that Park Chung-Hee treated the matter of joining Namnodang akin to his brother's joining the People's Party. Yi Chae-bok could very well have presented Namnodang as a successor to the People's Party, so that Park would essentially be following in his brother's footsteps. Namnodang did not exist while Park Sang-Hee was alive; it came into being twelve days after he was killed.

I am inclined to believe Park Chung-Hee consented to become a Namnodang member without attaching much importance to what Yi Chae-bok so eagerly sought. Park had reasons to be disgusted at American rule, and he did not need to be persuaded to act against it. Furthermore, he had no special reason to brush the reverend off. After all, Namnodang was not an outlaw organization at this time, and many other officers in his regiment were already members.[12] General Hodge himself had showed his goodwill toward the party by sending an army major as his representative to the party's inaugural conference on November 23, 1946.[13] This may explain why the conservatively oriented officers of the Constabulary did not regard Namnodang as their archenemy at this time. The Military Government was actually engaged in a war against the Communists on many fronts, but it had not officially

---

11 Cho Kap-je, *Pak Chŏng-hui*, vol. 1 (Seoul: Kkach'i, 1992), 167.

12 Chŏng Un-yŏn, *Sillok kun'in Pak Chŏng-hui* [Veritable Record of the Soldier Park Chung-Hee] (Seoul: Kaema, 2004), 144–145; Yŏm Chŏng-t'ae, a graduate of the third class of the Constabulary Academy, worked under Park Chung-Hee at the Eighth Regiment. He said there were numerous SKWP members among the officers in their regiment beginning with the Deputy Regiment Commander Yi Sang-jin, Park's classmate at the Manchukuo Military Academy. (P. 145). Chungang Ilbo, *Sillok Pak Chŏng-hui*, 69, provides the same information.

13 Kim Nam-sik, 310.

condemned the leftist camp as a whole. The resumption of the Soviet-American Commission sessions also required that the USMG tone down its attacks. The USMG's perspective toward Namnodang went through a drastic change several months later, but it was something Park could not have foreseen.

Thus, Park's disgust and aversion to U.S. rule stands out as the most likely cause for his joining Namnodang. It was his way of registering his antagonism against the new rulers. The fact that his brother was killed by American-controlled police gave him even more impetus to join Namnodang, which presented itself as the champion of resistance against American imperialism. The party stood for the protection of people's rights. If there was anything that the Koreans could agree on in 1946, it was American misgovernment of Korea. The United States showed no indication of wanting to help the Korean people recover from the fatigue of the colonial rule ending with the long war that had exhausted its people, land, and infrastructure. There was also the matter of American soldiers' behavior, which was repulsive to many Koreans. They were the plebeians and behaved that way. Park Chung-Hee had been trained in the Prussian manner.

Anti-Americanism in South Korea

Park was not alone in his views, it should be noted. The Koreans were deeply disappointed by the Americans. On August 11, 1946, just a few days before the first anniversary of Korean liberation, the "Korean Public Opinion Association" (Han'guk Yŏron Hyŏphoe) asked the Seoul residents on the streets what American policy they considered positive: 2 percent cited "sanitary facilities" while the remaining 98 percent could not think of any. On the negative side, 53 percent cited food policies and

31 percent industrial and residential policies.[14] The Korean disappointment was turning into anti-Americanism according to the Special Inter-Departmental Committee on Korea organized in Washington, D.C. The following is an excerpt from the committee's report to Secretary of State Marshall and Secretary of War Patterson dated February 25, 1947.

> The Korean people are daily growing more antagonistic in their attitude toward military government, toward U.S. objectives in Korea, and even toward the United States itself. These antagonisms have already caused riots and disorders involving loss of life. There is every reason to expect an increase in the use of tactical troops to suppress disorders with all the attendant complications in world public opinion. It is therefore obviously extremely unwise to rely solely on present ineffective program.[15]

The Committee consisted of representatives of the U.S. Army, Navy, and State Departments. It was the first time since the U.S. government had gotten involved in Korea that high-level authorities had studied the situation—and they found the situation abominable. Why had the U.S. government allowed such a development?

The principal reason for U.S. "misgovernance" was Korea's remoteness from the United States. It was remote not only geographically, but also economically, culturally, and politically. Americans had eagerly sought contact with the Hermit Kingdom in the late nineteenth century when it had shown signs of opening its doors, but they soon found

---

14 Ch'oe Yŏng-hui, "Silgi 30 nyŏn" [Real Record of Thirty Years], no. 124, *Han'guk ilbo* [Korea Daily], February 8, 1975, 5.

15 Memorandum by the Special Inter-Departmental Committee on Korea, February 25, 1947, to the Secretary of State (Marshall) and the Secretary of War (Patterson), U.S. Department of State, *Foreign Relations of the United States* (cited hereafter as FRUS), vol. 6 (1947), 611.

the country not worthy of attention. The first U.S. diplomats reaching Seoul reported that the Korean rulers had no backbone and the government officials were corrupt to the core; there were no resources to speak of; and people suffered from perpetual poverty. From that time on, the Americans, except for a small number of missionaries, simply stayed away from the peninsula. Korea became an American concern only in 1943, when President Roosevelt joined Winston Churchill and Chiang Kai-shek at Cairo—a meeting at which the leaders declared Korea would to be granted independence "in due course," without specifying a time. Having no direct interest in adding that country to its sphere of influence, the State Department proposed "*international* trusteeship" over Korea.

The surging hostility between the United States and the Soviet Union after that time made it totally impossible to implement "international trusteeship," which required very close cooperation among the trustees. However, no one had come up with an alternative. Americans were too busy with a host of other issues at the end of World War II. The U.S. government also needed to await a resolution of the internal conflict in China, because the strategic map in East Asia could not be drawn without it. President Truman hoped General Marshall could somehow resolve the conflict between Mao Zedong and Chiang Kai-shek, but the outcome was still uncertain. This was the situation until late 1947. Unknown to most Koreans, their future depended on how the Chinese civil war played out. The United States placed Korea in limbo, an indeterminate state, and the USMG simply drifted in the rising tides of the "Cold War." Yŏ Un-hyŏng succinctly summarized the situation in his letter of November 8, 1946, to General Hodge, as related by his political advisor to the State Department.

> Lyuh (Yŏ Un-hyŏng) attributes the prevailing exploitation of natural resources, disrepair and stagnation in South Korea to the absence of permanent officials bearing full responsibility and suggested that the civil government be turned over to the Korean people.[16]

The policy of "drift" resulted in a high rate of inflation and the shortage of food as reported by Arthur Bunce, General Hodge's economic advisor, to the Secretary of State on December 27, 1946. The two studies he had commissioned reported that (1) "Military Government in Korea has largely financed its operations through the printing of money and that the currency in circulation is increasing at a rate approaching one billion yen per month"; and (2) "Because of the large increase in population and reduction in grain production due to lack of fertilizers and other factors, the food situation for the coming year will be quite critical and will necessitate substantial imports of grains from the United States."[17]

This was the situation when the Special Inter-Departmental Committee on Korea proposed in February 1947 a massive three-year aid package to South Korea to rebuild the country as a showcase for democracy.[18] However, the "realists" in Washington D.C., including U.S. Army Secretary Robert Patterson and the State Department's Director of the Policy Planning Staff George Kennan, quickly shot the idea down. Kennan favored instead a plan in which the United States

---

16 The Political Advisor in Korea (Langdon) to the Secretary of State, Seoul, November 24, 1946, *FRUS, vol. 8* (1946), 770–775, quoted from p. 775.

17 The Economic Adviser in Korea (Bunce) to the Secretary of State, December 27, 1946, FRUS, vol. 8 (1946), 783–784.

18 Memorandum by the Special Inter-Departmental Committee on Korea, February 25, 1947, to the Secretary of State (Marshall) and the Secretary of War (Patterson), FRUS, vol. 6 (1947), 608–615.

would "cut our losses and get out of there as gracefully but promptly as possible."[19]

The South Korean Constabulary

It was in this atmosphere that Park Chung-Hee decided to join his former colleagues who had already established themselves in the South Korean Constabulary. I shall place these events in chronological order.

The resumption of Park's military career took place in September 1946, a full year after Korea was liberated from Japan, by his admission to the Korean Constabulary Military Academy in Seoul. It may have been humiliating for a veteran officer to take orders from the younger and less-trained men who outranked him solely by virtue of their earlier entrance into the constabulary, but Park is said to have endured the eighty days of retraining without complaint. His reputation as the gold-watch winner in the Manchukuo Military Academy and his distinguished record at the Japanese Military Academy preceded his admission, and everyone treated him with due respect. No one doubted that he would advance in rank very rapidly, because he was one of the dozen or so Korean military men who had received the best military training possible. At twenty-nine years of age, he was also older than most of the instructors. His classmates were of diverse backgrounds, but most had not received training that was as rigorous as Park's. Some were graduates of Chinese military academies that had provided a year or two of military training. Many others had served in the Japanese army as soldiers or noncommissioned officers. Some had served in the Kwangbok army that Park had encountered in Beijing; some had been trained in the

---

19 FRUS, vol. 6 (1947), 814; for Kennan's strategy as a whole, see John Lewis Gaddis, *Strategies of Containment* (New York: Oxford University Press, 1982), chapter 2.

Fengt'ien (Shenyang) or Sinjing military academies of Manchuria; and some had been trained at the military academy in Japan.

The U.S. occupation forces had started an officer's training program on December 5, 1945, by opening the Military English Language School. The American army needed interpreters and others to assist in maintaining law and order; the school provided a month-long English course with varying degrees of success.[20] Then on May 1 of the following year, the language school was converted into the Korean Constabulary Training Center, with those already enrolled in the language school becoming the first class. The training period was short, the first class receiving forty-five days of training and the second class eighty days' training.[21] Park was then commissioned a second lieutenant on December 14, 1946. Ordinance Number 86 of the U.S. Military Government, issued on June 15, 1946, stated that the Korean constabulary was a national agency established for the purpose of providing a reserve police force for the Government of Korea to maintain internal security. But the Korean men believed their mission was best defined by Ordinance Number 28, issued on November 13, 1945, which was not adulterated by tangled Soviet-American relations:

> In order to prepare for the eventual independence of Korea, to progressively provide the necessary forces to defend,

---

20 *Taehan Min'guk Yukkun Sagwan Hakkyo 30nyŏnsa* [Thirty Year History of the Republic of Korea Military Academy] ((Seoul: 1978), 63–65), provides an interesting account of the Language School. It admitted sixty students in the first year, selecting twenty veterans each from of the Kwangbok army, Japanese army, and the Manchukuo army. Aside from English, it also taught Korean history, automobile driving, small-arms weapons, and what can be translated as "staff work" in the military. Before it was closed in April 1946, the student body expanded to two hundred. Sixty-eight of the graduates eventually attained general's rank (p. 65).

21 Ibid., 69, for the length of training.

> protect and safeguard its sovereign rights and prerogatives among the Nations of the world, to assist civilian police agencies in the maintenance of civil peace and security and the defense of the rights of the people against civil disorder and to maintain freedom of religion, freedom of speech and property rights, to inaugurate the recruiting, organization, training and equipping of the requisite armed forces on land and sea, and to guarantee the evolution of administration of nationhood, the Office of the Director of National Defense of the Military Government of Korea is hereby established.[22]

Lieutenant Park's first assignment was the Eighth Regiment located in Ch'unch'ŏn, a stone's throw from the thirty-eighth parallel that constituted a border between the American and Soviet occupation zones. The only gunshots one heard, however, were those of the officers hunting for wild boar and other animals. The thirty-eighth parallel was not completely sealed, and there was a steady, if sporadic, flow of refugees from the north. There was also the traffic of merchants who smuggled goods between the two occupation zones.

Life at the command post on the front line was boring, but Park found delight in his immediate superior, the company commander, First Lieutenant Kim Chŏm-gon. Kim outranked him but insisted on using the Korean equivalent of "*vous*" form of addressing him rather than the familiar "*tu*." Kim showed Park respect not only because he was six years older, but also because he had much more knowledge and experience in military affairs. The scion of a landed family in the neighboring Cholla Province, Kim had gone to college in Japan but had been drafted into the Japanese army as a "student volunteer." Kim found the laconic and contemplative soldier to be not only a fountain of knowledge but also a model officer who molded his men into top shape. He could not

22 Ordinance Number 28, Section 1.

have hoped for a better officer.[23] The two became good friends, cementing their ties through occasional drinking.

However, within a few months in the spring of 1947, Park was transferred to the regimental headquarters to serve as acting operational staff officer. His superior training began to shine. Most of the officers of his regiment, including the twenty or so new officers assigned to the regiment, had virtually no military training to speak of. It fell on Second Lieutenant Park to write the training manuals. He trained the inexperienced officers in battle at the individual, squad, and platoon levels, transmitting the knowledge he had gained at the Japanese military academy. Then in July, Park planned and executed a three-day field exercise, mobilizing the entire regiment. This, according to Chŏng Yŏng-jin, was the first such exercise for the Korean constabulary. Overall, Park found the quality of the officers severely deficient, not only in knowledge and skill, but also in personal attributes.[24] The constabulary may have gathered men aspiring to be officers, but it had a huge task ahead if it was to forge a corps of officers out of the ragtag bunch of individuals it had collected.

It was during this period that Reverend Yi Chae-bok approached and "worked on" Park Chung-Hee and his superiors, that is to say, to enlist them into the left-wing South Korean Workers' Party. Kim Chŏm-gon testified later that he was one of those entertained by Park's "maternal uncle." No one at that time bothered to check the surname of Park's mother, which was Paek, very different from the "maternal uncle's." It was also at Ch'unch'ŏn, at a wedding of a mutual friend, that Park

23 Chŏng Yŏng-jin, vol. 3, 7–11.

24 Ibid., 12–13; Chŏng Un-yŏn quotes Yŏm Chŏng-t'ae to say that Park trained officers at the 3rd Battalion, stationed at Kangnŭng located east of Ch'unch'ŏn (p. 145).

met a twenty-one-year-old Ehwa Woman's University student. But the stay at Ch'unch'ŏn ended in September 1947, when he was promoted to captain and transferred to the Constabulary Academy in Seoul, where he was to serve as an instructor.

XI. THE SPECTER OF NAMNODANG

Miss Yi Hyŏn-ran, the Lover

Park Chung-Hee would have been very pleased with his appointment to the academy in September 1947. He had suffered much since the Japanese surrender of August 1945, but his patience had paid off. Those around him recognized who he was and treated him accordingly. He was now in Seoul, the capital, where all the important decisions were made. He was well on his way to becoming an army general as he had always wanted. To top it off, Miss Yi Hyŏn-ran had consented to become his bride. The two celebrated their engagement at a Seoul restaurant with a number of friends and moved in together at the officers' quarters in Seoul. She later recalled that the setup was quite plush. Her attendance at university classes became sporadic, and she eventually quit her studies, becoming a full-time housewife. She thought her fiancée's appearance rather unattractive, being so short and thin, but he had a dynamic personality and strong will to become a future defense minister.[1] He was also a very emotional man whose love for her knew no bounds. She was ecstatic at the way he showered affection on her.[2] But all this changed one day when he told her about his first wife. He had not been able to file for divorce before because of all the things that had happened in the intervening years, but he now wanted to do so. He also wanted to bring his eleven-year-old daughter to Seoul to raise her in his new family.

Yi Hyŏn-ran felt so shocked and betrayed that she ran away. He frantically chased after her and brought her home, saying that he could not live without her. But she could not forgive the man who had broken her

1 Cho Kap-je, *Na ui mudŏm e ch'im ul paett'ŏra* [Spit on My Grave], vol. 1 (Seoul: Chosŏn Ilbosa, 1998), 280–281. The author based his account here on Miss Yi's recollections told to a writer friend, Kang In-ok, in 1987 (see p. 279).

2 Ibid., 281.

heart and ran away again. He would have protested that his father had forced him to marry the woman and he had never loved the mother of his daughter, but nothing could mend her feelings of betrayal. She said their lives together spanned three calendar years, from 1948 to 1950, but they had spent only eight months together because of her frequent escapes.[3] Then, on November 11, 1948, she heard the shocking news that Park had been arrested for being a Communist. Captain Yi Hyo, who lived in the same compound, came to tell her the news, handing her a small sum of money. The Captain was drunk, as he needed the alcohol to buck up his courage to convey the bad news. Yi Hyŏn-ran could not believe that she had been living with a "Communist." She had left her home in Wonsan, North Korea, and crossed the thirty-eighth parallel for Seoul because she could not bear Communist dictatorship.[4]

A few days later, Major Kim Ch'ang-yong, the notorious "Snake" and chieftain of "Communist hunters" in the Korean army, visited and explained why Park had been arrested. He also handed her a note from Park.

> I don't know how to apologize, but please believe one thing I wish to tell you. I shaved and went to the Department of Defense ready to attend the graduation ceremony for the Seventh Class (of the Military Academy). Someone there whispered to me that I was to be arrested. I could have taken the Jeep and ran away from there but did not because I love you.[5]

She evidently believed him and chose not to disappear in his absence, but the situation did not improve. Park's relatives humiliated her by asking her not to visit him in prison for fear that his wife would

---

3 Ibid., 281.
4 Ibid., 280.
5 Ibid., 280–281.

discover their "illicit relationship." This was a sign that they regarded her as a mistress.[6] Furthermore, he could not file for divorce because he was unable to get his wife's consent for it. Yi Hyŏn-ran's patience ran out. On the evening of February 6, 1950, while Park was fast asleep, she snuck out of the residence for the last time, leaving a note for her man:

> I wish to thank you for everything you did for me. But my mind will not turn around. Please do not try to find me. I will kill myself if you do.[7]

One can only imagine how devastating this was for Park Chung-Hee. He needed her more than ever for mental and physical support. They did see each other later on one occasion during the Korean War, but only momentarily. She said she was walking on a Taegu street one day, smartly dressed in a one-piece outfit. She was married then and was two months pregnant. She turned around as she heard an army Jeep honking and saw Park Chung-Hee getting out of the vehicle. There was not a moment to lose; she ran as fast as she could away from him. A truck passed by between them just then, and he lost sight of her. Evidently, she had no doubt that Park was a Communist—she expected him to go to North Korea after the war started.[8] Much later, in 1987, eight years after he was assassinated, the sixty-two-year-old Yi Hyŏn-ran told her friend that she was sorry that she had hurt him so much. Her miserable life as a meat shop owner was a punishment she deserved for having been so

---

6 Ibid., 281; Yi Hyŏn-ran mentioned the name of Park's nephew, the son of the second brother Park Mu-hui, as the one who brought some ground hot pepper from the countryside as a gift and told her not to visit Park in prison (Cho Kap-je, *Pak Chŏng-Hui*, vol. 1 (Seoul: Kkach'i, 1992), 139).

7 Cho Kap-je, Spit on my grave, 281–282.

8 Ibid., 282.

severe and arrogant toward him, she said.[9] Park Chung-Hee would have been happy to have the pristine Yi Hyŏn-ran as the country's first lady.

Yi Hyŏn-ran hurt Park deeply, but we can say in retrospect that his love for her saved him and his future. Had he followed his instincts and driven away that day in the Jeep, he would have become a fugitive until he was arrested. He would not have been able to surface in South Korea, even if he had escaped execution. His life would not have been much better in North Korea, had he chosen to escape there. The Kim Il-sŏng regime there was not well disposed toward those who had served in the Manchukuo army—the troops that had pursued Kim's guerrilla units in Manchuria. It was his love for Yi Hyŏn-ran that stopped him from taking the fateful Jeep ride.

Park Chung-Hee was arrested in November 1948 not so much because of what he did, but because of the tidal change in South Korea's political environment. The U.S. Military Government had tolerated Namnodang, or the South Korean Workers' Party, as a legitimate political organization in spite of the Taegu uprising and the counterfeit incident, but the new Korean government could not be so ambivalent. Namnodang was a direct threat to the Republic of Korea (ROK), established on August 15, 1948, and hence was its archenemy. For that reason, all of the party members became enemies of the state, regardless of the member's beliefs, actions, or circumstances in joining the party.

Republic of Korea against Namnodang

The Republic of Korea (ROK) government could not be but hostile to Namnodang, because the latter had carried out an intense and even violent nationwide campaign against ROK's establishment since early

9 Ibid., 281.

1948. The Communists in North and South Korea charged that the general elections scheduled for May 10, 1948, were a step toward perpetuating the split of the nation, as if there were still hope for reunifying the two parts of Korea. Stalin had instructed his men on September 20, 1945, to establish a separate regime in North Korea, and by the fall of 1947, the North Korean People's Committee had taken steps to adopt a constitution for the government in North Korea.[10]

The Communist campaign against South Korea's general election then escalated in April 1948 to a revolt on Cheju Island, located south of the peninsula. As was the case at Taegu, the rebels attacked the police stations, killing policemen and destroying government facilities. They also attacked the landlords, merchants, and those associated with the right wing. The U.S. Military Government (USMG), still in power, sent additional police units from the mainland and when they were not enough, the right-wing youth groups. The latter, consisting mostly of the refugees from North Korea, vented their rage against Communism by brutally attacking anyone suspected of Communist ties and thus aggravating the situation. The swelled rank of rebels fled to the mountains and continued guerrilla attacks when the USMG transferred power in August 1948 to the newly inaugurated Republic of Korea (ROK) government, headed by President Syngman Rhee.[11]

---

10 See Yi Chŏng-sik, "Stalin's Korea Policy, 1945" [in Korean]; Yi Chŏng-sik, *Taehan Min'guk ui kiwon* (Seoul: Iljogak, 2006), 178–214.

11 For details, see John Merrill's excellent study, "The Cheju-do Rebellion," *Journal of Korean Studies*, (Seattle), vol. 2, (1980), 139–197. This article was published in Japanese as a book, *Saishūtō 4.3 hōki* [The April 3rd Chejudo Uprising], (Tokyo: Shinkansha, 1988).

The Revolt of the 14th Regiment

The Rhee government decided to dispatch the 14th Regiment of the former Constabulary, now converted to the ROK Army, to Cheju Island because it was located in Yŏsu, the port city nearest to Cheju Island. Little did the new authorities know that the decision would plunge the new government into a major crisis. This is because the Communist soldiers in the regiment precipitated a rebellion that shook the new regime to its foundations. The Yŏsu rebellion requires our special attention not only because it became a major turning point for the Korean nation, but also because it brought Park Chung-Hee's military career to a screeching halt. It took place three hundred kilometers away from where he lived, but it threw him literally to hell.

The root of the problem was the USMG's open-door policy regarding the South Korean Constabulary. American policy was to accept all able-bodied men willing to serve. An applicant's ideology or party affiliations were of no concern. As noted earlier, the USMG had treated the South Korean Workers' Party, or Namnodang, as one of the legally constituted political parties, and it did not consider the leftists as potential threats. Namnodang, therefore, enlisted as many of its members into the Constabulary as it could. It also carried out intensive campaigns to win over the troops. The Chŏlla Province, where the 14th Regiment was located, was a fertile ground for the party, because the landlords' exploitation of the peasantry there had been the harshest among all the provinces. The party had little need to indoctrinate the peasant-soldiers with Communist ideology. All it had to do was to describe the land reform that the Communist regime in the north had carried out in March 1946. The regime there had confiscated all farmland from the landlords and distributed it free of charge to the peasants. North Korean peasants did not have the right to sell the land given to them, but such land reform was something that the South Korean peasants could only dream of.[12] The 14th Regiment also included many who had joined the Constabulary to escape the police dragnet in Taegu after the revolt there.[13] The party undoubtedly benefited from the fact that some of the officers were Namnodang members.[14] It was only natural that the troops grumbled when the army headquarters ordered the regiment to Cheju Island to fight the rebels. Many soldiers had reasons to be more sympathetic to the rebels than the new government.

According to Kim Chŏm-gon, who participated in the suppression of the Yŏsu rebellion, the mutiny was directed by Master Sergeant Chi Ch'ang-su, who was the party's man embedded in the regiment's personnel office. He knew that the soldiers loathed the mission assigned to them, so he decided the time was right for a revolt. On October 18, the evening before departure, he ordered some forty of his comrades to take control of the armory and ammunition depot and to sound the bugle to call the regiment onto the drill ground.[15] Sargent Chi's message to his troops was incendiary:

> The police are coming to attack us; we must destroy them. We oppose the suppression of the people of the Cheju

---

12 South Korea carried out the land reform in 1949.

13 Kim Chŏm-gon, *Han'guk e issŏsŏui kongsan chuui t'ujaeng hyŏngt'ae yŏn'gu, 1945–1950* [A Study of the Pattern of Communist Struggle in Korea, 1945–1950] (PhD dissertation, Kyung Hee University, 1971), 245, footnote 6.

14 Ibid., 261.

15 Ibid., 264; it is quite likely that the startled officers showed up too and tried to disperse the troops, but the sergeant shot them on the spot, signaling what he meant to do. Kim Chŏm-gon indicates that three soldiers opposing the revolt were killed on the spot but did not say when the officers were killed. However, the tally of the damages inflicted by the revolt shows nine officers killed, including five shot by rebels at Sunch'ŏn.

> Island; we oppose the internecine struggle. The North Korean People's Army has started to march south crossing the 38th Parallel. We shall reorganize ourselves as the People's Liberation Army to meet them to fulfill our people's desire for unification. We must murder all officers who are the running dogs of American imperialism.[16]

Sergeant Chi's first target was the police. He then wanted to convert his troops into the People's Liberation Army, which would attack all challengers until it met and joined the North Korean forces. He set a grandiose mission for his men. From the outskirts of Yŏsu, the rebels moved into the city, destroying police stations, murdering police officers, and taking over other government buildings. Some six hundred left-wing students and others in the city joined the rebels in the massacre that followed. All those identified as "reactionaries," including businessmen, landlords, government officials, and others known to be right-wing supporters were summarily executed. Having thus turned the city of Yŏsu into a "people's republic," the rebels moved north onto the town of Sunch'ŏn, where they repeated the same carnage.[17] When the orgy of killing and burning stopped, 1,200 civilians had been killed and 1,150 wounded. More than 1,500 houses were either burned down or partially destroyed, leaving 9,800 people homeless.[18] The rebels could not advance beyond Sunch'ŏn, however, because the government dispatched other regiments to suppress them. They had to flee to the mountains and become guerilla fighters. The rebel losses included 392 killed and 1,500 captured.

16 Ibid., 264, footnote 12.
17 Ibid., 265–267; Kim Nam-sik presents the same account in op.cit., 450–456, based on Kim Chŏm-gon's work.
18 Ibid., 271.

No evidence has surfaced to prove that the Namnodang's headquarters ordered the insurrection. The only known party connection was in the form of post-facto approval by the Chŏlla provincial branch.[19] Sergeant Chi may have cast himself in the role of Vladimir Lenin directing the storming of the Winter Palace, but in reality, his rebellion did not extend beyond the small peninsula at the southern tip of Korea, where Yŏsu and Sunch'ŏn are located.[20]

The revolt of the 14th Regiment left an indelible mark on Korean history because the Yŏsu rebellion signaled the beginning of the end of the Communist movement in South Korea. It precipitated a massive and brutal hunt for all left-wing elements in South Korea, described in more detail later.

The decline and eventual fall of the Communist movement in South Korea also affected the outcome of the Korean War, which started in June 1950. Had Namnodang waited until the war and surfaced in the last days of June 1950, instead of October 1948 at Yŏsu, the war might have ended soon after the North Korean forces launched their attack against South Korea. Pak Hŏn-yŏng, the head of Namnodang, allegedly promised Stalin and Kim Il-sŏng in 1949 that the two hundred thousand South Korean party members would rise in support of the People's Army as soon as the invasion began, but he had not counted on the ROK regime destroying much of his organization before the war even began.

---

19 Ibid., 256–257, 270.

20 U.S. Army Captain James Hausman, member of the U.S. Military Advisory Group, who worked closely with President Syngman Rhee and his military staff, referred to the suppression of the Yŏsu-Sunch'ŏn rebellion as the beginning of the modernization of the South Korean Army. Only a part of the ROK forces had been issued M1 rifles at this time, but the U.S. Army in Korea supplied the entire suppression forces with M1 rifles, 81-mm mortars, light machine guns, and M8 reconnaissance vehicles (James Hausman and Chŏng Il-hwa, *Han'guk taet'ongryŏng ŭl umjigin Migun Taewi* [An American Captain behind the Korean President] (Seoul: Han'guk Munhŏn, 1995), 180–186. I am indebted to Professor Chae-Jin Lee for calling my attention to this book.

Thus, Sergeant Chi Ch'ang-su rendered a great service to the ROK regime and all of its supporters by launching his insurrection. In a strange turn of events, Pak Hŏn-yŏng paid the price for Sergeant Chi's bravado by being executed as an American spy in 1956 by the Kim Il-sŏng regime.[21] Had Chi not started the Yŏsu rebellion in October 1948, Pak Hŏn-yŏng might have been able to deliver some of the two hundred thousand party members he had promised.

The Purge

The Cheju revolt was a serious challenge to the new government, but the army leaders remained stoic. The commanders dispatched to the island attributed the revolt to the simmering enmity between the island natives and those from the mainland, including the police forces and the right-wing youth groups, whose dialects were substantially different from those of the islanders.[22] However, the mutiny of the Army's 14th Regiment at Yŏsu in October was a very different matter. What the Army confronted was not a people's revolt against the police but an internal mutiny. The integrity of the new government required the purging of all enemies within.

The purge was thorough, brutal, and inhumane—comparable to the purges under Stalin in the Soviet Union. In fact, protection of the accused was something unheard of in both the Chosŏn Dynasty and under the colonial government—the Korean justice system assumed that the suspect was guilty until proven innocent. Beating or torture of the suspect was the accepted norm, even when the crime committed was a minor theft. Here the investigators were dealing with enemies of the state. They also had personal reasons to be enraged, because the victims included their friends and colleagues. There was no mercy, regardless of rank or

21 On Pak Hŏn-yŏng's trial, see *Communism in Korea*, vol. 1, 436–452. On the 200,000 Communist uprising in South Korea, see ibid., 395–396, footnote 30.
22 Kim Chŏm-gon, 220–222.

position. It did not matter whether a person became a Namnodang member through the People's Party or the Communist Party. Nor did anyone pay any attention to the suspect's ideology or beliefs. The only thing that mattered was one's relationship with the dreaded party. It is strange in retrospect, but no one at that time appears to have remembered that Namnodang was a legal party until the establishment of the ROK in August 1948.[23]

In charge of the purge was Captain Kim Ch'ang-yong, a former Corporal in the Japanese Kantō Army Gendarmerie, who had specialized in the investigation of Communists in Manchuria. His nickname, "the Snake," says much about him; his first step in interrogation was to put the suspect through a series of tortures to make sure that the victim would not dare to hide anything. The process was cruel but effective in ferreting out the enemy.

The captain probably started with the more than 1,500 captured rebels.[24] All he needed initially were a few party members willing to name a few names. The party's entire organizational structure would be reconstructed step-by-step by following the linkage provided by these kernels of information. The investigation of officers proceeded more

23 The Legal Opinions Bureau, Department of Justice, U.S. Military Government, rendered the following legal opinion in June 1948. "South Korea Labor Party—Whether a crime to be a member (Opinion No. 1613, 29 June 1948). Problem: The adviser to the Department of Justice requested an opinion whether it is a crime to belong to the South Korea Labor Party (principal party in the communist South Korea Democratic People's Front) which has conclusively demonstrated that it is seeking to overthrow the Military Government." Opinion: Membership per se in the South Korea Labor Party is not an offense so long as the party has not been outlawed or judicially found to be seeking the overthrow of the government (United States Army Military Government in Korea, *South Korean Interim Government Activities,* no. 33 (June 1948), 154).

24 Kim Chŏm-gon, 271.

speedily because the police had been tracing left-wing activities in the army and had a jeepload full of dossiers.[25] By July 1949, the investigation had netted more than 4,700 members in various units of the army, including officers and soldiers.[26] Since the new army consisted of 50,490 troops including 1,403 officers, as of September 9, 1948,[27] the arrested constituted nearly 10 percent of the total force. General Kim Chŏng-ryŏl, who later became the prime minister under President Park Chung-Hee, estimated only 10 percent of those investigated were actually Namnodang members.[28]

Park Chung-Hee played no role in the Yŏsu-Sunch'ŏn uprising except as a staff officer in the Pacification Headquarters against the rebels, but the arrest of Yi Chae-bok and his assistant doomed him.[29] Yi Chae-bok, who had persuaded Park Chung-Hee to join the party, was at this time in charge of the Military Department in the Namnodang headquarters. The investigators found Park's name high up on the organizational chart.[30] He had just been appointed the section chief of

---

25 Paek Sŏn-yŏp, *Kun kwa na* [The Army and I], (Seoul: Taeryuk Yŏn'guso, 1989), 344. Captain Hausman also mentioned the police dossiers. Significantly, he mentioned Park Chung-Hee as one of the "Communist spies" listed in the dossiers; Hausman and Chŏng Il-hwa, *Han'guk taet'ongryŏng ŭl umjigin Migun Taewi*, 186. The word "*spy*" was probably a mistranslation of what Hausman said.

26 Paek Sŏn-yŏp, *Kun kwa na*, 269.

27 Han Yong-won, *Ch'ang Kun* [Founding the Army] (Seoul: Pakyŏngsa, 1984), 71, 106. As of late 1947, the Constabulary had between eighteen and twenty thousand men (Sawyer, 29, footnote 71).

28 Kim Chŏng-ryŏl, *Hangkong ui kyŏngjong* [A Warning Bell in Flight] (Ch'unch'ŏn and Seoul: Daehui, 2010), 104.

29 Chungang Ilbosa, *Sillok Pak Chŏng-hui*, 63; Kim Yŏng-sik was Yi Chae-bok's assistant. Chŏng Un-yŏn, *Sillok kun'in Pak Chŏng-hui* [Veritable Record of the Soldier Park Chung-Hee] (Seoul: Kaema, 2004), 140–141.

30 The description of Park Chung-Hee's position in the *Namnodang* organization varies according to sources. Kim Chŏm-gon called him the "ch'ong-ch'aek" or "the most responsible person," which would be the party secretary in the army. The MBC documentary, *Now We Can Talk about It*, episode number 5, "Yŏsu 14th Regiment Rebellion"; this TV documentary includes Kim's statement in front of the camera.

Operational Education in the army headquarters, but he was led to the torture chamber instead.[31]

Park as a Turncoat

All accounts agree that Park Chung-Hee was very compliant when arrested. "I knew this would happen," he was quoted to have said when he was given a pen and a stack of paper. He wrote about his brother and his encounter with Yi Chae-bok, but we do not know the full details of his statement. Some suggested that Park ordered the destruction of all documents related to his investigation when he took over the government in 1961, and this may be true. Kim Chŏm-gon, Park's superior and friend from the Eighth Regiment, testified that Park was the first one to reveal the Namnodang's organizational structure within the army.[32] He is also said to have provided the investigators with a detailed list of Namnodang members among army officers. In short, he cooperated fully with the investigation. However, another source indicated that the army had already obtained a list of virtually all the members through Yi Chae-bok's assistant prior to Park's arrest.[33]

Whether or not he was the first to identify Namnodang members within the army, his cooperation with the investigators definitely made him a traitor to Namnodang. We do not know how many officers were executed as a result of his revelations, but he certainly earned their contempt and hatred.

The documentary focused on the surviving witnesses talking about the indiscriminate killing by the army units sent to suppress the rebellion but mentioned nothing of the atrocities committed by the rebels.

31 *Sillok Pak Chŏng-hui*, 104.

32 Chŏng Un-yŏn, *Sillok kun'in Pak Chŏng-hui*, 141.

33 Ibid., 141.

The Nature of Park's Commitment to Namnodang

I concluded earlier that the likelihood of Park's joining Namnodang for ideological reasons was very slim. I also posited that the most likely reason for his acceptance of Yi Chae-bok's urging was his revulsion to American rule. That was in 1947, it should be recalled. It was now November 1948, and the intervening twelve to fifteen months had been the most turbulent period in Korea's modern history, including the violent conflict surrounding the establishment of the Republic of Korea and the later insurrection of the 14th Regiment. Park would have given much thought to the issues of the time. He also saw the hellish results of the revolts at Yŏsu and Sunchŏn as a staff officer in the Pacification Headquarters during this period.

One could argue that the establishment of the ROK government negated Park's reason for joining Namnodang, if my supposition about his motives is correct. As noted earlier, George Kennan had argued in September 1947 that the United States should exit South Korea as quickly as possible. The United States feared the American troops would be trapped in Korea in the event of a war against the Soviet Union and favored an early withdrawal. The United States, therefore, decided on abandoning the idea of establishing international trusteeship over Korea and encouraged the establishment of the Republic of Korea government. This was meant to be a "face-saving" device for withdrawing from Korea.[34] Thus, the U.S. rule of South Korea that Park had found

---

34 I have elaborated on these points in my "Road to the Korean War" article cited earlier. George Kennan stated in June 1949 that "[South Korea] is an exposed, unsound military position, one that is doing no good, and we are anxious to get rid of positions of that sort," June 16, 1949, at a hearing on "Korea Aid Act of 1949," Committee on International Relations, House of Representatives, *United States Policy in the Far East*, part 2, Selected Executive Session Hearings of the Committee, 1943–50, vol. 8 (Washington 1976), 59. This was in answer to Congressman John Davis Lodge's question: "Why do we want to get out?"

so repugnant ended on August 1948, when the ROK government was established. One could argue, therefore, that Park Chung-Hee no longer had a valid reason to remain a Namnodang member. The arrest enabled him to get rid of the burden, one could say, and hence he gladly revealed all he knew. One could present a retort, however, saying that the ROK was nothing more than an American puppet regime, and hence Park's motive for joining Namnodang remained valid.

Another alternative explanation would be that Park Chung-Hee had decided he had made a serious mistake when he joined Namnodang. He could very well have been repulsed by the destruction the party wrought on the people in Taegu, Cheju Island, Yŏsu, and Sunch'ŏn. Countless numbers of ordinary people were murdered or maimed, and many more were left homeless, yet nothing positive came from the carnage. Did the violence and destruction stop "American imperialists" from establishing a "puppet regime" in South Korea, as the party had argued? Did it help to unify the divided country? It was unclear whether the party leaders even knew what they were doing. These are highly plausible reasons for Park to have had second thoughts about being a Namnodang member. To the methodical and disciplined army officer accustomed to calculating the costs and benefits of strategies and tactics, the 14th Regiment's mutiny simply did not make sense. It was clearly a thoughtless outburst of short-sighted men. Park could not have known at that time, of course, that the party played no role in the mutiny. In any event, his remark, "I knew this was coming," was indicative of his disappointment with Namnodang.

Park Chung-Hee's colleague from the Manchukuo Academy, Pak Ch'ang-am, offered a variation on this theme. He said that Park Chung-Hee freely cooperated with the investigation because he was persuaded by a close friend from his Manchuria days, Ch'oe Ch'ang-ryun, who had gone through a harrowing experience in the North Korean army before escaping to the south.[35] Whether because of Kim Il-sŏng's hatred of those with Manchukuo army ties or for other reasons, Ch'oe and a number of his friends went through a very harsh ordeal in North Korea. Ch'oe, therefore, became an anti-Communist "evangelist" of a sort in South Korea, trying to persuade his friends to abandon Communism. Pak Ch'ang-am did not participate in the long conversation himself, but was at the scene where Ch'oe and Park Chung-Hee engaged in the lengthy discussion. Park Chung-Hee may not have totally changed his views that day, but Pak Ch'ang-am thought Park would have had serious second thoughts about Namnodang since then. One should also remember in this connection that Park's lover, Yi Hyŏn-ran, was a North Korean refugee. She opted to leave her home at the port city of Wonsan in North Korea for Seoul because of her hatred of the Communist regime. It is reasonable to assume that she told Park much about Soviet occupation of North Korea. She had no inkling that her lover was a Namnodang member and would have been candid about what she experienced.

These, I should emphasize, are hypotheses. Nevertheless, they are as plausible as the notion that Park Chung-Hee became a turncoat because of his fickle character. Perhaps the factors I have presented were at work simultaneously in his mind. On the other hand, some may reject all of these hypotheses. Park simply wanted to live in order to prolong his life with his beloved Yi Hyŏn-ran, one could argue. He wrote her saying that he had decided to go through the

35 Cho Kap-je, *Pak Chŏng-Hui*, vol. 1 (Seoul: Kkach'i, 1992), 137–138.

ordeal of interrogations because he loved her, did he not? What other proof is required? Love and the desire to prolong life prevailed over everything, and we have more solid evidence for this theory than others.

Park did reveal all he knew to the investigators. Still they demanded more and tortured him with electric shocks. This was a formality, one could say. The interrogator happened to be one of Park Chung-Hee's "students" at the Constabulary Academy, but there was no mercy shown. He had to name a name to stop the electric shocks; the truth did not matter. So he ended up pointing a finger at an innocent man, Captain Pak Won-sŏk. He is not known to have regretted his betrayal of *Namnodang*, but he could not forget the suffering he inflicted on the innocent man.[36] There was no way for him to know at this time that his naming of Captain Pak Won-sŏk saved his life.

The Court Martial

Park's trial took place on February 8, 1949, three months after his arrest. Presided over by Lt. Colonel Kim Wan-ryong, three officers headed by a colonel served as jurors. Sixty-nine suspects were indicted, all of whom were officers (except ten noncommissioned officers), including two lieutenant colonels and three majors. They were charged with joining the Namnodang, organizing secret cells within the army, and attempting to overthrow the government. After hearing statements from the prosecution and the court-appointed defender, the judgment by the chief judge and jurors was swift. Colonel Kim told

36 Chŏng Un-yŏn, *Sillok Kun'in Pak Chŏng-hui*, 158 footnote; *Sillok Pak Chŏng-Hui*, 65; President Park later appointed Pak Won-sŏk the Air Force Chief of Staff.

a reporter many years later that his court did not have much room for discretion. He had been instructed to pass death sentences to those considered to be the ringleaders.[37] Those sentenced to death in the morning would face the firing squads in the afternoon of the same day.[38] The Colonel regretted later that many good men were executed in the "rush to justice." One particular individual, Lt. Colonel Ch'oe Nam-kŭn, is mentioned in this context because he is known to have shouted "Long Live the Republic of Korea" (Taehan Min'guk Manse!) when he faced the firing squad.[39] This was the cry of a man wrongfully charged, because no Communist would have wished the new South Korean government well. Park Chung-Hee lost a good friend when Ch'oe was executed. He had known the man since their Manchukuo army days, and the two had maintained a close relationship. Ch'oe was not the only one executed. Many graduates of the Manchukuo and Japanese Military Academies, some quite close to Park, perished for having joined Namnodang. Some, however, managed to survive without even imprisonment. We shall have more to say about the case of Pak Won-sŏk.

Park's Guardian Angels

It is reasonable to assume that Park had held an important position in the Namnodang organization; otherwise, he would not have known what he told the investigators.[40] He does appear to have made efforts to recruit fellow officers to the party. Park reportedly tried to recruit Yi Chu-il, with whom he spent the long months in Beijing in the

37 Chŏng Un-yŏn, *Sillok Kun'in Pak Chŏng-hui*, 149.

38 The MBC documentary showed the photographs of the execution.

39 Chŏng Un-yŏn, 149; Major O Il-gyun was another one who did the same; ibid., 149.

40 Ibid., 140.

Kwangbok army compound,[41] and there may have been others.[42] In any event, Park's position in the party alone would have justified his execution by the 1949 standard. There is universal agreement among everyone involved with Park's case that he would have been executed had he not fully cooperated with the investigation.

Even when we take into account Park's full cooperation, however, the actions taken by the notorious "Snake," the primary investigator, were extraordinary. We have already mentioned Captain Kim Ch'ang-yong taking Park's letter to his lover. No one would have expected this cold-blooded man to serve as a suspect's messenger. He is also said to have taken the initiative to save Park Chung-Hee.[43] How did this happen? Did Park Chung-Hee melt the heart of the cold-blooded Snake? Was it because of Park's stellar reputation among army officers? Perhaps the Captain was impressed by Park's demeanor under pressure?

I believe Park was saved mostly due to the efforts of a man named Kim Chŏng-ryŏl. Kim was catapulted into action because Park Chung-Hee had named his close associate Pak Won-sŏk as a member of Namnodang. Fortunately, Kim Chŏng-ryŏl (1917–1992) left a detailed account of how he became involved in Park Chung-Hee's rescue. The relevant paragraphs are quoted from his autobiography, published in 2010.

---

41 Ibid., 147; Yi Chu-il was arrested and investigated but was set free by the court-martial.

42 Kim Yŏng-su noted in his study of Park Chung-Hee that he approached Captains Yi Pyŏng-ju and Yi Hallim, former classmates at Manchukuo Military Academy, for the same purpose; "A Study of Park Chung-Hee's Political Leadership," in Han'guk Chŏngshin Munhwa Yŏn'guwon (ed.), *Chang Myŏn, Yun Po-sŏn, Pak Chŏng-hui: 1960nyŏndae chuyo chŏngch'i chidoja yŏn'gu* (Seoul: Paeksan Sŏdang, 2001), 196.

43 Ibid., 154–155.

> It was in February 1949, soon after the Army Air Force Military Academy was established and I was appointed its commandant. I heard a loud pounding at the door of the official residence one evening and saw Pak Won-sŏk, my Dean of the Faculty, surrounded by a few stout young men and shouting at the top of his voice "I have done nothing wrong." I soon found out that the Army's purge team had sent for him for being a Red.[44]
>
> The next day I went to the Counter-Intelligence Corps (CIC) at Myŏngdong as I was told. There Major Kim Ch'ang-yong showed me a big chart taller than most men which turned out to be the organizational chart of the South Korean Worker's Party. There, at the bottom of the chart was Pak Won-sŏk's name just below that of Park Chung-Hee. He was the only one under Park.[45]

The Air Academy commandant knew the two men well and simply did not believe the charge. Coincidentally, in 1948, seven future founders of the ROK Air Force under Major Kim Chŏng-ryŏl had been sent to the military academy for American-style training for fifteen days, and they had been put under Company Commander Park Chung-Hee's charge. Park found the situation very awkward and uncomfortable because Kim Chŏng-ryŏl was three years ahead of him at the Japanese Military Academy and hence Kim was his superior, but he was now obliged to issue commands as his trainer. So Park resorted to inviting Kim Chŏng-ryŏl and another officer virtually every evening for drinking sessions to cover the awkwardness of the situation. In the process, Kim learned much about Park and came to respect him as a person. There was no possibility that he could be a Communist.[46]

---

44 Kim Chŏng-ryŏl, *Hangkong ui kyŏngjong* [A Warning Bell in Flight] (Ch'unch'ŏn and Seoul: Daehui, 2010), 103. The quotation here is slightly abridged.
45 Ibid., 105.
46 Ibid., 106.

Major Kim also knew his Dean of Faculty intimately. He was very familiar with Pak Won-sŏk's family background, his records at the Japanese Military Academy, where he was a year behind Park Chung-Hee, and his subsequent career. It was simply impossible in Kim's mind that either of them would be a Communist. So, Commandant Kim asked the CIC chief what would happen to the Dean if Park Chung-Hee were released as an innocent man. The answer, as expected, was that the Dean would be released too. So Kim went to see Chŏng Il-kwon, the army's Deputy Chief of Staff, who was the Snake's superior. But he said he could offer no help. "Kim Ch'ang-yong decided I was a Red and had been desperate to arrest me. I simply cannot do anything."

Major Kim, however, was undaunted. He went to Colonel Paek Sŏn-yŏp, the chief of the Intelligence Bureau, who was Snake Kim's immediate superior. They not only knew each other well, but Paek used to call Major Kim "*Hyŏngnim*," older brother, because he was three years older than Paek and because he was ahead of him in military life. The following exchange ensued:

> Isn't Kim Ch'ang-yong under your command?
>
> Yes, but…
>
> Don't you know Major Park Chung-Hee too?
>
> Yes, I know him well.
>
> I know you would have been much troubled about this matter, but Park Chung-Hee was arrested by the Counter-Intelligence, falsely accused of being a Communist. Pak Won-sŏk, our Dean of Faculty, was also arrested as Park Chung-Hee's cell member. Can you somehow release Park Chung-Hee?

> I simply can't do anything about it.
>
> What are you talking about? If the Intelligence Bureau chief cannot do anything about it, who can?
>
> Hyŏngnim! (Older Brother!) It's a mad situation. Kim Ch'ang-yong is going crazy because he can't get me arrested.[47]

Thus, Commandant Kim found Colonel Paek no different from Chŏng Il-kwon. Kim Ch'ang-yong, the CIC chief, suspected everyone and could not be touched. So the commandant pondered a while and headed straight for the home of the army's Chief of Staff, Ch'ae Pyŏng-dŏk, with whom he was as intimate as a brother. There, he explained the situation again and asked for his help, but what he got was a shout from him saying, "Hey! You think Park Chung-Hee is the only one? There are so many that are wrongfully arrested. How could I single out Park Chung-Hee and rescue him?" But Kim would not give up. Eventually, Chief Ch'ae relented and called Kim Ch'ang-yong to his home.

> The two talked to each other briefly. The Chief told me after Kim left: It looks certain that Park Chung-Hee is a *Nam-nodang* man, but he said there is a way to save him. Park will be required to go with the Counter-Intelligence Unit ten times when they arrest Communists. If he proved not to be a Communist, he would not hesitate to do it, and in any event, his reputation among Communists would be ruined. If he was a Communist, he would be driven out of their world for betraying them so many times. He would therefore go through a complete about-face. Kim Ch'ang-yong would release him if Park Chung-Hee agreed to cooperate.[48]

---

47 Ibid., 108.
48 Ibid., 109–110.

Early the following morning, Commandant Kim Chŏng-yŏl visited the Counter-Intelligence Unit at Myŏngdong and asked Kim Ch'ang-yong about Park's response. The answer was a definite "Yes."

Kim Chŏng-ryŏl's recollection is very credible, and his information coincides with Kim Ch'ang-yong's story of initiating the "rescue mission." Park Chung-Hee evidently went through the humiliating process as demanded, and Kim kept his promise to save him from execution. Kim Chŏng-ryŏl's passion for his Dean of Faculty saved Park Chung-Hee. Park had incriminated an innocent man under torture, but he ended up saving his own life.

The "deal" that Kim Ch'ang-yong, the Snake, made with the chief of staff persuaded everyone involved, including the Intelligence Bureau chief. Approving the "Snake's" proposal to save Park was very different from trying to influence him to release a suspect. When the CIC chief went to his immediate superior in charge of counterintelligence, Major Kim An-il, with a proposal to "save Park Chung-Hee," the Major was more than happy to oblige. He had been Park's classmate at the Constabulary Academy and knew him well. The two then went to Colonel Paek Sŏn-yŏp, the chief of the Intelligence Bureau, who would have been familiar with the efforts of Commandant Kim Chŏng-ryŏl. The martial court sentenced Park Chung-Hee to life imprisonment rather than execution, but this was only a formality. His sentence was quickly reduced to fifteen years and then suspended. He was back with Yi Hyŏn-ran by December.

Park Chung-Hee returned to his position as the head of the Operational Intelligence section and busied himself with the task of assessing the movements of the North Korean army. Lieutenant Yi Yŏng-kŭn, who worked under Park during this period, recollected that his section had much to "chew on." Numerous merchants traveled between North and South Korea carrying such medicines as Diachin and penicillin, which were unavailable in North Korea, and brought back dried pollack, which North Korean fishermen caught in abundance. North Korean refugees still trickled down to the south, somehow evading the guards at the border. The Intelligence Bureau also interviewed occasional defectors from the North Korean army, including a captain in the North Korean air force. The bureau also dispatched its agents to gather specific information.[49] When the data from these sources were aggregated and collated over a period of time, the intelligence officers were able to draw certain conclusions. On December 27, 1947, Major Park Chung-Hee, the section chief, filed the following report:

> A rapid change in North Korea is anticipated in the spring of 1950. Until then, the enemy will seek to build its foothold [in South Korea] to disrupt South Korean society to the end of bringing about internal collapse. It will then engage in rapid war preparation followed by an all-out attack at the 38th parallel to destroy the Republic of Korea.[50]

We do not know whether the above quotation was copied from the report itself or was based on Lieutenant Yi Yŏng-kŭn's memory, but the wording is rather ambiguous. We must presume that the above paragraph is a conclusion drawn after a more elaborate description and analysis of the information gathered. In any event, it reveals the kind of work that occupied Major Park Chung-Hee and that his unit believed the North Korean attack was imminent.

---

49 Ryu Kyŏng-hyŏn, "The Night before the War," no. 3, *Dong-a Ilbo*, June 14, 1975.
50 Ibid.

Major Park's restoration to his previous position may have led him to believe that the army headquarters had erased the "Communist episode" from his record and he could start with a clean slate, but this was not the case. In April or May 1950, he received an official notification that hit him like a thunderbolt: he was dishonorably discharged from the army.[51] All his training and efforts were for naught. He was no longer an army officer and simply did not have a future in the ROK Army. The bureau chief, Colonel Paek, tried to console Park and allowed him to work in the same office as before, even paying him informally from operational funds at his disposal, but Park Chung-Hee was a nonentity as far as the army was concerned. One wonders what went through his mind each day as he woke up. He could lose himself in work for a few hours each day, but the rest of his time would have been miserable. Park's friends avoided him, lest they be tainted by a man accused of being a Communist organizer. Despondent and gloomy, he could find solace only in alcohol. He may have wished his "guardian angels" had not rescued him. They may have saved his life, but he was a forsaken man. He had no lover, no friends, and no more dreams. Major Han Ung-jin, Park's classmate at the military academy, could not forget the evenings when Park crawled into his room at his boardinghouse drunk, sobbing, and moaning in anguish until he fell asleep. Major Han had replaced Kim Ch'ang-yong as the chief of the CIC and could associate with his old friend as no others could.

His mother's death in August 1949 deepened Park's despair. She is said to have died from the shock she received when the devastating news of her youngest son reached her. He was a turncoat and, worse still, an unfilial son. Park Chung-Hee was fated to die a broken man, a drifter trying daily to wash away his sorrow with alcohol.

---

51 Cho Kap-je, vol. 1 (1992), 170.

XII. THE KOREAN WAR

Wars mean death and destruction, and the Korean War was no exception. But when Kim Il-sŏng plotted the war in 1949, he undoubtedly anticipated it would be short, with a minimum of destruction. He may not have believed what Pak Hŏn-yŏng, the head of the Namnodang, or the South Korean Workers' Party, had told him about the rise of that party's two hundred thousand members in support of the North Korean attack,[1] but Kim had organized, with Stalin's active support, a massive force to overwhelm the South Korean army. He had an air force of 180 aircraft, all supplied by the Soviet Union, including 40 YAK fighters and 70 attack bombers,[2] while the South Korean Air Force had a single flight group of twelve liaison-type aircraft and ten advance trainers (AT6). The U.S. Advisory Group had approximately ten old F-51 (Mustang) planes under its control, but no South Korean pilots had yet qualified to fly combat missions.[3] The North Korean army had 150 Russian T34 (thirty-two-ton) tanks while the South Korean army had none.[4] Nor did the South Korean army have antitank guns or

---

1 Kim Il-sŏng referred to this situation on November 3, 1954, at the Plenary Conference of the Central Committee of the Korean Workers' Party: "We have a bitter experience on this matter. At the early part of the war when we had crossed [the thirty-eighth parallel] in counter assault, the enemy was pushed into a small corner along the Naktong River. If we had organized well and were able to mobilize even a small segment of the South Korean people, let alone the entire South Korean people, at this time to carry out their tasks and developed resistance movement, the enemy could not have helped but to withdraw. But we were not able to do so. We must learn from this experience." *Kim Il-sŏng sŏnjip* [Selected Works of Kim Il-sŏng], vol. 4 (Pyongyang, Chosŏn Rodongdang Ch'ulp'ansa, 1960), 192. This statement was made before Pak Hŏn-yŏng, the former chairman of the South Korean Workers' Party was executed on the charge of having been an American spy.

2 Roy E. Appleman, *South to the Naktong, North to the Yalu (June–November 1950)*, (Washington D.C., Office of the Chief of Military History, Department of the Army, 1961), 12.

3 Ibid., 17.

4 Ibid., 10, 16–17; in October of 1949, the South Korean Minister of Defense had requested 189 M26 tanks, but the acting chief of the U.S. Advisory Group (KMAG) held the view that the Korean terrain and the condition of roads and bridges would

antitank mines. Kim Il-sŏng also had reasons to believe that the South Korean army was no more than a ragtag army of uncommitted young soldiers. He had personally welcomed and inspected the two battalions of the South Korean army taken to North Korea in May 1949 by their commanders.[5]

Kim Il-sŏng was also on stronger ground than South Korea's President Syngman Rhee on the international front. Kim had the solid support of Joseph Stalin who, as noted, had provided a massive quantity of munitions and advisors, while the American officials repeatedly announced their disinterest in defending South Korea. Secretary of State Dean Acheson's January 1950 speech excluding the Korean Peninsula from the U.S. defense perimeter received much publicity, but General Douglas MacArthur had announced the same message to the world a year earlier. His statement, published on the front page of the *New York Times* on March 2, 1949, said the American defense line ran from the Japanese archipelago to the Okinawa islands and to the Philippines, clearly excluding Korea.[6] U.S. Senator Tom Connally,

---

not lend themselves to efficient tank operations; ibid., 16; Captain Hauseman contradicted Appleman's account by saying that Brig. General William L. Roberts, the head of the KMAG, complained about the U.S. Joint Chiefs of Staff's refusal to supply tanks to the ROK Army (James Hausman and Chŏng Il-hwa, *Han'guk taet'ongryŏng ŭl umjigin Migun Taewi* [An American Captain behind the Korean President] (Seoul: Han'guk Munhŏn, 1995), 194). General Roberts, according to Hausman, had served as commander of the 7th Tank Regiment at the Battle of the Bulge in 1944.

5 Two battalion leaders took their units across the thirty-eighth parallel in early May under the pretense of engaging in a military exercise. Some officers and soldiers fought their way back to South Korea when they discovered their leaders' intent; 239 of the 456 troops of the First Battalion, Eighth Regiment, returned to the south, and 143 of the 294 troops from the Second Battalion also returned. South Korea's CIC director, Major Kim Ch'ang-yong, had urged the investigation of the two commanders, and their case was pending (Chang Ch'ang-guk, *Yuksa cholŏpsaeng* [The Military Academy Graduates] (Seoul: Chung'ang Ilbosa, 1984), 221–222).

6 "MacArthur Pledges Defense of Japan," *New York Times*, March 2, 1949, 1.

the Chairman of the Senate Foreign Relations Committee, assured the world in May 1950 that "whenever she [Russia] takes a notion she can overrun Korea just like she will probably overrun Formosa when she gets ready to do it."[7]

Kim Il-sŏng would have been elated when his tanks pierced through the South Korean defense line on June 25, 1950, and occupied Seoul, the South Korean capital, within three days. He had a good prospect of destroying the South Korean regime and unifying the entire peninsula under his control. The only problem Kim encountered was the unexpected U.S. reversal of its Korea policy. Instead of remaining neutral to the development in Korea as expected, President Truman denounced North Korea as an aggressor and announced his decision to send American troops to defend South Korea. In hindsight, we can attribute Truman's decision to the massive scale of the North Korean attack. Its tank-led assault was too overwhelming for the United States to ignore. Stalin's hands behind the North Korean attack were obvious, as the North Korean regime simply lacked the capacity to produce or purchase such weapons. Truman, therefore, saw it as the harbinger of Stalin's plan to expand Communism worldwide.[8] Truman also could not accept South

---

7 The senator made the remark in response to a question put to him by an interviewer from the *U.S. News and World Report*: "Do you think the suggestion that we abandon Korea is going to be seriously considered?" He said: "I'm afraid it's going to be seriously considered because I'm afraid it's going to happen, whether we want it to or not. I'm for Korea. We're trying to help her—we're appropriating money now to help her. But South Korea is cut right across by this line [the Thirty-eighth Parallel]—north of it are the Communists with access to the mainland—and Russia is over there on the mainland. So 'whenever she takes a notion she can overrun Korea just like she will probably overrun Formosa when she gets ready to do it.' I hope not, of course" (*U.S. News and World Report*, May 5, 1950, 40).

8 On Truman's decision to intervene, see Glenn Paige, *The Korean Decision* (Glencoe, IL: The Free Press, 1968); James Matray, *The Reluctant Crusade: American Foreign Policy in Korea, 1941–1950* (Honolulu: University of Hawaii Press, 1985);

Korea's downfall with equanimity because it would have reinforced his domestic critics, who accused him of "losing China" to Communists just a year earlier. Kim Il-sŏng, therefore, had to face not only the South Korean forces but also the Americans, backed by the United Nations, which declared North Korea or the Democratic People's Republic of Korea, an aggressor. The North Korean "People's Army" appeared to be invincible in the summer of 1950, but the tide turned in mid-September, when General MacArthur landed his massive forces in Inchon to start the counterattack. Inchon is located in the middle of the peninsula, and North Korean forces south of there were cut off from their bases in the north, becoming an easy target for destruction. Kim Il-sŏng now faced the prospect of being driven out of the Korean Peninsula as the United Nations forces under MacArthur continued the push toward the north. Only the massive intervention by Chinese forces under Mao Zedong in October prevented North Korean defeat. Mao had decided that Korean unification under American aegis would jeopardize Chinese security. Mao's intervention changed the tide of the war, challenging the United States, whom many had considered invincible.[9] The massive infusion of Chinese "volunteers" and the U.S. decision not to expand the conflict beyond Korean borders prolonged the war until July 1953, when commanders of both sides signed a truce agreement at Panmunjom. The three-year war killed nearly one million South Korean civilians and 320,000 soldiers. It also uprooted five and a half million people, or 25

Stephen Pelz, "U.S. Decisions on Korean Policy, 1943–1950: Some Hypotheses," in Bruce Cumings, ed., *Child of Conflict: The Korean-American Relationship, 1943–1953* (Seattle: University of Washington Press, 1983); Kathryn Weathersby, "Soviet Aims in Korea and the Origins of the Korean War, 1945–50: New Evidence from Russian Archives," Working Paper #8: Cold War International History Project.

9 See Chen Jian, *China's Road to the Korean War* (New York: Columbia University Press, 1994).

percent of the population, and made them refugees.[10] North Korean and Chinese casualties were much heavier. North Korea also suffered the additional loss of more than a million people as they chose to abandon their homes in the North and flee to South Korea.

Back from Hell: Park Chung-Hee and the War

How did this war affect Park Chung-Hee? We noted earlier that he was a broken man in early 1950. He still commuted to work each day as before, but only because Colonel Paek and others took pity on him. It was fortunate that they did not believe him to be a Communist. But the war eliminated whatever lingering doubt anyone had held about Park Chung-Hee; he had chosen to cross the Han River and join the stream of soldiers and civilians who escaped from the capital city that was under North Korean attack. In fact, Park had no other choice; he had closed all doors to the Communists when he started to collaborate with the counterintelligence unit. No one had the time to question Park's motives, in any event. What mattered was that Park was with them when their forces were routed and their republic was facing crisis. The South Koreans also needed a man of Park's military caliber.

Colonel Chang To-yŏng (Chang Do Young), who had succeeded Paek Sŏn-yŏp as chief of the Intelligence Bureau only a week or so before the North Korean attack, gave us an account of how he restored Park Chung-Hee to the army. The sudden news of the North Korean attack and the speed with which the North Korean forces advanced tested the mettle of those at the highest echelon of the army. By the time the staff had digested the news and hurried to evacuate to the south,

10 David D. Cole and Princeton N. Lyman, *Korean Development: The Interplay of Politics and Economics* (Cambridge, MA: Harvard University Press, 1971), 22.

Colonel Chang was informed of the plan to blow up the only bridge over the Han River to prevent the North Korean forces from moving further south. The colonel hurried to the bridge to delay its explosion, but he was too late. The entire armed forces north of the river and millions of citizens were trapped, forced to endure Communist rule. Some of them, including the colonel and his staff, were fortunate to find a boat upstream and managed to cross the river.

It was in this agitated situation that the Colonel found Park Chung-Hee, the former major, among the G-2 staff that regrouped in the town of Suwon and then again at Taejon. The colonel had not known much about Park before, but he soon discovered that Park had led the men in his bureau to gather key documents essential for the G-2 operation, including maps and charts, before evacuation. There was no doubt about the respect and trust he commanded from those around him. He was a quintessential professional. Whatever reservations the Colonel had about Park dissipated, and he decided to have his military status restored. Chief of Staff Chŏng Il-kwon was initially reluctant to approve Colonel Chang's request for fear of stirring up unnecessary complications, but Chang persuaded both Chief Chŏng and the Minister of Defense to reinstate Park.[11] Park's reinstatement as an army major came on July 14, 1950, two days short of three weeks after the outbreak of the war. The ongoing war made his position as the section chief of operational intelligence within the army intelligence bureau ever more important. Park's promotion to lieutenant colonel came two months later, on September 15.

The record clearly shows that Park's conscientiousness and attention to detail was well suited for the field of intelligence. Even though

---

11 Chang To-yŏng, "I trusted Park Chung-Hee" (in Korean), *Shindong-a* (July 1984), 120–163. (136–137 on reinstatement).

the army dispatched him to be the chief of staff of the newly created 9th Division, he was called back six months later in May 1951, as a full colonel, to serve as the commandant of the army intelligence school. Then in December, the army headquarters transferred Park to the operational education bureau.

The army, as we have noted, restored Park Chung-Hee's status because of its dire need for his expertise. Similar circumstances also led to his promotion to the field officer's rank. The ROK army expanded rapidly particularly after the Chinese intervention in October 1950, and officers with experience were quickly promoted. General James A. Van Fleet's program to strengthen the ROK army's combat effectiveness also contributed to Park's promotion. Both the American and Korean commanders had recognized early in the war that the ROK army badly needed better training at all levels and adequate integral artillery in the ROK divisions, but van Fleet was the one who vigorously pushed for their implementation. The ROK army had only one 105-milimeter howitzer battalion to a division, while the American counterpart had three 105-milimeter and one 155-milimeter howitzer battalions. In mid-1952, during the height of combat, therefore, the U.S. army decided to provide weapons and training to their ROK counterparts to bring Korean artillery strength to the same level as U.S. divisions.[12] This, of course, required the appointment and training of high-level officers, who would serve as deputy division commanders in charge of artillery contingents. Park Chung-Hee was one of the sixteen selected in October 1952 to

---

12 Robert K. Sawyer, *Military Advisors in Korea: KMAG in Peace and War* (Washington, D.C., Office of the Chief of Military History, Dept. of the Army, 1962), 182–184.

receive the three-month intensive training in artillery, followed by a short period of practical training at the 5th U.S. Artillery Corps.[13]

Before Park's assignment as artillery corps commander and his promotion to brigadier general in November 1953, however, two episodes of interest took place. The first had to do with the presidential office's concern about Park's "Communist background"; the second was General Ryan's special mention of Park Chung-Hee's performance. As was the case in the United States, all appointments to the field officer's rank required presidential approval, and Park's case was no exception. The staff at the presidential office put Park and the other candidates through a routine security check, and naturally, Park's past ties with the South Korean Workers' Party (Namnodang) surfaced. General Paek quickly doused the fire, however, by guaranteeing Park's integrity.

General Ryan's case requires some background information. It so happened that General Maxwell Taylor, the U.S. Eighth Army Commander, was an artillery officer by training, and he did not believe the short period of training was adequate for the Korean officers. Taylor was also very skeptical about the Korean officers' basic intelligence and education. At least this is how Paek Sŏn-yŏp, the ROK Army chief of staff, interpreted Taylor's attitude. Understandably, Paek was irritated and told Taylor to test the newly trained artillery officers himself. Thereupon, Taylor sent General Cornelius Ryan, the head of the KMAG (Korean Military Advisory Group), to check the records at the U.S. Fifth Artillery Corps where the Korean candidates had received supplementary training and to examine the men. Ryan not only found the Korean officers qualified but found Park Chung-Hee particularly

---

13 Paek Sŏn-yŏp, 266.

impressive.[14] So for three years, from October 1952 to 1955, Park Chung-Hee concentrated on developing his skills as an artillery officer, receiving further training at Fort Sill, Oklahoma's artillery school. Park then commanded the fifth and seventh divisions respectively. He earned an additional star in March 1958 and became a major general.

Thus, Park Chung-Hee's intelligence, diligence, and luck enabled him to climb the ladder of success in the ROK army without difficulty. He rose from the rank of major to major general within a period of eight years. In the meantime, in 1951, he married twenty-six-year-old Yuk Yŏng-su (1925–1974), a young lady eight years his junior; their first daughter, Geun-hye, was born in 1952. Nothing in his vita suggested that he would be different from any other army general rapidly climbing the ranks. He was now one of a small number of elite officers. Park's assignments from July 1959, however, may have given him pause, as he was shifted from one administrative post to another. The assignment in Seoul (July 1959 to January 1960) was to head the 6th military district. The next assignment was to Pusan (January to July 1960) to head the newly created Logistical Command and then to Kwangju (July to September 1960) to head another military district. One could not become an army general by turning into a bureaucrat. Somehow, such line positions as corps commander and army commander eluded him. It is possible that he began to feel frustrated.

We have no record of Park's state of mind during this time in Seoul, but two leading journalists provided us much information about his thoughts and behavior in Pusan, the southernmost port city of the Korean Peninsula, where he served as commander of the logistical

---

14 Paek Sŏn-yŏp, *Kun kwa na* [The Army and I] (Seoul: Taeryuk Yŏn'guso, 1989), 266–267.

command. One of Park's classmates from his days in Taegu happened to be the chief editor of *Pusan Ilbo* (Pusan Daily News), and the two spent many evenings together sharing drinks and conversation. Since Hwang Yong-ju was an unabashed liberal and Park was the opposite, the two classmates often engaged in shouting matches. Yi Pyŏng-ju, who recorded the conversations from memory, was then the chief editor of the other major newspaper of the city, *Kukje Shinbo* (International News). Not being their classmate, Yi's relationship with Park was more formal, and he listened rather than talked. Park's remarks and Yi's observations were culled from different sessions.[15] It may be relevant to note that the author was imprisoned for two years and seven months under the Park regime, on the charge of abetting a Communist sympathizer. In fact, Yi argued, it was because he wrote hundreds of editorials against the police under the Rhee regime. His reflections on Park, in any event, were very cynical and critical. Park's first remark reproduced here is obviously about the elections in progress. The presidential election was scheduled for March 15, 1960, and the air was permeated with politics:

> "Why do they hold elections at all if they are going to have crooked ones! They are all rotten."[16]

> "Oh, the students should demonstrate. They should do it with their upmost if they are going to demonstrate at all."

When the talk was on a certain army general being court-martialed for usurping munitions, Hwang Yong-ju lamented: "There is no future in the nation if the moral of professional soldiers has fallen to that extent."

---

15 Yi Pyŏng-ju, "Major General Park Chung-Hee: That Incorrigible Egomaniac" [in Korean], *Wol'gan Chosŏn* [Monthly Chosŏn] (July 1991), 472–485; Cho Kap-je (1992), quoted much of Yi's article on pp. 269–275.
16 Yi Pyŏng-ju, "Major General Park Chung-Hee," 479.

General Park then pushed his chest forward and declared, "Don't worry about it. Here is a morally upright man."[17] Hwang occasionally tried to lecture Park on the basic tenets of democracy. Park would then wave his arm, saying, "Quit such nonsense about democracy. That's no use. Let's just drink."

5.15 and 2.26

Given the political context in Korea in 1960 and what happened the following year, it is extremely interesting that Park made references to the abortive military coups in Japan that had taken place in the 1930s. The 5.15 Incident refers to the Japanese naval officers' uprising of May 15, 1932, when they were angered by the Japanese government's agreement at the London Conference to reduce the size of the Japanese navy, resulting in the shooting death of Premier Inukai. The 2.26 Incident of 1936 involving army officers is better known, as discussed earlier in another context. The following is the continuation of Yi Pyŏng-ju's recollections.

> General Park looked as though he was infatuated with the ultra-nationalist officers of 5.15 and 2.26 incidents. Perhaps he patterned his behavior after those men; he tried to show himself as a man deeply concerned with national affairs. He normally did not speak much, but once he opened his mouth, he would express his concerns about the nation and the people. He was not breathing air; he was breathing patriotism and the love for the people.[18]
>
> On one occasion, General Park and Mr. Hwang engaged in a heated argument. After General Park extolled the Japanese

17 Ibid., 480.
18 Ibid., 480.

> officers involved in the 5.15 and 2.26 Incidents, Hwang shouted "What the heck are you talking about? They were the absolute believers in their emperor and Japan-centered anachronistic ultra-nationalists. Don't you know they brought Japan down?" General Park then retorted: "What's wrong with Japanese soldiers absolutely believing in their emperor? Why is ultra-nationalism bad?" When Hwang laid out his liberal views about the world being one and talked of the damages to come from self-centered world views General Park simply dismissed it as nonsense.[19]

The argument between the two went on, touching on the virtues of liberalism versus daring spiritual power (or the "can do!" spirit).[20] Park raised the issue: "You said earlier that the ultra-nationalist officers brought Japan down. But has Japan been ruined? It is doing well now, isn't it? Look at history straight. Japan rose again soon after it was defeated."

> Hwang: "Japan was ruined by the ultra-nationalists, but was restored by the liberals who had opposed the ultra-nationalists. Don't get it wrong.
>
> Park: "Liberalism? What do you do with liberalism? The ultra-nationalists' daring spirit is flowing underneath Japanese people today. That spirit produced today's Japan. You are the one that's wrong about Japan.
>
> Hwang: What you need to learn is not the daring spirit (or bald vision) but moral values. The daring spirit without moral values is nothing but savagery. Savagery.

---

19 Ibid., 480.

20 Park used the word *kibaek* here (*kihaku* in Japanese and *qipo* in Chinese), which can also be translated as "boldness of vision, daring" as a Chinese-English dictionary did. The English word *macho* or the expression *can do!* probably comes close to it.

Park: Moral value is a secondary problem. The daring spirit comes first.[21]

The above exchanges reveal a number of points. Yi Pyŏng-ju was right in saying that Park was infatuated with the officers' rebellion in the 5.15 and 2.26 incidents. He admired their daring spirit or boldness of vision, proactively eliminating what they perceived to be evil. Park saw no wrong in Japanese soldiers absolutely believing in their emperor and their ultranationalism. Very much like them, Park was devotedly patriotic, to the extent that Yi said Park was breathing patriotism. He also showed pride in being an upright person opposed to corruption. Park declared himself to be "a morally upright man." And that's why he found his army lacking and the Syngman Rhee regime abominable. Many graduates of the Japanese Military Academy would have echoed Park's views.

Park on Syngman Rhee

It is in this context that Park denounced President Rhee in harsh terms. The content of the conversation suggests this was around March 1960, when students began their demonstrations against the Rhee regime and demanded Rhee's resignation. The talk on Rhee started with Park's criticism of Yi Pyŏng-ju, our reporter. Park said, "I found Hwang Yong-ju's editorial clearly against Rhee but yours was ambivalent. Perhaps you are too warm-hearted?" Yi responded: "Well, I resent him too but somehow I feel uncomfortable hearing about him leaving office. That's probably why I was ambivalent."[22]

21 Ibid., 480.
22 Ibid., 481.

Park reacted with a stronger voice:

> "No. That's not right. There is no room for sympathy. Wasn't it enough for him to occupy that position for twelve years? Even then he wanted to stay on for another term, and resorted to illegal practices. It simply does not make sense. First of all, it is wrong to think that he alone can handle things right (or he is indispensable). He must be condemned in the style of Spring and Autumn writers (of ancient China) to warn the later generations.[23]
>
> I felt General Park was right, but I explained that I simply could not cruelly condemn the man who spent his seventy years fighting for Korean independence.
>
> Park responded to me in an icy tone.
>
> "You say he spent his whole life fighting for independence? All he did was to give some lectures to the compatriots abroad or submit petitions to American presidents. Can you really say that Korea became independent because of their independence movement? It is all bogus, their talk of having engaged in independence movement.[24]

As the discussion became heated, Hwang Yong-ju interjected, admonishing Park for his harsh comments. Hwang said there may have been bogus fighters, but there were also true fighters. It was because of them that the Korean people could keep their pride today.

Hwang's statement incensed General Park even more.

> "They enabled us to keep our pride? Who were those that shamed us by organizing political parties like the

---

23 Ibid., 481.
24 Ibid., 482.

mushrooms sprouting after the rain? Weren't they those who claimed to have engaged in independent movement?"

Hwang: "Well, that's another story."

"What do you mean that's another story. All they did was to engage in factional struggles while claiming to engage in the independence movement. That habit led the country into confusion after its liberation. Can you still say they allowed us to keep our pride?"[25]

Readers of the above account may find some of Park's comments ironic, particularly his denunciation of Rhee's intent to stay in power even after twelve years. Park's rule lasted even longer than Rhee's—eighteen years. Park reportedly prepared for retirement before the end of his last term as president, but many accused him of plotting to be a generalissimo, or a lifetime dictator. Park's statements here are very important though, because he repeated many of the same points later in his publications. His seven-month stay in Beijing obviously gave him some insight, and one might say authority, on the factional struggles among exiled leaders. His evaluation of Rhee and his cohorts abroad was among the harshest one will encounter anywhere.

Syngman Rhee, as Yi Pyŏng-ju's narration indicated, had been a well-known nationalist leader. He established himself as a passionate fighter against the decadent old kingdom in the 1890s and suffered more than five years of imprisonment before he was released in 1904. Sent to the United States by patriotic leaders to plead for Korean independence in 1905, he met President Theodore Roosevelt briefly to submit a petition on behalf of the Koreans. He then earned a doctorate in international politics from Princeton University under President Woodrow Wilson in

25 Ibid., 482.

1910 and became a widely known Christian educator at the Seoul YMCA until 1913, when he exiled himself to the United States to avoid Japanese colonial suppression.[26] In 1919, when the exiled revolutionaries organized the Provisional Government of the Republic of Korea, Rhee was chosen to be the president. These facts were well known, but Park raised an important question as to whether Rhee and his cohorts abroad actually contributed to the cause of Korean independence. That question requires us to consider how Korea became independent in 1948.

The Role of the Nationalists

As regrettable as it may have been for the Korean people, they did not win their independence through their struggle against the Japanese empire. The old Chosŏn kingdom did not have the power or strength to resist the Japanese takeover of Korea in 1905, nor did the people acquire the strength to wage a war against the Japanese. Some of the Korean nationalists did wage battles against the Japanese army in Korea and Manchuria between 1907 and the early 1920s, and then again in the 1930s, but they were no match for a modern army strong enough to wage a war against the United States. Only when the United States and its allies defeated Japan in 1945 was it possible for Korea to regain independence. The victorious powers thus won the right to decide the fate of the Japanese colonies, including Korea. Thus seen, the most important factor for Korean independence was the attitude and policies of the United States and her allies.

But why did the United States and its allies opt for Korean independence? Why did President Franklin D. Roosevelt (FDR) and Generalissimo Chiang Kai-shek of China pledge their support for

26 See Robert T. Oliver, *Syngman Rhee: The Man behind the Myth* (New York: Dodd Mead, 1955); Chong-Sik Lee, *The Prison Years of a Young Radical* (Seoul: Yonsei University Press, 2001).

Korean independence when they met with Prime Minister Churchill of Great Britain at the Cairo conference of November 1943? Prime Minister Churchill, as is well known, was an imperialist who staunchly opposed any notion of liberating colonies, regardless of which power possessed them. He simply did not want the "germ of liberation" to spread, lest it lead to the fall of the British Empire. I have already related Chiang Kai-shek's support for Korean nationalists. But why did Roosevelt show an interest in Korea? The United States had had very little contact with Korea after Japan took over Korea's foreign relations in 1905, and neither *Korea* nor *Chosŏn* appeared on any world maps. The only Americans who paid any attention to Korea were the Christian missionaries, but they assiduously avoided politics in order not to jeopardize their primary task of proselytizing and spreading evangelical messages. They knew the Japanese authorities were watching them very closely and hence avoided anything that would provoke the Japanese.

This is why the Korean nationalists in the United States were so important. From 1919, many Koreans living there devoted themselves to the task of drawing American attention to the injustices perpetrated in Korea. The Korean population in the United States was less than several thousand, and most, about five thousand, worked in sugar plantations on the islands of Hawaii earning a dollar a day, but these workers pooled their resources for the cause of Korean independence. Sŏ Chae-p'il, the veteran of the reformist movement of the 1890s and the first Korean to earn a medical degree in the United States, and Syngman Rhee, the first Korean to earn a Ph.D there, became expatriate leaders. They inundated American mass media with their appeals and propaganda, presented their case to various international conferences, and made "presentations" to U.S. presidents and Congress at various times. They even succeeded in winning the support of Mrs. Eleanor Roosevelt, FDR's wife, who was sympathetic to the cause of oppressed peoples.[27]

We cannot establish a direct link from these activities to FDR's concern about Korea at Cairo, but neither Roosevelt nor the State Department would have paid attention to the Korean issue without the prolonged and intense efforts of the Koreans abroad. They simply did not let the State Department or the president forget the Korean people's desire for independence and tried their best to keep the Korean issue alive in the American mass media. It is not an overstatement to say that the Cairo Declaration on Korea was the fruit of their efforts. Park Chung-Hee's dismissal of Rhee and the other nationalist leaders abroad, therefore, was unwarranted.

But why did Rhee become so unpopular? Why did he find himself the object of denunciatory demonstrations in 1960? Why did Park oppose him with such vehemence? Did he not play a major role in founding the Republic of Korea in 1948? Did he not lead the South Korean people through the most difficult years after the North Korean invasion?

The principal problem was Rhee's unshakable belief in his indispensability. Having accomplished much, he firmly believed he was the only one who could attain Korean unification. He also feared others would be too weak to defend Korea's integrity before the United States. Unfortunately for him, however, nature would not let him stay young forever; neither would the democratic system allow him to stay in power for long. The combination of these factors provided power-hungry politicians an opportunity to usurp power from Rhee, and they relished it.

27 For details about Rhee's activities in the United States, see Robert T. Oliver, *Syngman Rhee: the Man behind the Myth* (New York: Dodd Mead, 1960); see also Chong-Sik Lee, *The Politics of Korean Nationalism*, chapters 7, 10–12.

The result was a dictatorship of the worst kind during the last two years of Rhee's third term (1956–1960).[28] The vicious politicians hid behind President Rhee and an organization called the Liberal Party to do everything possible to extend their rule. Park Chung-Hee's fury against Rhee, therefore, is quite understandable.

Yi Pyŏng-ju's account of Park Chung-Hee's mind-set in Pusan makes it easy to accept the notion that he began to prepare for a coup against President Rhee there. The straw that broke the camel's back was the Liberal Party's use of armed forces in the presidential and vice-presidential elections. Rhee might have been reelected to his fourth term of office even if Cho Pyŏng-ok, his opponent in the 1960 presidential election, had not died on February 15, just a month before the election was scheduled.[29] Everyone was aware, however, that Rhee's running mate for vice president, Yi Ki-bung, simply did not have a chance of defeating the opposition candidate Chang Myŏn, who was the incumbent vice president. Unfortunately for Yi Ki-bung, he could not ride Rhee's coattail; he had to be elected by popular vote. Therefore, Rhee's Liberal Party resorted to all available means, legal or illegal, to ensure Yi Ki-bung's election. Rhee was eighty-five years old that year, and everyone believed it highly likely that the next vice president would quickly succeed him.

Rhee's party had used the army for electoral purposes before, but there was a stronger need in 1960 to mobilize their votes. The seven hundred thousand votes of the armed forces personnel were too important to be left alone. All pretenses were thrown out the window, and the

---

28 See Hahn-Been Lee, *Korea: Time, Change, and Administration* (Honolulu: East-West Center Press, 1968), chapter 5, particularly 98–108.

29 Cho Pyŏng-ok died at the Walter Reed Hospital in Washington, D.C., sparing Rhee the suspicion of malfeasance.

army chief of staff Song Yo-ch'an toured various units himself to ensure that the army delivered the votes for Rhee and Yi Ki-bung. The party also assigned politically appointed high-ranking army officers to various units to ensure its victory. It is in this connection that Kim Chong-sin's witness account is important. He was a reporter in Pusan, attached to the army units there. He attended a dinner that General Song hosted just before the election, inviting high-ranking military officers and a number of journalists. The host tried to create a jovial mood, and everyone joined in the laughter except the stone-faced Park, who kept on drinking in silence. Then the journalists jokingly complained to the chief of staff that General Park, the logistical command's chief, had lately distanced himself from the press. General Song, in turn, mockingly admonished Park not to be so aloof. And this was when the reporter heard Park's muttering, which shocked him. One could not translate the Korean expletive without breaking the code of propriety, but it referred to a part of the male body with a four-letter word added to it. Park's voice was low, to be sure, but Kim was sure that General Song had heard him, as Park had intended.[30]

The same journalist recorded another event he witnessed, and together with his expletive against General Song, one can easily detect in hindsight that Park was ready to strike. Either of these events was offensive enough for the ruling party to punish him, and a man without a remedial plan would not have chosen such a path. Here is Kim Chong-sin's account of the second incident:

> It was two or three days before the balloting. I was sitting in a corner of the [Logical Command's] commander's

30 Kim Chong-sin, *Yŏngsi ui hoetbul* [The Flare at Midnight] (Seoul: Hanrim, 1966), 34–36.

> office working on my notes. General Park was engaged in serious conversation with his Chief of Staff Brigadier Hwang P'il-ju, warming their hands in the office stove. Colonel "P" in charge of supervising the election in the Pusan area army personnel walked in. He wielded great influence at this time as he had the backing of a top man of the Liberal Party.
>
> He said, as soon as he saluted the General, "Your Excellency. Please do not be obdurate and cooperate [with us]. Please call together the officers under you and encourage them [to mobilize the troops for the election.]"
>
> It appeared from what he said he had tried this before. The two Generals suddenly stopped talking. Park then stared at the stove in silence, his hand holding a cigarette trembling. Colonel "P" continued in a voice of issuing a command. "Your Excellency. Please consider my position and help me. Just once, please call the unit commanders and talk to them.
>
> General Park abruptly raised his head. "I cannot do such a thing. I am the one who must supervise my subordinates. How could I commit such a foul act?" His voice became colder. "What's the purpose of having such an election? Do as you wish!" He glared at the Colonel and then pulled out the bundle of ballots on his desk. He tore them all into pieces and threw them into the stove.[31]

Another issue that angered Park was the collusion between politicians and the army. This had been the cause of the Japanese officers' revolt in 1936, and Park was very sensitive about it. But, according to Kim Se-jin, who interviewed many senior officers to write his book on Park's coup d'état, Rhee's party used the army as a source of political funding.

---

31 Ibid., 41–43.

> Rhee asked more than mere loyalty from the favored officers. He asked for financial contributions that were used to shore up the sagging political popularity of the President. The military, which dispensed over 40 percent of the national budget and roughly 400 million dollars of annual aid from the U.S. in arms and other commercially valuable goods, became the major supplier of political funds for Rhee's vast political machine.[32]

Rhee's defenders would argue that he had nothing to do with corruption. It was the leaders of the Liberal Party who clamored for political funds; their needs multiplied as the popularity of the octogenarian president plummeted after the election for his third term in 1956. But Rhee could not evade the responsibility for what was going on. He was the president of the government, and he headed the deplorable party. He should have known better than to force himself on the young republic when he was eighty-five years old. The aged politician would have been astonished, in any event, if he had learned how the army raised the money:

> Among many unlawful plans to raise money, the most frequently used method was the outright marketing of such commercially valuable war materials as petroleum, automobiles (i.e., trucks) and their parts, and most vital foodstuffs. A more ingenious method—and one which yielded a tremendous amount of money—involved the diverting of monetary allowances designated for the purchase of secondary foodstuffs for 600,000 soldiers. Also, kickbacks were openly demanded, not only for granting a contract, but also for allowing goods of inferior quality to pass inspection.[33]

32 Kim Se-Jin, *The Politics of Military Revolution in Korea* (Chapel Hill, N.C., University of North Carolina Press, 1971), 75.
33 Ibid., 75.

The “secondary foodstuffs” Kim mentioned here did not refer to fruits or desserts. He was referring to the contents of the bowl of soup the soldiers received at each meal with a bowl of rice: meats, eggs, vegetables, and so on. On paper, the soldiers consumed a certain amount of beef, chicken, or pork each day, but there was a saying in the military barracks that the “cows walked through our soup pot with rubber boots on,” meaning the cows left no trace in the soup. Bean sprouts often substituted for more expensive meats or vegetables. The Liberal Party was not the only culprit. The generals and others took “their share.”

Kim Se-jin’s denunciation did not stop with the president or the generals. Corruption became pervasive.

> The gravitation of the senior officers into the world of politics and financial irregularities led them to increasingly shady operations. In order to be protected from the often harassing National Assembly, from the Government Auditing Office—the watchdog of government expenditures—and from the JMPM (Joint Military Provost Marshall), the high-ranking generals had to make increasingly greater financial concessions to Rhee and his party, further compromising their personal integrity and political neutrality. The financial and material misappropriation rapidly spread at all levels of the military; low-ranking officers began to imitate their superiors. Indeed, the corruption within the military was rampant.
>
> In the final analysis, corruption and graft, the decline of morale and the compromise of leadership, and the friction between the junior and senior officers were largely the results of violating political neutrality by the military and the abetting of factional struggles by Rhee.[34]

34 Ibid., 76.

Why did corruption within the military become so rampant? Were the Chinese right in saying "Good iron does not become a nail; a good man does not become a soldier?" Were the men in the military service exceptionally corrupt, or were there other factors at work? The answer to these questions is negative. Military men were not exceptional. It had to do with the government's policy. Inflation had been one of the principal concerns of the Rhee government in fighting the war against Communist North Korea, and it tried not to aggravate the situation by raising the salary of government employees, including the seven hundred thousand military personnel. That, of course, did not stop the steady rise in prices when the country was at war, and a monthly salary of a lieutenant could not pay for more than two bowls of noodles. His family had to manage with the monthly allotments of food grains alone. Kim Se-jin described this situation:

> The ridiculously low pay scale for the ROK Army in the early 1950s was the reason for the military personnel's itchy fingers. In 1952, privates received only the dollar equivalent of fifty cents a month, and captains received the equivalent of six dollars a month.[35]

Even sixty dollars would not have been enough for the captain. American soldiers fresh out of training camp at this time earned more than seventy dollars a month, and most had no family to support.

It is doubtful that many generals approved of the Liberal Party's use of the army for politics. But Park Chung-Hee and Yi Chong-ch'an, the commandant of the War College, were the ones best known for openly

---

35 Ibid., 76, footnote 30; "Park rectified the situation after he took over the government. The combined annual income in salary and allowances averaged $1,500 for generals and $650 for junior officers."

defying the Liberal Party.[36] President Syngman Rhee announced his resignation on April 19, 1960, ending his long political career and plunging South Korea into turmoil. Vice President Chang Myŏn, who had been Rhee's ambassador in Washington, D.C., emerged as the new head of the government in August, but he had neither the charisma nor the political experience or the political organization behind him to control the floodgate of demands for freedom opened by the student revolution. What irked the public more was the internal wrangling of the Democratic Party, which had replaced Rhee's Liberal Party. The loss of its presidential candidate, Cho Pyŏng-ok proved to be fatal for the Democrats. The so-called new and old factions within that party washed their soiled laundry in public, and even the liberal elements in Korean society began to shy away from them. This is when Park Chung-Hee launched his coup d'état. He had long studied the strategy of military revolt since his days at Manchukuo Military Academy, where Lieutenant Kanno had lectured him on the abortive 2.26 revolt. He knew how to neutralize the incumbent chief of staff Chang Do-yŏng; all he had to do was dangle a carrot in front of his eyes. He did see great risks ahead, but he plunged ahead in the early morning of May 16, 1961.

The Specter of Namnodang

In planning the coup, Park worried about the reaction of the United Nations commander.[37] The Korean War had brought the U.S. Army back into Korea, and the Americans naturally had a keen interest in the top-ranking Korean army officers. President Truman's decision to intervene against the North Korean invasion in 1950 drastically changed

---

36 Sungjoo Han, *The Failure of Democracy in South Korea* (Berkeley: University of California Press, 1974), 59.
37 Cho Kap-je (1992), 267.

the U.S. role from that time onward, particularly because President Syngman Rhee placed the ROK army under United Nations command. Unfortunately for Park, General Carter Magruder, the commander of the U.S. Eighth Army who concurrently held the title of UN commander, happened to hold a very negative view of him.

Ironically, Park's past surfaced as an issue because General Yi Chong-ch'an, the new defense minister under the Chang Myŏn government, had recommended Park Chung-Hee to be the new army chief of staff.[38] Premier Chang then consulted General Magruder, who would have had to work closely with the Korean army chief. Magruder was startled by the ROK army headquarters' response when he inquired about the recommended candidate: General Kim Hyŏng-il, the Deputy Chief of Staff, told him that Park Chung-Hee was a "leftist." Magruder reportedly exclaimed, "How could you have such a man in such an important position?" Not only was Park not appointed the army's chief of staff, he was exiled from his position as chief of operations in the army headquarters. Instead, Park was made the deputy commander of the Second Army in Taegu.[39] Some of his colleagues thought this to be the preliminary step toward his retirement, because his new position carried little responsibility.[40] Namnodang cast a long shadow on Park's career.

---

38 Chŏng Un-yŏn, *Sillok kun'in Pak Chŏng-hui* [Veritable Record of the Soldier Park Chung-Hee] (Seoul: Kaema, 2004), 161. This author heard about this episode from General Han Mu-hyŏp, who had worked under Park Chung-Hee in the intelligence bureau. General Yi Chong-ch'an, who was then the commandant of the war college, recommended Park Chung-Hee, according to Han.

39 Ibid., 160–163; his new appointment took place on December 8, 1960.

40 This was what Kim An-il, Park's longtime friend, thought. (Chung'ang Ilbo, *Sillok Pak Chŏng-hui*, 72).

One might attribute General Kim Hyŏng-il's remark about Park being a "leftist" to jealousy or malice, because Kim was in competition for the chief-of-staff position. But Kim was not alone in holding a negative view of Park. General Chŏng Kang, Park's classmate from the Constabulary Academy agreed. He confided to a reporter later that he thought Park to be a "dangerous man" and was quite startled when he discovered that Park Chung-Hee headed the junta that overthrew the democratic regime. He was afraid that Park Chung-Hee, as the new head of the government, would submit South Korea on a platter to Kim Il-sŏng in North Korea.[41]

General Chŏng did not know it, but General Magruder shared the same fear when he heard of the coup and was ready to order the ROK's armed forces to suppress the junta. Seoul's streets were about to turn into a battleground unless Park was willing to abandon the coup attempt and face another court-martial. There was a distinct possibility of Park's coup ending just as Japan's 2.26 Incident of 1936 had, when the young officers surrendered their arms after attempting a coup against the civilian government in power. While Park commanded a determined group of officers and men, his force of 3,750 could be no match to the 720,000-troop ROK army, navy, and air force. Park's junta had little chance of winning against an all-out assault, particularly because many general officers of the army opposed the coup.

General Magruder was determined to act against Park's forces, but not because he wanted to uphold the constitutional order in the Republic of Korea. Politics in South Korea was clearly out of his area of responsibility. Park, as a general officer, had violated military rules when he mobilized units of the ROK army and Marine Corps without prior

41 Chŏng Un-yŏn, *Sillok kun'in Pak Chŏng-hui*, 143.

authorization as specified by U.S.-ROK agreement, but this did not constitute sufficient ground for the U.N. commander to intervene. But an insurrection by a "Communist general" was a totally different matter, because Magruder was charged with the responsibility of defending the ROK from Communist enemies. The United States had already expended over fifty-five thousand lives and enormous sums of money and energy to defend South Korea and had pledged to defend it through the Mutual Defense Treaty of 1953. Magruder would have been derelict in his duty had he chosen not to prevent the Communist takeover of South Korea.

What went through Magruder's mind and what developed afterward is recorded by Kim Chŏng-ryŏl. Kim had been the Air Force Academy commandant when Park Chung-Hee was under arrest, but later served as the ROK government's defense minister. He had welcomed Magruder to Korea in that capacity in 1959, and the two had gotten to know each other well to the extent that they were on a first-name basis. (Kim Chŏng-ryŏl was known to his American friends as "Mike.") This is why the two met again on May 18, two days after Park's coup. We begin with Magruder's summation of the situation as Kim recorded it.[42]

> About 2,700 junta men under Major General Park Chung-Hee are now occupying Seoul. He is a Communist according to our information. He is not showing it now, but he will show his colors sooner or later. So, we are questioning the character and the future of the coup.

42 Kim Chŏng-ryŏl, "5–16, Park Chŏng-Hui Magrudŏ hoedam naemak" [The Inside Story of Park Chung-Hee-Magruder Meeting], *Shin-dong-a* (September 1993), 430–455. Kim Chŏng-ryŏl's conversation with Magruder was in English, but I had to translate it back from the Korean version Kim had recorded.

> As you know, we have a good example in the 1958 coup in Iraq. The West did not know much about General Kassim when he overthrew the monarchy, but he was a Communist. What happened there after that? Kassim led the revolution to the socialist direction. So we ended up with a Communist regime after the monarchy.[43] We are not sure whether the same thing is happening in Korea right now, but we are worried about it. So it is unfortunate, but we have decided to suppress the junta through force in order to cut the buds off before Communism takes over.

General Kim knew the army enough to ask Magruder about the opinion of the incumbent ROK chief of staff, General Chang Do-yŏng, but Magruder's terse answer surprised Kim: "We don't trust Chang." Chang was too wishy-washy to be trusted. The dialogue continued:

> What would you do if Park Chung-Hee was not a Communist?
>
> What are you talking about, Mike? Park not being a Communist?
>
> What are you going to do if Park is not a Communist?
>
> If Park is not a Communist? What a strange question!

Magruder's eyes narrowed in bafflement, but he mulled over Kim's repeated question and said, "If so, we must think it over."

General Kim then told Magruder in an authoritative voice, "Park Chung-Hee is not a Communist."

---

43 At age three, King Faisal II succeeded his father, Ghazi I, who was killed in an automobile accident in 1939. Faisal and his uncle, Crown Prince Abdul-Illah, were assassinated in July 1958 in a coup that ended the monarchy and brought to power a military junta headed by Abdul Karem Kassim. Kassim reversed the monarchy's pro-Western policies, attempted to rectify the economic disparities between rich and poor, and began to form alliances with Communist countries, Infoplease online by Pearson Education.

Magruder responded in surprise: “Of course, I believe what Mike says regardless of what hundreds of others tell me!”

Kim then explained how Park came to be suspected of being a Communist and assured Magruder that he was not one. The American general then asked Kim what should be done. Kim Chŏng-ryŏl mulled over the question a moment and suggested that Magruder talk to Park Chung-Hee himself before making any decisions. Kim had saved Park Chung-Hee from certain death in 1949. Twelve years later, he dispelled Namnodang’s specter from the United Nations commander.

Park Chung-Hee had been informed of Kim’s meeting with Magruder and was anxious to hear what had happened. The American response toward the coup had been his concern even when he was plotting it, but Magruder and the U.S. acting ambassador Green had already issued a statement on the sixteenth against Park’s junta. Park, therefore, was pleased with Kim’s results and agreed to meet Magruder the next morning, May 19. Nevertheless, Magruder’s office called Kim at 11:00 a.m. the following morning to say that Park had not shown up for the meeting, nor had he called to explain why he was not there. Colonel Pak T’ae-jun, Park’s secretary, told the bewildered Kim that the Chairman of the Supreme Revolutionary Council had gone down to Pusan, three hundred miles south of Seoul, to attend a mass rally in support of the military revolution.[44] Park obviously wanted to send Magruder an unspoken message that he was not going to be intimidated. American presence in Korea may have been important to him, but the American commander was not going to bully him again. It was bad enough that Magruder had driven him away from army headquarters five months earlier. In the meantime, Park had arranged with Yun

44 Kim Chŏng-ryŏl, 442.

Po-sŏn, the incumbent president, to support the junta. Yun did not have executive power under the new constitution, which made him only the titular head of the state with very limited powers, but Yun's statement was enough to legitimize the junta regime.

The content of the conversation between Generals Magruder and Park Chung-Hee has not been released to the public, but it is not very difficult to surmise. There is no doubt that Magruder tried to confirm what Kim Chŏng-ryŏl had told him, that is, Park was not a Communist. Park, on the other hand, did his best to assure Magruder and his deputies that he was indeed against Communism in every way and close cooperation with the United States was his first priority. Magruder and Park would also have discussed the reasons for Park's extraordinary step against the democratic regime and his aspirations as a junta leader.

The statement the junta issued on May 16, 1961, known as the "Hyongmyong Kongyak" [the Junta's Pledge], must be viewed with this background in mind. The junta obviously anticipated General Magruder's concern. The first item was the junta being against Communism. The second was about following or observing the United Nations charter and cooperating particularly with the United States. Park Chung-Hee's outrage that had led to the coup, thus, was relegated to the third position, followed by economic aims. The inclusion of the term "*chaju kyŏngje*," or autonomous economy, draws one's attention. The Pledge then referred to the obligatory mention of national unification: "All efforts must be concentrated on nurturing the strength that can effectively confront Communism to fulfill the national desire for unification." Implicit in the statement is the criticism of the past efforts against Communism, but more important, what Park Chung-Hee wanted was to develop South Korea's economy as a means of confronting North Korea.

The Magruder-Park conversation would also have touched on the sixth and the last item in the Pledge. Magruder probably asked Park how long he intended to rule South Korea and when he would restore democracy. His promise was that he would yield power to politicians whenever his task was accomplished. One should note that items 3, 4, and 5 were not objectives that could be accomplished within a year or two. Indeed, they would require decades. But it was not Park's only conditional phrase. He would yield power only when "fresh and conscientious"[45] politicians emerged. Needless to say, he did not indicate who was to decide on such qualifications. The U.S. government had to change its position, and Washington even invited Park to the White House in November, where President John Kennedy greeted South Korea's new president.

---

45 "Ch'amsin hago do yangsim jŏk'in" chŏngch'iin."

CONCLUSIONS

Why did Park Chung-Hee launch his political career in 1961 by lambasting Korean history? Why did he follow up two years later by saying, "Our five thousand years of history was a continuation of degeneration, crudity, and stagnation" and "We should set ablaze all our history that was more like a storehouse of evil"? Why should anyone pay attention to such an outlandish statement by a young military man?

I contend that these statements not only deserve our attention but are essential to understanding Park Chung-Hee's mind-set. Indeed, Park's interpretation of Korean history constitutes the key to his drive to overcome barriers from his childhood. It was Park's disgust and indignation against Korea's past that pushed him through elementary school to his success as an adult. Twentieth-century Korea was fortunate that Park Chung-Hee directed his seething anger to the positive result of developing his country's economy. Park's goal was not only to undo the wrongs of the past but also to transform the national character that the old regimes had fostered. His characterization of the Korean people's behavior pattern was indeed extreme: "While the powerful abused their authority, engaged in corruption and accumulated wealth, the people came to accept intrigues, slander, and false accusations as a means of advancing in the world."

The germ of Park's anger, or his sociopolitical consciousness, was planted very early in his life. The young child could not help but notice the wide discrepancy in wealth and lifestyle between his immediate family and that of his third uncle, his father's younger brother. His uncle's family could enjoy rice, the most valued and preferred staple food of the Koreans, while his family had to be content with barley or millet, the coarse and cheapest grain. His uncle's family lived in the lowland surrounded by rice fields, while his family had to live on high mountain ground surrounded by graves, with very little to eat. Something was definitely amiss given the fact that his father was the first son, who should have inherited the family estate from his grandfather.

We do not know whether anyone in the family solved this puzzle for him or if he solved it himself while growing up. His mother gave him a clear clue by repeatedly teasing him, saying that he would not have been born had his father been executed for joining the Tonghak rebels. But who were the Tonghak rebels? Why did they rebel? Why had his father gotten involved in such a rebellion? Park Chung-Hee was too bright a child not to ask these questions. He may have had to wait until he reached the Taegu Normal School to understand the history involved, but he was astute enough to raise questions about Korean history.

Park's misgivings and doubts about the Chosŏn kingdom would have intensified when he read Yi Kwang-su's account of Admiral Yi Sun-shin. It would have enlightened him to discover that Korea was once a kingdom, which had been invaded by Japan in the late sixteenth century. While the admiral made his mark by his bravery, strategy, and loyalty, he appeared on the scene only in 1597, five years after Hideyoshi's army had overrun the Korean territory with impunity. Why had King Sŏnjo and his cabinet officers not stopped the invaders? Where was the Korean army? Why did that army let the Japanese traverse the peninsula from the southern end to the northern border, virtually without resistance? Why hadn't the Koreans used their geographical barriers to stop the Japanese? Why was there such a contrast between the invading Japanese army generals and their

Korean counterparts? A Korean child would have shed tears as he read about the Japanese invasion.

The admiral, in the end, saved the kingdom from the Japanese, but what humiliation and suffering he endured at the hands of backbiting, jealous, and selfish politicians! Park admired the admiral, while harboring disgust and anger for the court politicians, who represented the ruling elite. Park Chung-Hee could not but share Teacher Kim Yŏng-ki's fury against Korea's past rulers.

Park Chung-Hee attributed much of the Chosŏn Dynasty's problems to its class system, which resulted in both the rulers and the subjects becoming unproductive, unscrupulous, and corrupt. His opening statement on the subject was as follows:

> General Yi Sŏng-gye founded a new [Chosŏn] dynasty in 1392 after overthrowing the previous regime, but his reforms did not alter the fundamental structure the [previous] Koryŏ dynasty had. Yi's new regime divided the people into two classes as before, the *yangban* and the commoners, giving the former monopoly of power.[1]

Not only did the yangban have a monopoly of power; they were also exempt from taxes, military duties, and other obligations. Whatever the government needed had to be imposed on the commoners, whose lives inevitably became harder as years went by. And since the civil service examinations for government positions were limited to the yangban class, their sole occupation had become preparation for these examinations, disparaging all nonintellectual activities as demeaning. Soon,

1 Park Chung-Hee, *Kukka wa hyŏngmyŏng kwa na* [The Nation, Revolution, and I] (Seoul: Hyangmunsa, 1963), 66, 67–68.

Korean society was inundated with an idle population.[2] The monopoly of power inevitably bred abuse and corruption, and the Confucian ideology became nothing but a shell, as Park told his teacher Kishi. In time, the system simply ignored the welfare of the people and the state.

Under this system, the farmers had no incentive to work hard or be productive because the yangban, as landowners, took away as much of the crops as possible. What the yangban landowners did not take away was then taken by unscrupulous government officials, greedy for more. Many commoners found it too onerous to bear the financial burden for the rest of society and even voluntarily chose to become slaves in yangban households. By doing so, they not only escaped the tax and corvée burdens the state imposed but were also exempted from military duties.

This system in the end made people lethargic, without any desire to accomplish anything new.[3] It also prevented the emergence of men with an adventurous or enterprising spirit. The structure simply would not tolerate such an individual, who could disturb the social and political equilibrium. What it encouraged instead was a slave mentality; commoners would either ingratiate themselves to the powerful or abandon all effort. Escapism became the norm, and people became prone to tears and self-pity.[4]

---

2 Hong Tae-yong (1731–1783), the eighteenth-century reformer, described the situation: "Our country attaches so much value to the name (honor) and status that those belonging to the *yangban* class would not engage in labor of any kind even if they face starvation. They will sit with folded arms and will not take up hoes or spade. If someone of their class chooses to engage in such work, he will be scorned and ridiculed as if he has fallen to become a slave," quoted by Kang Chae-ŏn, *Kindai Chōsen no henkaku shisō* [Transformative Thoughts in Modern Korea] (Tokyo: Nihon Hyōronsha, 1973), 23, from Hong's collected works entitled *Tamhŏnsŏ*. Tamhŏn was Hong Tae-yong's pen name.

3 Park, *Kukka wa hyŏngmyŏng kwa na*, 71.

4 Ibid., 96.

This reprehensible class system was abolished as early as in 1884, but much of the legacy remained, in Park Chung-Hee's opinion. First and foremost, he had personally experienced a farmer's life of poverty. Secondly, Korea's abominable national character remained unchanged. Park's hope was to alter the national character by eliminating poverty.

Park Chung-Hee also criticized Korea's ancestors for their lack of backbone. They not only allowed big powers abroad to push them around but willingly followed foreign culture, to the extent of forgetting their national identity.[5] In their long history of suffering under foreign pressure and conquests, Korea's ancestors never once pushed out to the outside world to show the nation's strength. And even worse, Korea suffered aggression not only because the peninsula's geography imposed limits, but also because Koreans regarded themselves as weaklings, suited only to submit to great powers. What Korea needed, according to Park, was to attain independence (*chaju*) and progress (*paljŏn*) by rooting out this inveterate disease (*kojil*) of this evil legacy.[6]

By the time Park Chung-Hee reached these conclusions, however, he was well on his way to escaping the confines of such an environment. It was not because the environment had turned in his favor, however. His family still lived in the primitive mountain village, and his commute to the elementary school required eight miles of walking each day. But he discovered that his efforts made a difference; he had qualities that enabled him to outperform other children in the same class. The elementary school under Japanese colonialism did not differentiate on the basis of students' family backgrounds. Park could not only escape from dire poverty but could dream impossible dreams of grandeur.

---

5 *Kukka wa hyŏngmyŏng kwa n*a, 245.

6 Ibid., 246.

The Father

Park Chung-Hee suffered from the poverty "imposed by his father," but he inherited qualities that served him well. While we know very little about Park's first two brothers and sisters, his third brother was clearly gifted. A mountain-town boy with only four years of education in Kumi, Sang-Hee taught himself enough to become a reporter for national newspapers, as well as a local leader. Relatives and neighbors probably considered it only natural that Sang-Hee's younger brother was as smart as he was. Chung-Hee's intelligence, in combination with the confidence he gained in childhood, took him far.

We also know that Park Chung-Hee gained self-confidence early in life. Perhaps his mother's love was enough to bestow this trait. Or he may have gained confidence while playing with the children in his village. But his experiences at elementary school were crucial. A class leader under the Japanese educational system had the status equivalent to a platoon leader in the army. Park would line up classmates in military style in the school yard, command them to march to class, bark orders to the class when the teacher entered the room, and even occasionally serve as the teacher's assistant. It was clearly a leadership role that gave him confidence. There is little doubt that Park Chung-Hee enjoyed his role as class leader. He devoted many lines to this experience in his short biography, written many decades later.

One could say that he had inherited his rebellious streak from his father, who had paid an exorbitant price for joining the Tonghak movement against the Chosŏn Dynasty. His father was definitely not the type to succumb to despair or panic under duress. He did not even allow a menacing tiger to make him lose his wits. We cannot say whether this was an inborn quality or something he acquired through learning, but it served Park Chung-Hee well, just as it helped his father to survive.

Napoleon Bonaparte

It is easy to understand why Park as a sixth-grade child was fascinated by biographies of Napoleon Bonaparte. Napoleon reached military and political heights in spite of his adverse family and political background, and Corsica shared many similarities with colonial Korea. Napoleon not only refused to succumb to the hurdles placed before him but turned them into stepping stones for higher achievement. All that mattered were one's determination and effort. Napoleon did not allow his environment to dictate his course. Park admired Napoleon's perseverance and fortitude, but above all, his daring spirit. The phrase "Impossible is not in my dictionary" was an expression well known to all elementary schoolchildren of this time. Park had even more reason to admire Napoleon after becoming familiar with the spineless and corrupt rulers of Korean history. Napoleon, in any event, spurred Park Chung-Hee on.

Poverty

Park's statement about poverty having been his teacher and benefactor is easy to accept. But it does not convey the depth of suffering he had to endure. The tears he shed walking to the railroad station in Taegu would have left a deep imprint in his heart. The school found it impossible to delay the submission of required payment any further, but Park knew too well that his family simply had no means of producing the measly sum of money. His grades declined precipitously, as he had to miss classes for the lack of money, and his teachers found him *fumajime* or frivolous. We will never know how close Park was to giving up his pursuit of success, but there was a strong chance of his becoming victimized by despair.

It is not difficult to see, therefore, why Park set the elimination of poverty as his primary goal when he attained power in 1961. The liquidation of all farmers' usurious debts became the first step in this endeavor; Park knew all too well how families suffered from ubiquitous debt, from which there was no escape. Park's government then moved on to the development of South Korea's industries. The farmers' livelihood had to be improved within the framework of overall growth in the country's economy. That in turn enabled the government to electrify entire rural communities and bring them modern amenities. Then, in 1970, Park launched the New Community Movement, which completely altered the way of life in rural communities.

Park and Japan

Young Koreans of the twenty-first century might be surprised by my assertion that Park Chung-Hee did not regard Japan as his enemy, or that he never bad-mouthed Japan, even in private. Teachers and the media have emphasized how brutal and exploitative Japanese rule was over Korea; Koreans today might find it difficult to believe that any person growing up under Japanese colonial rule did not always hate the Japanese. How could a slave not hate his oppressor? Koreans might argue that not hating the Japanese was *prima facie* evidence that Park Chung-Hee was a collaborator and a traitor. Granted, Park Chung-Hee might not have known any better as a child and, therefore, could be forgiven for his innocence then, but should he not have known better when he had grown up?

Such reasoning, however, ignores the influence of political and social environments on people's thinking and behavior. The Old Testament showed how the Hebrews, in spite of their misery, had adjusted to life under Pharaoh. Faced with Pharaoh's army overtaking them in their exodus, they exclaimed to Moses, "Didn't we say to you in Egypt, 'Leave us alone; let us serve the Egyptians?[1] The Hebrews wanted to live and die in Egypt, where they had "pots of meat and ate all the food" they wanted.[2] When they had no water to drink in the desert, they were ready to stone Moses to death.[3] All this happened even after Jehovah had rained calamities on Pharaoh's land and parted the waters of the Red Sea to aid the Hebrews' escape. The Hebrews had been accustomed to the routine of their daily lives under Pharaoh and resented Moses for leading them away.

Korea under Japan was vastly different from Moses's Egypt in many ways, but there were some similarities. Even though Japanese rule was only two or three generations old when Park Chung-Hee was growing up, the colonial government had implanted no other thought on him than to ascend the ladder of success and become the Rikugun Taishō, the Army General. Japanese rule of Korea was something most of his generation accepted as a given condition; Koreans grumbled about the limitations the Japanese had imposed on them, as the conversation among Park's classmates at Taegu showed, but they had resigned themselves to accept what they had been given. Park Chung-Hee would have been aware of the obstacles to becoming a general, but the thought of treating Japan as his enemy did not occur to him, nor did his classmates hold such a view.

The thought of "fighting the system" or going against it does not come naturally in any society. One needs strong and even calamitous stimuli to do so. Park Chung-Hee's family background also did not encourage him to deviate from his goal. As noted earlier, the only occasion that might have raised doubts in Park's mind about his chosen path was at Panbishan, where Park encountered the Chinese troops fighting their Japanese aggressors. This was the first time in Park's life that he encountered a challenge against what he had been taught and believed. Until then, Park Chung-Hee was a captive of the environment in which he was raised. In any event, he was not alone in not treating Japan as his enemy.

Park's search for glory took him to the Manchukuo and Japanese military academies that changed his life. The Manchukuo academy restored his self-confidence and put him on the threshold of a new life as a soldier. The Japanese military academy cemented Park's outlook and character. This is where he was pounded into a soldier. Park already had the physical and mental toughness to endure the worst of hardships, and here his spirit was fortified to lead other men. His military career also afforded him an opportunity to observe the dynamic transformation of Manchuria from an agrarian land into a major industrial center. Park had learned about the Meiji Revolution before, but in Manchuria, he saw directly how such a transformation was accomplished.

Japan was also important to Park Chung-Hee because it broadened his horizons. The discovery that there was a wider world beyond the skies of Kumi, Munkyŏng, and Taegu would have been significant enough, but Japanese imperialism enabled Park Chung-Hee to see and experience Manchuria, Japan, and northwest China in turmoil. He was away from Korea for only six years, from 1940 to 1946, but what he saw and learned exceeded what most Koreans would experience in their lifetime. The effect of Park's experiences in Beijing and in the far corner of

China near the Mongolian border should not be minimized. There Park witnessed the Chinese fighting against Japanese aggressors and the fall of the Japanese empire. A state must be built on a sound foundation, but it must also be managed prudently. The Japanese empire had appeared to be ready to conquer all of Asia, but its leaders had been reckless. Their empire had collapsed like a castle built of sand. What followed in China was a continuation of the long civil war between Chiang Kai-shek's Nationalist Army and Mao Zedong's Communist forces. Chiang's army dominated the scene with its U.S.-trained forces and better armament, but in the end, it was no match for the Communists. Chiang's Nationalists were too steeped in corruption to defeat the Communists, who had better discipline and socioeconomic programs. There were clearly lessons to be learned. Park's indignation against the corruption in the South Korean army must be seen in this light.

Did Park Chung-Hee's experiences add up to his being a pro-Japanese renegade, as some Koreans of the twentieth century charged? If he was at the front line confronting the Chinese Communist forces in 1945, why did he not desert the Manchukuo Army and join the anti-Japanese forces, as some Koreans of this period did? It should be remembered in this regard, however, that the number of deserters reaching the Korean nationalist camps in China was very small. It did not exceed a few hundred, if that many, out of the thousands recruited. One had to be at the immediate front line to have a chance of escaping from the Japanese or Japanese-controlled army units, and desertion involved a very high level of risk. More important, Park Chung-Hee's background was different from the others'. Not everyone suffered from the Chosŏn Dynasty as the Park family had, nor was everyone a son of a Tonghak rebel. We should also remember that Park Chung-Hee was a cold, calculating realist.

He did not have the luxury of taking chances with his fate. Ultimately, one could say that Park was a careerist under Japanese colonial rule, squarely focused on improving his status and ability.

All of these experiences turned Park Chung-Hee into an army officer well versed in East Asian politics and history, but he had not encountered any situation that would have required him to change his personality. Park demanded and received obedience from his classmates at the elementary school; he would either slap those who did not obey his commands or cajole them, as with the student who lagged in math lessons. Park then prepared himself to be a soldier at the Taegu Normal School, where he won Colonel Arikawa's approbation and recognition. Discipline and obedience, of course, were the foundation of any army, but Japanese military academies could not teach cadets "how to die" unless they instinctively obeyed every command issued. Nothing in army life mitigated Park's authoritarian traits, nor did his personality change after he left the army. Park's straight posture, his Spartan lifestyle, and his relentless pursuit of established goals reflected his soldier's mentality. He offered incentives for others to follow him but did not tolerate dissent or opposition. He was not about to yield to those who found it painful to follow his established course. The harsh rule Park imposed on his country was an extension of his personality. He believed it was the only way for South Korea to surmount the crisis it faced, but a large segment of the population found his style of leadership unacceptable. Park's policies nurtured a large sector of the better-fed and better-educated middle-class elements; they now wanted not only to enjoy the fruits of their labor but also demanded opportunities for political participation. The result was the clash that eventually led to Park's undoing.

Park and the United States

Park had a different relationship with the United States. He was a cosmopolitan figure by contemporary standards, but he was not ready to encounter the Americans after the Japanese surrendered. Park's generation, it should be recalled, had been indoctrinated by the Japanese empire to regard Americans as devilish animals (*bei-ei kichuku*). The Koreans welcomed the American forces in September 1945 as liberators nonetheless, but doubts remained. It was necessary for the United States, therefore, to earn the trust and respect of the Koreans by their deeds. But by 1947, as the interdepartmental committee in Washington reported, the United States had failed the test, mostly because the U.S. government could not formulate a long-range policy toward Korea. The decision makers in Washington could not do so because Korea was part of the Asian continent, and the civil war in China was still in flux. The "policy of drift" that resulted inevitably brought about political instability, lack of food and other supplies, and a high rate of inflation that made life very difficult for the Koreans. Under such conditions, Park Chung-Hee could not help but be indignant toward the United States.

Added to this was the confrontation between the U.S. Military Government (USMG) and the (Korean) People's Committees, in which Park's brother was involved. Then came the startling news of the policemen under the USMG shooting his brother to death. It was in this distressed condition that Park Chung-Hee joined the South Korean Workers' Party (SKWP) that had hoisted anti-American struggle as its principal goal. Park had to endure terrible punishment for that decision. His aversion to the United States intensified when General Magruder exiled him from the Korean army headquarters to a remote post. Had General Kim Chŏng-ryŏl not intervened, the same American general would have squashed Park's junta. Park Chung-Hee had good reason to be wary or even resentful of the United States.

History since then has shown that Park Chung-Hee's relationship with the United States fluctuated. Park was a realist and would not let his personal feelings sway national interest. President John Kennedy's invitation to the White House and his successor Lyndon Johnson's visit to Seoul substantially improved mutual relations. Johnson's request for South Korea's participation in the Vietnam War also proved to be beneficial to the Park regime and the Republic of Korea. But there was much strain in Park's relations with the Nixon and Carter regimes. Park was focused on protecting South Korea's security against North Korea's belligerency, while Americans worked on creating a new international environment that would require less direct U.S. involvement.

Americans considered Richard Nixon's initiative to build "a structure of peace" through détente with China an epoch-making and brilliant move, but both the Soviet Union and North Korea considered it a threat against their regimes. The former considered the Sino-American détente an attempt to isolate and encircle it, while North Korea considered it an attempt to dampen China's resolve against U.S. imperialism and to weaken its support of North Korea's confrontation against South Korea. Hence, both the Soviet Union and the Democratic Republic of Korea hardened their stance against the United States and South Korea.

President Carter's Korea policy, moreover, reflected his ideological prism, which Park could not accept. Carter believed that the U.S. presence in South Korea was superfluous and wanted to withdraw all U.S. combat troops. This, he evidently assumed, would moderate North

Korea's behavior. But Park found such hope illusory. Disagreements and even conflicts with the American president proved to be inevitable.

Park Chung-Hee was placed in a vise between the détente policy of the United States and North Korea's belligerence. He responded domestically by declaring a state of emergency in 1971 and launching a development plan for heavy and chemical industries, as a prelude to manufacturing for the defense industries. But the public focused their anger against the Yushin constitution, which had turned Park into a perpetual dictator.[7] Subsequently, over the next decades, the heavy and chemical industries served as the primary engine for South Korea's sustained growth. The Yushin system, however, created an atmosphere that led to the assassination of Park's wife in 1974 and Park himself in 1979.

7 Please see the "epilogue" for more discussion of these events.

Epilogue

Authoritarianism and Economic Development: The Regime of Park Chung-Hee, 1961–79

Major General Park Chung-Hee overthrew Korea's democratic regime in May 1961 and instituted a junta government. In 1963, Park was elected president under a new constitution and ruled the country until he was assassinated in 1979. Park's regime (1961–79) presided over South Korea's phenomenal economic growth. While the aim of this book was limited to the study of Park's experience before the coup, readers may wish to know more about how Park accomplished his goal of transforming the country. The following is a brief account of what transpired in Korea before Park's coup.

During its early years, the Republic of Korea (ROK) made fitful economic progress. Most South Koreans were pessimistic about the possibility of real economic development. South Korea was poor in natural resources, and American aid was insufficient to fully offset the economic burden of maintaining a large army to confront the belligerent North Korea. President Syngman Rhee's primary concern was the reunification of Korea: for him, focusing on the economic development of South Korea alone would have been tantamount to abandoning the unification effort. Rhee insisted that the United States provide arms to continue the war to reunify the country and refused to send official representatives to the truce talks at Panmunjom in 1953.

The Rhee regime faced an enormous task in reconstructing the war-torn economy, however, and the years between 1953 and 1958 were devoted to reconstruction with aid provided by the United States and the UN reconstruction agency. The government pursued a policy of import-substituting industrialization, attempting to increase industrial production by emphasizing light industrial products for domestic consumption. Light manufacturing, including textiles, food, beverages, tobacco, wood, leather, and paper, dominated the early stages of South Korean industrialization. GNP rose by an average of 5.5 percent a year from 1954 through 1958, with industrial production leading the advance at an annual growth rate of nearly 14 percent.

By 1958, however, the economy had lost its momentum. The saturation of the domestic market, growing unemployment, and difficulties in obtaining foreign exchange for necessary imports led the government to review the wisdom of its import-substituting development strategy. The government was also concerned with arresting inflation and coping with sharply reduced aid from the United States. However, political factors were also responsible for the slowdown. Rhee (1875–1965) was aging; his chosen right-hand man was in ill health. By 1958, Rhee's underlings were paying more attention to political survival than to economic development. In 1960, for the first time in South Korean history, the government adopted a comprehensive seven-year economic development plan, but not much was done before the regime was toppled by the student revolt of April 1960. Economic discontent and the increasing use of the police to suppress opposition, in addition to the election rigging, had precipitated the revolt. The transitional regime under Premier Hŏ Chŏng facilitated the general election, which brought in the democratic regime under Chang Myŏn, but as noted before, political turmoil overshadowed all efforts at economic stability. Park Chung-Hee and his cohorts carried out a coup on May 16, 1961.

Park and the young military men, however, were similar to former president Rhee in their political and administrative inexperience. The junta they led found the task of managing a national economy daunting. Its policies led to inflation, economic stagnation, and mixed results in the agrarian program. It also faced the problem of discord and corruption within its ranks. Some of the junta members attacked the concentration of power in the Central Intelligence Agency established under Kim Chong-Pil, Park's nephew-in-law. Park's three years of military rule clearly did not justify the military coup. On February 27, 1963, General Park, in a highly emotional speech, admitted the failure of the junta to bring about a "human revolution" in Korea and promised to retire from politics.[1]

But Park reversed himself quickly and ran for the office of president, which the new constitution of December 1962 had instituted. The general election of October 1963 revealed that Park Chung-Hee faced a skeptical public. While he won 46.64 percent of the total votes cast, his opponent, Yun Po-sŏn won 45.1 percent, a margin of only 1.54 percent. Park was more popular in the rural sector, where he won by 59 percent versus Yun's 41 percent. In the urban sector, where opinion leaders including students, intellectuals, merchants, and industrialists dominated, Park won only 37 percent of the vote. Election figures for the unicameral National Assembly, held simultaneously with the presidential election,

---

1 For details, please see Chong-Sik Lee, "Korea: In Search of Stability," *Asian Survey* (January 1964): 656–665.

were much more disappointing for Park Chung-Hee. The party he and Kim Chong-pil created for the election, the Democratic-Republican Party, won only 35 percent of nine million votes, while the two major opposition parties shared most of the remainder.

Firmly in control of political power, however, President Park recruited professionals to manage the economy. Park's most important decision was to create the Economic Planning Board (EPB), which came into being in May 1964. It was directed by the deputy prime minister, who was given broad fiscal, financial, and economic powers. The EPB controlled both budget and planning functions and became the central clearinghouse for all economic policy. Park's new development policy was based on an overall strategy of export-oriented industrialization. Park deserves credit for providing firm political support for the work of professionals and for making some crucial developmental decisions.[2]

Park Chung-Hee undoubtedly solicited ideas from his colleagues and others before establishing the EPB, his headquarters for economic development, but this is where Park's Manchurian experience manifested itself. The EPB was a replica of the Fourth Section of the Kantō-gun headquarters of the Japanese army in Manchuria, described earlier by Mutō Tomio. It was, Mutō said, "the crucible (motoshime) of Manchukuo; all major policies, whether they originated in the Japanese or Manchukuo government would not be translated into action without that section's approval."[3] What Kantō-gun leaders wanted was an

2 The account below is based on my earlier work, "South Korea: Challenge of Democracy," Steven M. Goldstein (ed.), *Minidragons: Fragile Economic Miracles in the Pacific* (New York: Ambrose Video Pub. Inc., and Boulder, Colorado: Westview, 1991), 112–134.

3 Mutō Tomio, *Watakushi to Manshūkoku* [I and Manchukuo] (Tokyo: Bungei Shunju, 1988), 414.

economy based on a capitalist system, wherein the zaibatsu, the financial and industrial conglomerates, would operate under strict supervision.

Some of the measures undertaken by the EPB in the period that followed Park's election were revolutionary in the Korean context. In May 1964, the EPB devalued the currency, the won, by 90 percent and established a unitary exchange rate. The EPB then floated the won the following year. Exports had more than doubled between 1961 and 1963, and they rose another 50 percent in 1964; government emphasis on exports began to play a dominant role in economic and investment policies. In 1965, the EPB drafted a more aggressive second five-year plan and began to liberalize import restrictions. It put through an interest-rate reform that revitalized the banking sector by attracting private savings with high interest rates.

In line with the strategy of export-oriented industrialization, the government also provided businesses with powerful incentives to export: they were given preferential treatment in obtaining low-interest bank loans, import privileges, which included permission to borrow from foreign sources, and tax benefits. These incentives were particularly important because of the large differential between bank loans and private loans. Because of their scarcity, imported products commanded high prices in the domestic market. Import privileges were doubly profitable because they were accompanied by government-guaranteed foreign loans, which bore very low interest rates relative to domestic rates. Would-be entrepreneurs needed virtually no capital to start businesses, and the opportunities were enormous. Businessmen responded eagerly to the incentives, meeting the government's export target. Park's strategy was thus to guide, encourage, and support private entrepreneurs. If his politics could be characterized as "guided democracy," his economics were "guided capitalism."

Under strong and direct encouragement from the state, some of South Korea's most successful businesses grew into *chaebŏl*, or huge conglomerates. The *chaebŏl* emerged as the distinctive hallmark of South Korean industrialization, dominating the nation's economy. In the years to come, conglomerates including Hyundai, Samsung, and LG would become the most recognizable symbols of South Korea's place in the world economy. The two Chinese characters that form the word *chaebŏl* in the Korean language form *zaibatsu* in Japanese. These organizations not only share the same Chinese word; their historical origins are also similar. Both South Korean and Japanese conglomerates began with small nuclear enterprises that benefited from government contacts and patronage. Both were given government protection, which enabled them to monopolize certain spheres of activity and thereby accumulate capital to finance diversification into other areas. One crucial difference between *chaebŏl* and *zaibatsu*, however, was that the Japanese conglomerates had their own banks and financed their operations internally, while the *chaebŏl* had to depend on government-guaranteed external financing; the government prevented them from acquiring banks for fear of their disrupting the free flow of capital. The *chaebŏl* were therefore more vulnerable than their Japanese counterparts to governmental pressures and the vicissitudes of international markets.

Park's development programs required enormous amounts of capital. Since the United States was no longer willing or able to sustain its previous level of assistance, the Park regime resorted to "financial diplomacy" elsewhere. In late 1964, Park paid a state visit to the Federal

Republic of Germany, which led to government aid and commercial credits. The normalization of relations with Japan in 1965 brought Japanese funds in the form of loans and compensation for the damage South Korea had suffered during the colonial era. The availability of foreign funds and Korea's increasing exports boosted South Korea's credit rating, enabling the country to borrow more on the open international market.

While foreign loans played the key role in the initial stages of economic development, the success of South Korea's export drive derived from other factors as well, including the availability of an educated labor force, a highly trained bureaucracy, and the favorable international market. South Korea made stunning advances in education after its liberation in 1945. From 1945 to 1965, enrollment in elementary schools rose from 1.3 million pupils to 3.6 million, and in high schools from 50,000 to 164,000. Enrollments in vocational high schools increased fivefold, in institutions of higher learning by a factor of eighteen. The explosive rise in education reflected the success of the Rhee government's policy in meeting the aspirations of South Koreans.

It was not only schools and colleges that provided education to workers. The armed forces performed that task as well. The Korean War and the continuing confrontation with North Korea necessitated the maintenance of large armed forces, and by necessity the army, navy, and air force provided supplementary education to their recruits. Furthermore, the armed forces provided technical training not easily accessible to the young from rural areas, such as learning to drive vehicles of various kinds, operating communications equipment, and serving as medical aides. Since the ROK's armed forces never fell below six hundred thousand, and since a large number of the troops were discharged each year, Korea had available a large pool of young people ready to work in modern industries.

The bureaucracy and financial institutions also played important roles. The Korean bureaucrats had little experience in managing an economy when Syngman Rhee was inaugurated in 1948, but they acquired much training and experience by the time Park took power. The government had been obliged not only to mobilize and feed the soldiers, but also to look after the country's economy in wartime. When the battle lines were stabilized in the middle of the peninsula, the government started the task of reconstructing the economy and managing large sums of foreign aid from the United States and the United Nations Reconstruction Agency. Korea's financial institutions also had to work in tandem with the government to manage the funds. Both institutions, therefore, had considerable experience in economic management. Furthermore, Park's export drive fortuitously started when the world economy was booming. The world market was exploding between 1965 and 1975, the decade in which South Korea's exports expanded. The availability of the American and Japanese markets was of crucial importance to South Korean advancement. The United States absorbed a large share of South Korean products. The United States was the largest purchaser of South Korean products until 1973, when Japan overtook them. Japan was also a major source of public and private loans to South Korea, providing $674 million in commercial loans and $416 million in government loans between 1965 and 1973.

Another factor helping South Korean exporters in the 1960s was the absence of competition from other developing countries. South Korean industries were using entry-level technologies that were relatively easy to acquire and learn. Many Japanese industries were preparing to install advanced technology, and they were eager to sell their old plants and technologies to South Korea. Korea's rapidly growing exports were typical of a country in the early stages of growth. Manufactured goods constituted less than 20 percent of total exports before 1962 but increased to 44.5 percent in 1963 and 73.5 percent in 1968. Within this category, light industrial products supplied the largest share of South Korea's exports. The emphasis was on items that would benefit from low wages and an unskilled labor force, in particular textiles, clothing, and footwear. At the same time, South Korean entrepreneurs were gaining more experience and preparing to diversify their commodities and markets.

In 1972, however, President Park's development policy took a major turn toward heavy and chemical industries. The principal impetus for this turn was the sudden change in the U.S. policy toward East Asia, but South Korea also needed to upgrade its industries to meet the stiff competition from China and other Asian countries that had a more abundant supply of cheap labor.

The U.S. policy change was the result of the prolonged Vietnam War that had exhausted America's resources. President Nixon indicated in his speech of July 1969 the weariness of the United States in defending its allies. His decision to unilaterally withdraw one of the two U.S. divisions from Korea in 1970 also strongly suggested the possibility that South Korea may not be able to count on U.S. support in confronting North Korea. While South Korea must continue to depend on the United States for advanced weaponry, it was necessary to produce as much of its own weaponry as possible. This meant the need for heavy and chemical industries. The result was the third five-year economic development plan (1972–1976), which called for the development of heavy and chemical industries. More than 50 percent of industrial investment in the early years of the 1970s went into developing chemicals, petroleum products, and basic metals. The new policy had a direct impact on export structure. Electrical products and electronics, iron and steel, metal works, and ships began to figure prominently in South Korea's exports. In 1980, heavy and chemical industries accounted for 44 percent of all export value and nearly half of all industrial exports. Four years earlier, the ratio had been less than 30 percent.

There were, however, adverse consequences. The allocation of exorbitant sums of capital to industries that required long gestation periods increased inflationary pressure. Small- and medium-sized manufacturers producing light industrial products suffered the most, and depressed output led to a shortage of consumer goods, exacerbated by increasing consumer demand brought about by rising wages and the advance in living standards. Price controls imposed on producers of consumer goods further discouraged the manufacturers. Meanwhile, the inflow of foreign loans to finance the new heavy and chemical industries rapidly expanded the money supply, further fueling inflation. Officially, according to a Bank of Korea report, consumer prices rose only 14.4 percent in 1978; however, most observers agree that the actual rate was near 30 percent.

The December 1978 general election for the National Assembly revealed Park's government to be a fragile system held in place by sheer force. The president's declaration of a state of emergency in 1971 and the proclamation of the *Yushin* constitution of 1972 were unpopular, as the new constitution made Park a perpetual dictator with the power to appoint one-third of the members of the National Assembly. These measures assured political stability to the regime but heightened the discontentment among the populace, including the labor, students, and the intellectuals. The government harshly suppressed all forms of opposition, but it was clearly fighting a losing battle. The opposition's New Democratic Party (NDP) won a handsome plurality with 34.7 percent of the votes, an increase of 2.2 percent from the 1973 vote, while the government party's share declined to 30.9 percent. Independent candidates won 27.2 percent of votes, and most of them joined the NDP. The majority of voters clearly wanted a change.

The election results strengthened the cause of the opposition leader, Kim Young-Sam, and in June 1979, he launched a scathing attack against the policies of the Park government. The government retaliated by removing Kim from the National Assembly, a measure that only intensified the highly charged political atmosphere. The workers and students soon joined in the struggle against the Park regime by taking to the streets, thus presenting the government with a dilemma. Applying more pressure to the opposition would create martyrs, making the situation even more explosive. Loosening control might foster the spread of demands for reform, rendering it impossible for the government to contain the opposition. Park's lieutenants were evidently divided on which measures would best manage the crisis. While they were deliberating these measures, the director of the KCIA, Kim Jae-Kyu, shot President Park and the director of the presidential security forces dead on December 12, 1979. Kim later told a military court that his victims wanted to resort to brutal force to suppress the demonstrators. The *Yushin* system may have been necessary to meet the crisis created by Nixon's policy of reducing the U.S. role in Asia, but the system did not provide a safety valve for social and political pressures. It might have been maintained through dexterous manipulation of all the political and economic mechanisms, but managing all the variables proved to be impossible.

* * *

Many scholars and pundits have already analyzed Park Chung-Hee's role in South Korea's economic development. But attention should be paid to an obvious but nonetheless very startling fact: South Korea's per capita income expanded from $100 to $20,000 within the lifetime of most of the adults now living. This was the result of their sweat and blood, to be sure, but it could not have been accomplished without the leadership of a man who emphasized the need for the "can-do" spirit. Many critics then and later criticized him, however, for his disregard of human rights and for ignoring the plight of the unprotected laborers. One wishes those sacrifices had not been necessary for the successes achieved.

APPENDIX

Appendix 1: Korean Names and Words

Readers of this book would undoubtedly notice that so many Koreans appearing in the book are named either Kim or Park (or Pak). This is because, according to South Korea's official census data of 2000, 21.6 percent of the Korean households' surnames are Kim, 14.8 percent are Yi (Lee or Rhee), and 8.5 percent are Park (or Pak). There are more than two hundred surnames in Korea, but for some unknown reason, these three surnames constitute nearly half (or 44.9 percent) of the total household surnames. I have not encountered any plausible explanation of why this is the case.

Transliteration of Korean names and words into English presents a slight problem because the two languages are different in many ways. The sounds for Korean consonants, for example, are not pronounced in the same way as in English. The sound "K" in Kim, for example, sounds more like "G" rather than "K" to the untrained ears although it is not exactly like "G." My linguist friend, Professor Chin-W. Kim, said in his publication that the Korean phonetic symbol ㄱ should be pronounced "between vowels as in begin, weak and lax [k] elsewhere as in cookie." Most Koreans named Kim use that spelling, although some choose Gim or Gym.

Park Chung-Hee spelled his surname as "Park," but it could have been "Pak" too, which is the way the McCune-Reischaur (M-R) system would transliterate that surname. But Park Chung-Hee chose to spell it "Park," and I used his spelling here for him and for his immediate family. English readers would probably pronounce his surname more correctly by spelling it Park rather than "Pak" because Pak could be mispronounced as "Pack," which designates another surname spelled either "Paek" as in the M-R system or "Paik." If this is too confusing, simply ignore this paragraph.

Where does the McCune-Reischaur system come from? George M. McCune was a Korean specialist at the University of California; Edwin O. Reischauer was a Japanese historian at Harvard. They came up with the system in 1937. South Korea now has another system, which the government adopted in 2000. If you followed that system, Park Chung-Hee would become "Bag Jeong Hee."

What does the diacritical mark over "o" as in "Chŏng" mean? The vowels "o" and "ŏ" are distinctly different in the Korean language. The same goes for "u" and "ŭ." The ŏ sound is like the "u" sound in "until." My name, Chong-Sik Lee, does not have a diacritical mark on it simply because it is difficult to put that mark on with most computers.

By the way, my name is pronounced Yi Jung-Shik in Korea. This is because the surname comes before the given name in Korea. My surname is pronounced "Yi" in South Korea and "Ri" in North Korea. Korean dictionaries up to about 1950 listed that character as "Ri," but the South Korean government chose to use "Yi," which was the way the people in Seoul pronounced it.

If it is "Yi" in South Korea, why did I choose "Lee" as my last name? I suppose it is because I wanted to use a name familiar to Americans and other English-speaking peoples. Transliterating one's name in English presents a problem for most Koreans. (This is not the case for the Japanese, whose language's five vowels are easy to handle for English speakers. Yamamoto is Yamamoto, and there is no ambiguity.) Syngman Rhee, the first South Korean president, chose "Rhee" rather than Yi or Lee. In fact, he struggled with the choice when he first entered the United States in 1904. His name first appeared in print as E Sung Man. In other words, he had chosen "E" rather than Yi. It then became Yee Sung Man and Ri Sung Man. He used a few other spellings before he settled on Syngman Rhee. His surname is the same as mine in Korean, by the way.

President Park Chung-Hee spelled his name "Park Chung Hee." I added the hyphen to signify that "Chung-Hee" is his first name, as I did for all Korean first names. Korean given names consist of two Chinese characters in most cases. Siblings share at least one of the two characters as did Park Chung-Hee and his brother Sang-Hee. Some families, such as Hŏ, use only one Chinese character for the given name. Hŏ Chŏng, the former acting prime minister, is a good example.

Another vowel in Korean, "ŭ" carries a "half-moon" mark, as I call it; ŭ is like the "u" in min<u>u</u>te.

The Japanese use ō and ū for their long vowels. The "o" sound in Tokyo should carry long vowel marks on both of them, but it is never done. Toshiba and Toto are other familiar cases. Toshiba should be Tōshiba; Toto should be Tōtō, but the long vowel mark is omitted for convenience's sake.

I would like to offer my thanks and congratulations to anyone who had the patience to read this far.

Appendix 2: Sangmo-dong, Park Chung-Hee's Birthplace

Those few who wish to trek the eight kilometers from Park Chung-Hee's home to his elementary school will be disappointed; they will find neither the thatched-roof house nor the mountain road. The house was burned down during the Korean War, and urbanization since then has wiped out all traces of the rice fields, forests, and even the mountains along the road. While a replica of the house has been built, it is constructed of lumber and cement instead of tree branches and mud mixed with straw. In the past, Korean kitchens had nothing but dirt floors, but the kitchen in the replica is covered with concrete. Park's room was rebuilt presumably to replicate the original, but it does not evoke the look and smell of the house that his wife loathed.

Even from such a replica, however, I could see why Park's wife was disappointed by her *sijip*, or husband's home. Park's room was even smaller than the prison cells I have seen. Even Park Chung-Hee, who was of small stature, could not stand up in the room because of the low ceiling. It's best that the builders did not install electricity, as there was none when Park lived there. In front of the reconstructed house is a well and a hand pump for water, with a sign indicating that the Park family had the pump when they lived there, which seems questionable. A poor family could not have installed such a pump for their own use. Whatever the case may have been, the Sangmo-dong house is now a shrine surrounded by a small bamboo grove, tiered lawn in the back, and a few persimmon trees. In the front of the house is a big parking lot for tourists. Across the street are a seven- or eight-story apartment building and a number of small stores catering to what appears to be a growing urban neighborhood. The apartment building, incidentally, is way below the Parks' shrine. Even the top of the building does not reach the level of their house. That shows how steep the Park family's climb was each day to reach their hovel.

The shrine-like appearance of the reconstructed house seems an inaccurate recreation of the original, which I saw in an old photo. In addition, the streets and traffic signals on the way to Park's old elementary school also ruin the historical accuracy of Park's old town. While the old school remains—with a statue of Park standing in front of the huge four-story building—one would risk injury walking along the road from the many cars zooming by. What once were rice fields and forests are now wide, modern, four-lane streets, lit with neon signs and with complexes of tall buildings lined up on both sides. The planners neglected to construct sidewalks on some of the streets.

Our car passed under a railroad bridge, where young Park Chung-Hee saw the trains pass every morning. Park would have crossed the railroad track at that point too. His school was only a five-minute drive from the tracks; he might have started running from that point to the school so as not to be late. The Kumi Railway Station still stands on the left not far from there.

It is not only the Park family's neighborhood that has changed. Sangmo-dong used to belong to the county of Sŏnsan in north Kyŏngsang Province, but it is now a part of the city of Kumi, which underwent phenomenal growth during Park's presidency. The center of a once-fertile farming region has been transformed into an industrial city. The Nakdong River still runs through Kumi, but while it was once used for agriculture, it now provides water for the production of textiles, electronic products including LCDs, and other industries. President Park launched Kumi's first industrial park in 1968 with Samsung, LG, and other large companies, and construction has since continued. In 2010, a fourth such complex was being built. Kumi had a big celebration in 1999 marking the export of $100 million worth of products, but only six years later, in 2005, they exceeded $300 million dollars of exports. That figure has probably doubled by 2010.

As our Hyundai SUV drove down the superhighway from Munkyŏng, where Park taught briefly, to Kumi, I saw a modern city looming, with tall, new, white buildings everywhere. My eyes popped just as Judy Garland's did upon seeing the Emerald City in the movie *The Wizard of Oz*. What she saw was a figment of the imagination created by moviemakers, but what I saw was real. It was the city of Kumi that Park Chung-Hee had created. That superhighway, incidentally, is like the yellow brick road that Garland and her friends hopped along to the wizard's castle. In the mid-1960s, many Koreans opposed the very idea of building such a "wasteful road." There would not be enough traffic to justify such a massive investment, they argued. But that superhighway and so many others in South Korea today facilitated the country's growth. While such roads weren't painted yellow, they were the groundwork for Korea's golden egg.

Appendix 3: "How I Found Banbishan"

Banbishan is where the young Lieutenant Park Chung-Hee spent thirteen months between 1944 and 1945, and I was determined to visit the place to see whether it would provide me some useful information. Professor Kim Yong-Ho of Inha University knew what I wanted and offered to take the trip with me when I was in Seoul. So we took off together in October 2009. I knew the general location from a map provided in a Japanese book, *Manshū kokugun* [The Manchukuo Army], but nothing more. An Internet search for Banbishan led me to a town near the Great Wall, but I knew it was not where Park spent his first year after graduating from the Japanese Military Academy. The travel agency in Seoul assured us, however, that the local guides would find the right place for us. So Professor Kim and I took off from Inchon, stayed a night in Beijing, and headed for Chengde, which used to be known as Rehe, Jeho, or Jehol, the summer resort of the Qing emperors. A visit to Rehe would be worth the cost and trouble of our trip even if we could not find Banbishan, we had figured. The city is known in Korea as Yŏlha, made famous by Pak Chi-won's travelogue *Yŏlha Ilgi* or *Rehe Diary*. (All these different spellings for the city would be confusing to the uninitiated, but it is simply a matter of different transliteration systems for the Chinese.[1])

It took us about six hours by car from Beijing to reach Chengde traveling on a well-built and well-maintained modern highway although it turned out to be a very foggy day. A part of the road was superhighway,

1 Under the Wade-Giles system of transliteration, invented by two men by the name of—you guessed it—had decided for some reason that the Chinese word for "hot" should be "je" while the Chinese government people decided it should be "re," which is closer to the way the Chinese people pronounce it. The Koreans, for whatever reason, decided to pronounce it "yŏl." Clear enough?

no different from the kind you see anywhere else. We were accompanied by a driver and a guide from Beijing. Very sophisticated and colorful ultramodern apartment and government buildings greeted us as we entered Chengde wiping out our annoyance and concern over the chauffer's driving. For some reason, as we approached Chengde, he slowed down the car, pulled out his handphone, and started to text with one hand. We kept telling him to stop the car and text or not do the texting at all, but he did not listen to us. The food at an elegant-looking restaurant near our hotel was too greasy for us, the visitors, but the new local guide enjoyed it. The city or the province required that visitors must have a guide from Chengde even though we already had a guide from Beijing. So we now had a Chinese-Korean guide from Beijing and a part-Mongolian Chinese lady guide from Chengde.

The next morning, the five of us, including the driver, the guide from Beijing, and the other guide from Chengde, took off for Banbishan, the Half Wall Mountain. Neither of the guides had ever heard of Banbishan, and none of the maps listed the place. I remembered a town called Kuojiatun in the vicinity of Banbishan in the Japanese book, and it became our target.[2]

The two-lane highway to Kuojiatun was simply beautiful; it had been completed just four years before in 2005. The road went through the valleys between the mountains and rolling hills, and we saw farm villages once in a while. Occasionally, the road was filled with vendors of melons of all kinds, lined up on both sides of the highway. After we passed a big city called Xinglong, we could see men and women

---

2 Those who are interested in such things should note that *Kuojiatun* means the Kuo Family Hamlet. *Kuo* in Chinese is pronounced "Kwak" in Korean. So it is the Kwak family hamlet in Korean.

sweeping the highway quite far from the villages with their long brooms made of reed. In about four hours, we found Kuojiatun and saw a mid-sized van with a big sign in red letters on the front windshield saying "Kuojiatun-Banbishan." We had reached Kuojiatun and found our Banbishan!

That sign, by the way, was the only one we ever saw anywhere that mentioned Banbishan. None of the road signs did—not even at the entrance of the hamlet. It took a number of inquiries on the way to find the bumpy and narrow dirt road that took us to our destination. We encountered a brand-new station wagon and a jeep on the muddy road, but the occupants had never heard of Banbishan. It branches off from the dirt road at a tiny bridge over a stream, but evidently, no one paid any attention to the small hamlet, which produced nothing but corn. The village with about a dozen neat brick row houses was divided into two sides, half of them on one side of the street and the others on the other side. The space in between was not paved, and there was no drainage for the rain. One had to stay in the car or put on a pair of rubber boots to wade through the pools of water. All we saw as we entered the hamlet was a hog on the road.

Then several men and women showed up. A young woman offered us boiled corncobs. The town's Communist Party secretary had the only tiled single house, which had a beautiful ceramic tile floor, and he invited us into the guest receiving room or the living room of their three-room house. That's probably where the chairman held meetings with other people of the hamlet. He and his wife were very hospitable. They sent for the "oldest man of the hamlet" to answer my questions. But the gentleman did not know anything about the Manchukuo Army that had been stationed in the hamlet years ago. He was too young for me. I needed a person who was at least seventy-five years old, but he looked only about sixty.

At least we found our Banbishan and came to know about the topography of the area. Yes, we found the Half Wall Mountain. The mountain range north of the hamlet abruptly ended with a cliff. There was a small Buddhist temple at the bottom of the cliff that looked like a hut with Buddhist decorations. The stream we crossed was the Little Luan River, which supplied water for the cornfields of the hamlet. The fields between the low-lying mountains were not large enough to sustain the population of more than a hundred, hence, the small size of the hamlet. The dirt road led north to Inner Mongolia from there, but we decided to take the same road that took us through Kuojiatun. We stopped at a noodle shop in that bustling town where we saw lots of traffic, including buses with signs of destinations prominently displayed on their windshields.

But our mission was not complete because I had to see the town of Banbishan we had found on one of the maps. I must emphasize the word *town* here, because this Banbishan is different from the hamlet of Banbishan we visited. One of the Web sites on Park Chung-Hee had a map with the town of Banbishan as the place where Park spent his youthful days. Even though I knew it was the wrong Banbishan, I had to know what kind of place the second one was.

The town of Banbishan was located southwest of Chengde on the way to Beijing, so we went back to Chengde to tour the city and stay another night. A long wall surrounded the mountainous compound where the emperors spent their summers. There was a huge Tibetan temple on the mountainside facing the imperial compound across the river; the Qianlong emperor had it built in honor of a Tibetan Dalai Lama who visited him. He knew how to make his visitor comfortable; he needed to pacify the Tibetan chief too.

The town of Banbishan was located near the Great Wall, and we had to take a different route from Chengde that went through very rugged terrain. The highway was paved, but our van could not pick up any speed because of the steep, winding mountain roads. On top of that, there were many big trucks carrying heavy loads. The mountains were beautiful, but the sun began to set when we arrived in the town of Banbishan. We all exclaimed when we saw a fading sign that said "Banbishan Clinic." We then visited the Communist Party branch of Banbishan across the street. This being Saturday, no one was in the office. It was a small market town outgrown with lots of people. It was where the local farmers traded their products. The main street was paved, but it had trash and garbage all over. All kinds of small shops lined the street—the beauty shops, groceries, bike shops, and so on. The town had an old-town look, and the people there did not look very refined either. I would choose the hamlet of Banbishan any day over the town that had the same name.

Some may wonder how there could be two places with the same name in the same province. But the two places used to belong to different provinces. They are now placed in the same Hebei Province. It was only an odd person like me who even noticed; having two Banbishans did not seem to have bothered anyone else. On the way out of the town of Banbishan, we saw a mountain that ended with a cliff. That's why the town is also named the Half Wall Mountain. We had to cross the Great Wall again as we headed for Beijing. It was very chilly as we passed through the checkpoint at the wall. That's where Pak Chi-won wrote poems about the Great Wall in 1780.

About the Author

By the time Chong-Sik Lee reached Los Angeles to attend the University of California there in 1954, he had already lived through the Japanese invasion and occupation of Manchuria and Central China, the Second World War, the Chinese civil war, and the Korean War. The political turmoil led him to learn and speak Korean (his native language), Japanese, Chinese, and English. He graduated from UCLA, studying under Professor James S. Coleman and Henry E. McHenry, and earned a PhD in political science from the University of California, Berkeley, where he studied under Professor Robert A. Scalapino. He has since then taught at the University of Colorado, Dartmouth College, and the University of Pennsylvania, where he concentrated on East Asian politics and international relations. Since his retirement from the University of Pennsylvania in 1999, he lectured at Yonsei University in Seoul as the George L. Paik Professor and at Kyung Hee University's Graduate Institute of Peace Studies. He is currently a Professor of Political Science Emeritus, University of Pennsylvania and Eminent Professor at Kyung Hee University in Seoul, Korea. His list of visiting professorships includes the University of Iowa, Korea University, and Princeton University.

He has published numerous books and articles in English and Korean, many of which also appeared in Japanese translations. His first book was the *Politics of Korean Nationalism* (1963). His coauthored work with Professor Scalapino, *Communism in Korea* (1973), earned them the Woodrow Wilson Foundation award of the American Political Science Association in 1974 as the best book in politics, government, and international relations published in the United States during the previous year. He was also awarded the first Wi-am Jang Ji-yŏn Award in Korea in 1990 for his academic achievement.

He lives in Berwyn, Pennsylvania, with his wife, Myungsook Woo, a pianist devoted to flower gardening and tennis.

✲ ✲ ✲

Interviews:

Interview with Choe P'illip, May 5, 2009.

Interview with Chŏng Yŏng-jin, June 6, 2009

Interview with Kim Chae-ch'un, May 4, 2009, Seoul.

BIBLIOGRAPHY

Akira Iriye. *After Imperialism: The Search for a New Order in the Far East, 1921–1931* Cambridge, MA: 1965.

———. *Across the Pacific*. New York: Harcourt, Brace and World, 1967.

Appleman, Roy E. *South to the Naktong, North to the Yalu (June–November 1950)*. Washington, DC: Office of the Chief of Military History, Department of the Army, 1961.

Asada Kyōji, and Kobayashi Sadao, eds. *Nihon teikoku shugi no Manshū shihai: 15nen sensōki o chūshin ni* [Control of Manchuria by Japanese Imperialism: Centered on the 15-year war period]. Tokyo: Jichōsha, 1986.

Calvet, Henri. *Napoléon*. Paris: Presses Universitaires de France, 1943.

———. *Napoléon* [Japanese trans. by Inoue Kōji]. Tokyo: Hakusui-sha, 1952.

Ch'oe Yŏng-hui. *Kyŏkdong ui haebang 3nyŏn* [The Turbulent Three Years after the Liberation]. Ch'unch'ŏn: Hallim University, 1996.

Ch'unwon munhak [Ch'unwon Literature]. Vol. 6. Yi Sun-shin. Seoul: Sŏnghan, 1978.

Chandra, Vipan. *Imperialism, Resistance, and Reform*. Berkeley: Institute of East Asian Studies. University of California, 1988.

Chang Ch'ang-guk. *Yuksa cholŏpsaeng* [The Military Academy Graduates]. Seoul: Chung'ang Ilbosa, 1984.

Chang Chun-ha. "Clean Waters of Chialing Pours into the Muddy Yangtze: My Reflections." *Sasangge* [The World of Thought] (December 1960), 252–267.

Chang To-yŏng. "I Trusted Park Chung-Hee." [In Korean.] *Shindong-a* (July 1984), 120–163.

Chen Jian, *China's Road to the Korean War*. New York: Columbia University Press, 1994.

Cho Kap-je. "Pak Chŏng-hui wa kŭui shidae" [Park Chung-Hee and His Era]. *Wŏlgan Chosŏn* [Monthly Chosŏn], (January 1987) (1), 222–254.

———. *Na ui mudŏm e ch'im ul paett'ŏra* [Spit on My Grave]. Seoul: Chosŏn Ilbosa, 1998.

———. *Park Chŏnghui ui kyŏljŏngjŏk sun'gandŭl* [Decisive Moments of Park Chung-Hee]. Seoul: Kip'irang, 2009.

Cho Tŏk-song. "The Anti-Japanese Student Movement toward the End of Japanese Rule." *Sasangge* (November 1964), 82–90.

Choe Yong-ho. *The Civil Examinations and the Social Structure in Early Yi Dynasty Korea, 1392–1600*. Seoul: Korean Research Center, 1987.

Choi Byŏnghyŏn, trans. *The Book of Corrections: Reflections on the National Crisis during the Japanese Invasion of Korea, 1592–1598*. Berkeley: Institute of East Asian Studies, 2002.

Chŏng Chae-gyŏng. *Wiin Park Chung-Hee* [Park Chung-Hee, the Great Man]. Seoul: Chipmundang, 1992, 12–24.

Chŏng Un-yŏn. *Sillok kun'in Pak Chŏng-hui* [Veritable Record of the Soldier Park Chung-Hee]. Seoul: Kaema, 2004.

Chŏng Yŏng-jin. *Ch'ŏngnyŏn Park Chŏng-hui* [Young Man Park Chung-Hee]. Seoul: Riburo (Libro) Books, 1997.

Chōsen Ginkōshi Kenkyūkai, ed. *Chōsen Ginkōshi* [History of the Bank of Chōsen]. Tokyo: Tōyō Keizai Shinpōsha, 1987.

Chōsen Sōtokufu (Korean Government General). *Shisei 30nen shi* [A 30 Year History of Administration]. Seoul, 1940.

Chōsen Sōtokufu Nōrin-kyokucho. "Hanbai hiryÙ shÙhi jisseki ni kansuru ken, August 26, 1943" [Chief, Agr. and Forest Bureau, Korean Government-General, on the Actual Consumption of Fertilizers Sold], a document of Naimusho Kanrikyoku, the Ministry of Interior, Control Bureau.

Chōsen Sōtokufu, Nōrin-kyoku (Korean Government-General, Bureau of Agriculture). *Nōka keizai gaikyō chōsa: Kosaku nōka, 1933–1938*. Seoul: 1940.

Chungang Ilbosa. *Pirok Chosŏn minjujuiui inmin konghwaguk* [Democratic People's Republic of Korea, the Secret Records]. Seoul: Chungang Ilbosa, 1992.

Clubb, O. Edmund. *China and Russia: the Great Game*. New York: Columbia University Press, 1971.

Cole, David D., and Princeton N. Lyman. *Korean Development: The Interplay of Politics and Economics*. Harvard University Press, 1971.

Committee on International Relations. House of Representatives. *Korea Aid Act of 1949. United States Policy in the Far East*. Part 2, Selected Executive Session Hearings of the Committee, 1943–50. Vol. 8. Washington, 1976.

Drake, H.B. *Korea of the Japanese*. London: John Lane the Bodley Head, Ltd., and New York: Dodd, Mead and Co., 1930.

Endō Yoshinobu. *Kindai nihon guntai kyōikushi kenkyū* [Study of the History of Modern Japanese Military Education]. Tokyo: Aoki shoten, 1994.

Friday, Karl. "Bushido or Bull? A Medieval Historian's Perspective on the Pacific War & the Japanese Military Tradition." *The History Teacher* 27, no. 3 (1994).

Gaddis, John Lewis. *Stratégies of Containment*. New York: Oxford University Press, 1982.

Godechot, Jacques. "Napoleon Bonaparte." *Encyclopedia Britannica* online.

Gragert, Edwin H. *Landownership under Colonial Rule: Korea's Japanese Experience, 1900–1935*. Honolulu: University of Hawaii Press, 1994.

Haboush, JaHyun Kim. *A Heritage of Kings*. New York: Columbia University Press, 1988.

Han Sŭng-dong. "The Days with the Kwangbok Army." [In Korean.] *Shin-ch'ŏnji* [The New World], (May 1948): 116–119.

Han, Sungjoo. *The Failure of Democracy in South Korea*. Berkeley: University of California Press, 1974.

Han'guk Hyŏngmyŏng chaep'ansa [History of Revolutionary Trials], 1962. (The editor of this collection is noted as The Editorial Committee for the History of Revolutionary Trials.)

Hausman, James, and Chŏng Il-hwa. *Han'guk taet'ongryŏng ŭl umjigin Migun Taewi* [An American Captain behind the Korean President]. Seoul: Han'guk Munhŏn, 1995.

Hur Nam-lin. "Politicking or Being Politicked: Wartime Governance in Chosŏn Korea, 1592–98." Paper presented at Association for Asian Studies (March 2006).

Hurst, G. Cameron. "Death, Loyalty and the Bushido Ideal." *Philosophy East and West* 40, no. 4 (1990).

Itō Takeo. *Mantetsu ni ikite* [Having Lived in South Manchuria Railway Company]. Tokyo: Keisō shobō, 1964.

Iwata Masakazu. *Okubo Toshimichi*: *The Bismarck of Japan*. Berkeley: University of California Press, 1964.

Jansen, Marius B. *The Making of Modern Japan*. Cambridge, MA: Harvard University Press, 2000.

Jeon Hyeon-su, ed. and trans. *Switikof ilgi, 1946–1948* [Diary of Terenty F. Shitikov, 1946–1948]. Seoul: Kuksa py'ŏnch'an Wiwŏnhoe, 2004.

Kamada Sawaichirō. *Chōsen shinwa* [New Stories on Korea]. Tokyo: Sōgensha, 1950.

Kang Chae-ŏn. *Kindai Chōsen no henkaku shisō* [Transformative Thoughts in Modern Korea]. Tokyo: Nihon Hyōronsha, 1973.

Keikidō Keisatsubu [The Police Department, Kyŏnggi-do]. *Ch'ian jŏkyō* [Security Conditions], 1939 (the section of special police).

Kim Ch'ang-guk. *Kankokujin ga chi'nichika ni narutoki* [When a Korean Becomes a Japanophile]. Tokyo: Heibonsha, 2000.

Kim Chin-hwa Reports in His *Ilje ha Taegu ui ŏnron yŏn'gu* [A Study of Taegu Journalism under Japanese Imperialism]. Taegu: Hwada Ch'ulp'an, 1978.

Kim Chŏm-gon. *Han'guk e issŏsŏui kongsan chuui t'ujaeng hyŏngt'ae yŏn'gu, 1945–1950* [A Study of the Pattern of Communist Struggle in Korea, 1945–1950]. PhD dissertation, Kyung Hee University, 1971.

Kim Chŏng-ryŏl. "5–16, Park Chŏng-Hui Magrudŏ hoedam naemak" [The Inside Story of Park Chung-Hee-Magruder Meeting]. *Shin-dong-a* (September 1993), 430–455.

———. *Hangkong ui kyŏngjong* [A Warning Bell in Flight]. Ch'unch'ŏn and Seoul: Daehui, 2010.

Kim Chŏng-ryŏm. *Ah, Park Chung- Hee*. Seoul: Chungang M & B, 1997.

Kim Chong-sin. *Yŏngsi ui hoetbul* [The Flare at Midnight]. Seoul: Hanrim, 1966.

Kim Ku. *Paekbom Ilji* [Autobiography of Kim Ku]. Seoul: Kinyŏm Saŏop Hyŏphoe, 1968.

———.. *Paekbŏm ilji: Kim Ku Chasŏjŏn* [Memoirs of Paekbŏm: Autobiography of Kim Ku]. Seoul: Koryŏ Sŏnbongsa, 1947.

Kim Mun-sik. "Iljeha ui nongŏp konghwang kwa nongch'on bunhae" [Agricultural Depression and the Disintegration of Farming Villages under Japanese Imperialism." *Nongŏp kyŏngje yŏn'gu*, 12, no. 1 (September 2005), 1–23.

Kim Nam-sik. *Sillok Namnodang* [Veritable Record of the South Korean Workers' Party]. Seoul: Shin Hyŏnsil-sa, 1975.

Kim Pyŏng-hee, autobiography on Internet. http://home.megapass.co.kr/~gimbyngh/hoigorog00.html.

Kim Se-Jin. *The Politics of Military Revolution in Korea*. Chapel Hill, NC: University of North Carolina Press, 1971.

Kim Yŏng-su. "A Study of Park Chung-Hee's Political Leadership." In Han'guk Chŏngshin Munhwa Yŏn'guwon, ed. *Chang Myŏn, Yun Po-sŏn, Pak Chŏng-hui: 1960nyŏndae chuyo chŏngch'i chidoja yŏn'gu*. Seoul: Paeksan Sŏdang, 2001.

Kindleberger, Charles P. *The World in Depression, 1929–1939*. Revised and Enlarged Edition. Berkeley: University of California Press, 1986.

Kishi Yonesuke. *Ryūten kyōiku rokujū nen* [Sixty Years of Meandering Education]. Kawasaki, 1982, private publication.

Kō Mei-shi. *Ikiru koto no imi* [The Meaning of Living]. Tokyo: Tsukuma Shobō, 1974.

Komori Tokuji. *Akaski Motojirō*. Taipei: Taiwan Nichinichi Shinpo-sha, 1928.

Kuksa P'yŏnch'an Wiwonhoe [The Committee for the Compilation of National History]. *Yun Ch'i-ho ilgi* [The Yun Ch'i-ho Diary]. Vol. 4. Seoul: T'amkudang, 1975.

Kuno Osamu, and Tsurumi Shunsuke. *Gendai Nihon no shisō* [Contemporary Japanese Thought]. Tokyo: Iwanami, 1956.

Kusayanagi Daizō. *Jitsuroku Mantetsu Chōsabu* [Veritable Record: Research Department, South Manchuria Railway Company]. Tokyo: Asahi Shinbunsha, 1979.

Kwon Yŏng-ki. "Kongkae kŭmji. Taegu Sabŏm sŏngjŏkp'yo us pimil" [Not for the Public: The Secret of the Taegu Normal School]. *Wŏlgan Chosŏn* [Chosŏn Monthly] (May 1991): 351–361.

Lasswell, Harold D. *Power and Personality*. New York: Viking Press, 1962, 39. (Original edition by W.W. Norton, 1948.)

Lee, Hahn-Been. *Korea: Time, Change, and Administration*. Honolulu: East-West Center Press, 1968.

Lee, Chong-Sik. "The Korean Communists and Yenan." *China Quarterly* (January-March 1962): 182–192.

———. "The Road to the Korean War: The United States Policy in Korea, 1945–48." G. Krebs and C. Oberlander, eds. *1945 in Europe and Asia*. Munchen, Germany: Iudicium, 1997: 195–212.

———. *Counterinsurgency in Manchuria: The Japanese Experience, 1931–1940*. Santa Monica, CA, 1967.

———. *Japan and Korea: The Political Dimension*. Stanford: Hoover Institution Press, 1985.

———. *Revolutionary Struggle in Manchuria*. Berkeley: University of California Press, 1983.

———. *The Prison Years of a Young Radical*. Seoul: Yonsei University Press, 2001.

Leonard, Thomas M., ed. *Day by Day: The Forties*. New York: Facts on File, 1977.

Lew Young-Ick. "The Conservative Character of the 1894 Tonghak Peasant Uprising." *The Journal of Korean Studies* 7 (1990): 149–180.

Li Teng-hui. *Bushido kaidai* [Exposition of *Bushido*]. Tokyo: Shōgakukan, 2003.

Manshikai (Assoc. for the History of Manchuria), ed. *Manshū kaihatsu yonjūnen shi* [Forty-Year History of the Development of Manchuria]. Tokyo: Kenkōsha, 1964.

Manshūkokushi Hensan Kankōkai [Editorial and Publication Committee]. *Manshūkokushi* [History of Manchukuo]. Tokyo: Manmō dōhō Engokai, 1971.

Matray, James I. "Captive of the Cold War: The Decision to Divide Korea at the 38th Parallel." *Pacific Historical Review*. Vol. L (1981): 145–168.

Matray, James. *The Reluctant Crusade: American Foreign Policy in Korea, 1941–1950*. Honolulu: University of Hawaii Press, 1985.

Matsumoto Sannosuke. *Kindai nihon no chiteki jyōkyō* [Intellectual Condition of Modern Japan]. Tokyo: Chūō Kōronsha, 1974.

Matsuoka Takao. "The Formation and Development of Immigration and Labor Policies after the Establishment of Manchukuo." [In Japanese.] In Manshūshi Kenkyūkai, ed. *Nihon teikokushugika no Manshū* [Manchuria under Japanese Imperialism]. Tokyo: Ochanomizu Shobō, 1972.

McCune, George M., and John A. Harrison. *Korean-American Relations*. Vol. 1. Berkeley: University of California Press, 1951.

Memmi, Albert. *The Colonizer and the Colonized*. Translated by Howard Greenfield. Boston: Beacon Press, 1965.

Merrill, John. "The Cheju-do Rebellion." *Journal of Korean Studies*. Vol. 2 (1980): 139–197.

Miyata Setsuko. *Chōsen minshū to "Kōminka seisaku"* [The Korean Masses and the "Policy to Turn Them to Imperial Subjects"]. Tokyo: Miraisha, 1985.

Mutō Tomio. *Watakushi to Manshūkoku* [I and Manchukuo]. Tokyo: Bungei Shunju, 1988.

Naimushō [Ministry of Home Affairs]. *Chōsen oyobi Taiwan no genkyō* [The Present Condition in Korea and Taiwan] (July 1942). Reprinted in *Taiheiyō senka no Chōsen oyobi Taiwan* [Korea and Taiwan during the Pacific War], Kondō Ken'ichi, ed. Tokyo, 1961.

Naimushō Keihokyoku. *Tokkō geppō* [Ministry of Home Affairs, Police and Security Bureau, Special High Police Monthly Report], (September 1941).

Nihon Koksai Seiji Gakkai. *Taiheiyō sensō eno michi* [The Road to the Pacific War]. Tokyo: Asahi Shinbunsha 3 (1962): 85–87.

Nitobe Inazō. *Bushidō*. Trans. Yanaihara Tadao. Tokyo: Iwanami Shoten, 2004.

Ogata Sadako. *Defiance in Manchuria*. Berkeley: University of California Press, 1963.

Oliver, Robert T. *Syngman Rhee: The Man behind the Myth*. New York: Dodd Mead, 1955.

Paek Sŏn-yŏp. *Kun kwa na* [The Army and I]. Seoul: Taeryuk Yŏn'guso, 1989.

Paige, Glenn. *The Korean Decision*. Glencoe, IL: The Free Press, 1968.

Pak Yŏng-jae, Pak Ch'ung-sŏk, and Kim Yong-dŏk. *19segi ilbon ui kŭundaehwa* [Modernization of Japan in the 19th Century]. Seoul National University Press, 1996.

Park Chung-Hee. "Na ui sonyŏn shijŏl" [My Childhood Days]. Reprinted in *Wŏlgan Chosŏn* [Chosŏn Monthly] (May 1984): 84–95.

———. *Chidojado* [The Leader's Way]. Seoul: Supreme Council of National Reconstruction, 1961.

———. *Kukka wa hyŏngmyŏng kwa na* [The Nation, Revolution, and I]. Seoul: Hyangmunsa, 1963.

———. *Minjok ui chŏryŏk* [Underlying Strength of the Nation]. Seoul: Kwangmyŏng, 1971.

Park Chung-Hui. *Kukka wa hyŏngmyŏng kwa na* [The Nation, Revolution, and I]. Seoul: Kwangmyŏng, 1963.

Park, Eugene. *Between Dream and Reality: The Military Examination in Late Chosŏn Korea, 1600–1894*. Cambridge, MA: Harvard University Press, 2007.

Pelz, Stephen. "U.S. Decisions on Korean Policy, 1943–1950: Some Hypotheses." In Bruce Cumings, ed. *Child of Conflict: The Korean-American Relationship, 1943–1953*. Seattle: University of Washington Press, 1983.

Ranseikai [Orchid Star Society]. *Manshū kokugun* [The Manchukuo Army]. Tokyo: private publication, 1970.

Rikushi Dai 57ki Dōkiseikai, ed. *Chiru sakura: Rikushi 57ki senbot-susha kiroku* [The Falling Cherry Blossoms: A Record of War Casualties among the 57th Class of the Military Academy]. Tokyo, 1999.

Ryu Yŏn-san. *Manju Arirang* [Manchuria Arirang]. Seoul: Dolbegae, 2003.

Satō Seizaburō. "Response to the West: The Korean and Japanese Patterns." Albert M. Craig, ed. *Japan: A Comparative View*. Princeton: Princeton University Press, 1979, 105–129.

Sawyer, Robert K. *Military Advisors in Korea: KMAG in Peace and War*. Washington DC: Office of the Chief of Military History, Dept. of the Army, 1962.

Scalapino, Robert A. *The Japanese Communist Movement, 1920–1966*. Berkeley: University of California Press, 1967.

Sherwood, Robert E. *Roosevelt and Hopkins: An Intimate History*. Rev. Ed. New York: Grosset and Dunlap, 1950.

Shin Hyŏn-jun. *No haebyŏng ui hoegorok* [Recollections of an Old Marine]. Seoul: K'at'orik ch'ulp'ansa, 1989.

Shin Pŏm-sik, ed. *Park Chŏng-hui taet'ongryŏng sŏnjip* [Selected Works of President Park Chung-Hee]. Vol. 1. Seoul: Chimunkak, 1969.

Shin Sang-ch'o. "The Escape from the Chinese Communists." [In Korean.] *Shin-Dong'a* [New East Asia] (March 1965): 318–345.

Sono Ayuko. "Waga chichi Boku Seiki" [My Father Park Chŏng-Hui]. Interview of Park Kŭn-hae by Sono Ayuko. (April 1980), 114–128.

"Sōshi no jisseki" [Accomplishment of Creating Names]. Kōto Hōin, Kenjikyoku [Korean Government General, High Court, Prosecutor's Bureau]. *Shisō ihō* [Ideological Report Series], no. 25 (December 1940), 47–48.

Suzuki Kenichi. "Rikugun Shikan gakkō ni okeru kokushi kyōikuno suii" [Transition in Teaching National History at the Military Academy]. *Kinki daigaku kyōiku ronsō* [Kinki University Education Essays]. Vol. 11, no. 2 (January 2000), 33–52.

Taehan Min'guk Yukkun Sagwan Hakkyo 30nyŏnsa [Thirty Year History of the Republic of Korea Military Academy]. Seoul, 1978.

Takano Kunio, ed. *Kindai Nihon guntai kyōikushiryo shūsei* [Collection of Historical Materials on Modern Japanese Military Education]. Tokyo: Kashiwa Shobō, 2004.

Tang Tsou. *America's Failure in China*. University of Chicago Press, 1963.

Tsurumi Shunsuke. *Senjiki Ninhon no seishinshi, 1931–1945* [Spiritual History of Japan during the War, 1931–1945]. Tokyo: Iwanami, 1982.

Tucker, Mary Evelyn. "Religious Dimensions of Confucianism: Cosmology and Cultivation." *Philosophy East and West*, 48, no. 1 (January 1998).

U.S. State Department. *Foreign Relations of the United States*, 1942, Vol. 3 (Europe).

U.S. Army Military Government in Korea. *South Korean Interim Government Activities.*

Underwood, Horace. "Korean Boats and Ships." *Transactions of the Korean Branch of the Royal Asiatic Society*, XXXIII (1934)

Wagner, Edward W., *The Literati Purges: Political Conflict in Early Yi Korea* (Cambridge, Institute for Asian Studies, Harvard University, 1974.

Wagner, Edward. "The Ladder of Success in Yi Dynasty Korea." *Occasional Papers on Korea*, 1 (April 1974): 1–18.

Weathersby, Kathryn. "Soviet Aims in Korea and the Origins of the Korean War, 1945–50: New Evidence from Russian Archives." Working Paper #8: Cold War International History Project.

Yi Chŏng-sik. "The People's Republic and the Post-Liberation Politics." [In Korean), *Han'guksa shimin kangjwa* (Citizen's Lectures on Korean History), No. 12 (1993), pp. 15-45.

Yi Chŏng-sik, *KuHanmal ui kaehyŏk tongnip t'usa Sŏ Chae-p'il* [Sŏ Chae-p'il: The Fighter for Reform and Independence at the end of the Old Korea]. Seoul: Seoul National University Press, 2003.

———. *Taehan min'guk ui kiwon* [The Origins of the Republic of Korea]. Seoul: Iljogak, 2006.

———. *Yi Sungman ui kuhanmal kaehyŏk undong* [Syngman Rhee: From a Revolutionary to a Christian Nation-Builder]. Taejeon: Paichai University Press, 2005.

———. *Yŏ Un-hyŏng*. Seoul: Seoul National University Press, 2008.

Yi Ki-baek. *New History of Korea*. Translated by Edward Wagner with Edward J. Shultz. Seoul: Ilchogak, 1984.

Yi Kyu-t'ae. *P'yŏngjŏn Taesan Shin Yong-ho* [Biography of Taesan Shin Yong-ho]. Seoul: Kyobo Mun'go, 2004.

Yi Man-gap. *Han'guk nongch'on ui sahoe kujo* [Social Structure in Korean Farming Villages]. Seoul: Han'guk Yŏn'gu Tosŏgwan, 1960.

Yi Min-won. "The Establishment of the Tae-Han Empire." Kuksa P'yŏnch'an Wiwonhoe [The Committee for the Compilation of National History]. *Han'guksa* [Korean History]. Vol. 42 (Kwach'ŏn, 1999), 13–38.

Yi Mok-u. "Taegu sip-il p'oktong sakŏn" [The Taegu October First Riot Incident]. *Sedae* [Generation], (October 1965), 226–233.

Yi Pyŏng-ju. "Major General Park Chung-Hee: That Incorrigible Egomaniac." [In Korean.] *Wol'gan Chosŏn* [Monthly Chosŏn] (July 1991): 472–485.

Yi Tŏk-il. *Tangjaeng ŭro bonŭn Chosŏn yŏksa* [Korean History Seen from the Perspective of Factional Struggles]. Seoul: Sŏkp'il, 1997.

Yŏm In-ho. "The Korean Independence Party's Movement to Expand the Kwangbok Army South of the Great Wall after Liberation." [In Korean.] *Yŏksa munje yŏn'gu* [Studies on Historical Problems], 9, no. 1 (1996): 163–313.

Yu Sŏng-yong. *Chōbiroku* [Chingbirok]. Translated by Park Chong-myŏng (Boku Shō-mei in Japanese). Tokyo: Heibonsha, 1979.

Yu Yŏng-ik. *Tonghak nongmin pong-gi wa Kap-o kaengjang* [The Tonghak Farmers' Uprising and the Kap-o Reform]. Seoul: Ilchokak, 1998.

Yukawa Kōhei. "Boku gichō tono ichijikan" [An Hour with Chairman Park]. *Bungei shunjū*. (January 1962): 324–335.

Zenkoku Keizai Chōsakikan Rengōkai Chōsen Shibu [The Korea Branch, the Federation of All-Nation Economic Study Organizations]. Shōwa 16–17nen han. *Chōsen keizai nenpō* [Korea Economic Annual Report, 1941–1942]. Tokyo: Kaizōsha, 1943.

INDEX

32036979R00234

Made in the USA
Lexington, KY
05 May 2014